Designing and Implementing Linux Firewalls and QoS using netfilter, iproute2, NAT, and L7-filter

Learn how to secure your system and implement QoS using real-world scenarios for networks of all sizes

Lucian Gheorghe

BIRMINGHAM - MUMBAI

Designing and Implementing Linux Firewalls and QoS using netfilter, iproute2, NAT, and L7-filter

First published: October 2006

Production Reference: 2181006

Published by Packt Publishing Ltd.
32 Lincoln Road
Olton
Birmingham, B27 6PA, UK.

ISBN 1-904811-65-5

www.packtpub.com

Cover Image by www.visionwt.com

Credits

Author

Lucian Gheorghe

Reviewer

Barrie Dempster

Development Editor

Louay Fatoohi

Assistant Development Editor

Nikhil Bangera

Technical Editor

Niranjan Jahagirdar

Code Testing

Ankur Shah

Editorial Manager

Dipali Chittar

Indexer

Mithil Kulkarni

Proofreader

Chris Smith

Layouts and Illustrations

Shantanu Zagade

Cover Designer

Shantanu Zagade

About the Author

Lucian Gheorghe has just joined the Global NOC of Interoute, Europe's largest voice and data network provider. Before Interoute, he was working as a senior network engineer for Globtel Internet, a significant Internet and Telephony Services Provider to the Romanian market. He has been working with Linux for more than 8 years putting a strong accent on security for protecting vital data from hackers and ensuring good quality services for internet customers. Moving to VoIP services he had to focus even more on security as sensitive billing data is most often stored on servers with public IP addresses. He has been studying QoS implementations on Linux to build different types of services for IP customers and also to deliver good quality for them and for VoIP over the public Internet. Lucian has also been programming with Perl, PHP, and Smarty for over 5 years mostly developing in-house management interfaces for IP and VoIP services.

I would like to thank everyone who is reading this book and the people that run netfilter, iproute2, and L7-filter projects. Your feedback is very important to me, so drop me a line at lucian.firewallbook@gmail.com. The book is far from being perfect so please send me errata information on the same email address (I would love to receive erratas from readers because it will convince me that people who read this book actually learned something :-))

I want to dedicate this book to my father, my mother, and my sister—I love you very very much. Many thanks go to the team at Globtel who were like second family to me, to my girlfriend for understanding me and standing by me, to Louay and the rest of the team at Packt Publishing for doing a great job, to Nigel Coulson, Petr Klobasa and the rest of the people at Interoute for supporting me, to Claudiu Filip who is one of the most intelligent people I know, and last, but not least, to the greatest technical author alive—Cristian Darie.

About the Reviewer

Barrie Dempster is currently employed as a Senior Security Consultant for NGS Software Ltd, a world-renowned security consultancy well known for its focus in enterprise-level application vulnerability research and database security. He has a background in Infrastructure and Information Security in a number of specialized environments such as financial services institutions, telecommunications companies, call centers, and other organizations across multiple continents. Barrie has experience in the integration of network infrastructure and telecommunications systems requiring high-caliber secure design, testing, and management. He has been involved in a variety of projects from the design and implementation of Internet banking systems to large-scale conferencing and telephony infrastructure, as well as penetration testing and other security assessments of business-critical infrastructure.

Table of Contents

Preface

A networking firewall is a logical barrier designed to prevent unauthorized or unwanted communications between sections of a computer network. Linux-based firewalls besides being highly customizable and versatile are also robust, inexpensive, and reliable.

The two things needed to build firewalls and QoS with Linux are two packages named netfilter and iproute. While netfilter is a packet-filtering framework included in the Linux kernels 2.4 and 2.6, iproute is a package containing a few utilities that allow Linux users to do advanced routing and traffic shaping.

L7-filter is a packet classifier for the Linux kernel that doesn't look up port numbers or Layer 4 protocols, but instead looks at the data in an IP packet and does a regular expression match on it to determine what kind of data it is, mainly what application protocol is being used. IP2P is an alternative to L7-filter, but has been designed for filtering only P2P applications while L7-filter takes into consideration a wider range of applications.

What This Book Covers

Chapter 1 is a brief introduction to networking concepts. It covers the OSI and TCP/IP networking models with explanations of their layers, TCP and UDP as Layer 4 protocols, and then rounds off the chapter with a discussion on IP addresses, Subnetting, and Supernetting.

Chapter 2 discusses possible security threats and vulnerabilities found at each of the OSI layers. The goal here is to understand where and how these threats can affect us and to stay protected from attackers. It then rounds off the discussion by sketching out the basic steps required to protect the services that run on our system.

Chapter 3 introduces two tools needed to build Linux firewalls and QoS. We first learn the workings of netfilter, which is a packet-filtering framework, and implement what we have learned to build a basic firewall for a Linux workstation. We then see how to perform advanced routing and traffic shaping using the IP and TC tools provided by the iproute2 package. The chapter ends with another example scenario where we implement the concepts learned in the chapter.

Chapter 4 discusses NAT, the types of NAT, how they work, and how they can be implemented with Linux by giving practical examples. It also describe packet mangling, when to use it, and why to use it.

Chapter 5 covers Layer 7 filtering in detail. We see how to install the L7-filter package, apply the necessary Linux kernel and iptables patches, and test our installation. We then learn the different applications of L7-filter and see how to put them to practical use. We also see how to install and use IPP2P, which is an alternative to the L7-filter package, but only for P2P traffic, and finally we set up a test between the two packages.

Chapter 6 raises two very popular scenarios, for which we design, implement, and test firewalls and a small QoS configuration. In the first scenario, we configure Linux as a SOHO router. Being a relatively smaller network with few devices, we learn how to adapt to what we have learned in the earlier chapters to suit this environment and build a secure network. We implement transparent proxies using squid and iptables so that children/minors cannot access malicious or pornographic web content. Our firewall setup implements NAT to redirect traffic from certain ports to other hosts using Linux. This configuration is tested by checking the NAT table and seeing how the kernel analyzes our rules.
As part of QoS, we split the bandwidth between the devices in a SOHO environment using HTB. Assuming a 1Mbps connection, we design a policy to split it between the 4 devices creating 4 HTB child classes for the 4 devices. In the end, we test our QoS configuration using the `tc class show` command.
In the second scenario, we configure Linux as router for a typical small to medium company.

Chapter 7 covers the design of a firewall system for a hypermarket having its headquarters in one location, one store in the same city, and several stores in other cities. The hypermarket has an application that uses MSSQL databases in each location, which are replicated at the headquarters. All locations have IP Analog Telephone Adapters with subscriptions at the main provider (the HQ provider). In this example we use, just like in the real H.323 as the VoIP protocol. We set up all remote locations to have an encrypted VPN connection using `ip tunnel` to connect to the headquarters. Users are shown how to create a QOS script with HTB that controls bandwidth usage based on priorities.

The next firewall taken up is that for a small ISP setup that has one internet connection, an access network, a server farm, and the internal departments. The setup of firewall scripts for each of them and methods to handle the tricky wireless server are covered. The QoS is handled by the intranet server, the wireless server, and the Core router.

Chapter 8 covers the design of a three-layered network deployed at a large provider of Internet and IP telephony services, the three layers being Core, Distribution, and Access. It explains network configuration first on the core and distribution levels and then moves on to building firewalls. The huge size of the network also means that there is a need to tackle newer security threats. We have four Cores running BGP under Zebra and each one is peculiar in its own way. There are three data services that this ISP can provide to its customers: Internet access, national network access, and metropolitan network access. This chapter will show you how to handle QoS so as to limit this traffic as needed.

Conventions

In this book, you will find a number of styles of text that distinguish between different kinds of information. Here are some examples of these styles, and an explanation of their meaning.

There are three styles for code. Code words in text are shown as follows: "To limit upload, we will mark packets in the PREROUTING chain of the mangle table".

A block of code will be set as follows:

```
#Drop SSH packets except from admins
$IPT -A INPUT -s ! 1.2.3.16/28 -p tcp --dport 22 -j DROP
```

When we wish to draw your attention to a particular part of a code block, the relevant lines or items will be made bold:

```
tc filter add dev eth0 protocol ip parent 1:0 prio 5 u32 match ip src
1.2.3.34 flowid 1:100
```

New terms and **important words** are introduced in a bold-type font. Words that you see on the screen, in menus or dialog boxes for example, appear in our text like this: "In the **IP: Netfilter Configuration** section you will find the options needed for NAT".

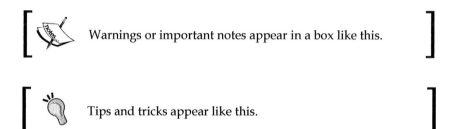

Warnings or important notes appear in a box like this.

Tips and tricks appear like this.

Reader Feedback

Feedback from our readers is always welcome. Let us know what you think about this book, what you liked or may have disliked. Reader feedback is important for us to develop titles that you really get the most out of.

To send us general feedback, simply drop an email to feedback@packtpub.com, making sure to mention the book title in the subject of your message.

If there is a book that you need and would like to see us publish, please send us a note in the **SUGGEST A TITLE** form on www.packtpub.com or email suggest@packtpub.com.

If there is a topic that you have expertise in and you are interested in either writing or contributing to a book, see our author guide on www.packtpub.com/authors.

Customer Support

Now that you are the proud owner of a Packt book, we have a number of things to help you to get the most from your purchase.

Downloading the Example Code for the Book

Visit http://www.packtpub.com/support, and select this book from the list of titles to download any example code or extra resources for this book. The files available for download will then be displayed.

The downloadable files contain instructions on how to use them.

Errata

Although we have taken every care to ensure the accuracy of our contents, mistakes do happen. If you find a mistake in one of our books—maybe a mistake in text or code—we would be grateful if you would report this to us. By doing this you can save other readers from frustration, and help to improve subsequent versions of this book. If you find any errata, report them by visiting `http://www.packtpub.com/support`, selecting your book, clicking on the **Submit Errata** link, and entering the details of your errata. Once your errata have been verified, your submission will be accepted and the errata added to the list of existing errata. The existing errata can be viewed by selecting your title from `http://www.packtpub.com/support`.

Questions

You can contact us at `questions@packtpub.com` if you are having a problem with some aspect of the book, and we will do our best to address it.

1
Networking Fundamentals

When it comes to theory, some of you out there might find it boring to read; so the first thing that may go through your mind is to skip this chapter. Don't do it. Even if you think that you know all the theoretical concepts, a recapitulation is good anytime.

Network professionals talk about protocols, devices, and software in terms of which OSI Layer they function at. When people talk about high-performance Layer 3 switches these days, they talk about switches that can perform OSI Layer 3 tasks and they expect you to know which tasks are at that layer. A simple deduction makes you realize that classic switches perform OSI Layer 2 functions.

Layer 3 switches are beyond the scope of this book, but that was a simple example of why you should know the OSI layered model, which is purely theoretical. Further in this book, you will learn about "Layer 7 filtering" which refers to how to filter what is on OSI Layer 7, which I'm sure you will find very attractive to read and implement.

By definition, a network is a group of two or more computer systems linked together, with the ability to communicate with each other.

The types of networks commonly used are:

- **LAN (Local Area Network)**: A network in which the computers are close together (the same building).
- **WAN (Wide Area Network)**: A network in which the computers are at very long distances.
- **MAN (Metropolitan Area Network)**: A city-wide network.
- **CAN (Campus Area Network)**: A network in a campus or a military base.
- **SAN (Storage Area Network)**: A high-performance network used to move data between servers and dedicated storage devices.
- **VPN (Virtual Private Network)**: A private network built over the public network infrastructure (over the Internet).

- **HAN (Home Area Network)**: A network in a personal home. This term is rarely used; most people use the term LAN in this matter.

Computers in a user home network (a HAN) are usually connected to the building switch and form a LAN with the other users' computers. This switch is connected to a MAN or a CAN that is connected to the largest WAN, which is the Internet.

The OSI Model

In order for computers to communicate, they must speak the same language or protocol. In the early days of networking, networks were disorganized in many ways. Companies developed proprietary network technologies that had great difficulties in exchanging information with other or existing technologies; so network interconnections were very hard to build. To solve this problem, the International Organization for Standardization (ISO) created a network model that helps vendors to create networks compatible with each other.

In 1984, ISO released the Open Systems Interconnection (OSI) reference model, which is a well-defined set of specifications that ensures greater compatibility among various technologies.

In fact, OSI is a description of network communication that everyone refers to. It is not the only network model, but it has become the primary model for network communication. You will see further in this chapter, that the TCP/IP model is only a reduced version of the OSI model.

The OSI model consists of seven layers, each illustrating a particular network function.

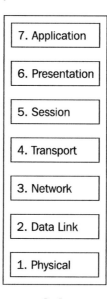

Information contained in one layer usually has headers and trailers and data encapsulated from an upper layer. **Encapsulation** is the process of placing the data from an upper layer between headers and trailers so that when data is received by a layer, after it is analyzed, the protocol at that layer removes the headers and trailers and gives the data to the upper layer in the format that the upper layer understands.

At Layer 7 (application) of the OSI model we have the user interface (a web browser for example). Layer 6 (presentation) handles how data is presented (e.g. HTML). While accessing a web page, a computer may be sending/receiving emails. Keeping data from different applications separate is the job for Layer 5 (session) of the OSI model. At Layer 4 (transport) we find protocols that transfer the data (TCP for example), while at Layer 3 (network) we find logical addressing, which is used for path determination (e.g. IP). At Layer 2 (data link), we find network protocols such as Ethernet, and at the lowest layer, Layer 1 (physical), we find the cabling specifications (e.g. RJ-45).

This was a quick overview on the OSI layers. Now, let's have a closer look at these layers in order for us to understand the communication process.

OSI Layer 7: Application

The OSI application layer refers to communication services to applications. When programmers design an image editor for example, they don't have to think about adding OSI Layer 7 capabilities to that software, because it has no need for communication with other computers. On the other hand, when creating an FTP client, they must add communication capabilities to that software.

At Layer 7 we usually find Telnet, FTP, HTTP, SMTP, SNMP, or SSH.

When we say, for example, Layer 7 filtering, we refer to filtering application data, regardless of what port or computer it may come from.

OSI Layer 6: Presentation

The purpose of the presentation layer is defining the data formats in which data is represented. Data formats are usually standard formats like ASCII, JPEG, GIF, TIFF, MPEG, etc. OSI Layer 6 also defines encryption as a presentation layer service.

The importance of defining data formats is obvious. For example, when sending email, you usually send it plain text (ASCII) or HTML. If the receiving application doesn't know these data formats, your email will not be displayed correctly.

OSI Layer 6 provides a service to the upper OSI layer (application). It formats the data to be sent across the network in a manner that the receiving application is able to understand and/or manipulate.

OSI Layer 5: Session

The session layer defines how to start, control, and end conversations. These conversations are called sessions. OSI Layer 5 ensures inter-host communication, meaning that it establishes ways to manage sessions between applications.

An application may communicate with several other applications (on other PCs) at the same time. For each communication channel, Layer 5 starts a separate session that provides a service to the upper layer (presentation). The session layer ensures that a series of messages is completed. For example, if only half the data is received on a particular session, Layer 5 will not pass the data to the upper layer if the application is built this way. For example, suppose you go to an ATM machine, log in, print your account status, and insert an amount you want to extract from your account, but a communication error happens right then. The ATM will not give you the cash before it debits your account; instead, it will wait for the confirmation from the central system that the account was debited with that amount and then gives you the cash.

At the session layer, we find SQL, NFS, RPC, etc. Usually, the operating system is responsible for OSI Layer 5.

OSI Layer 4: Transport

The transport layer ensures the management of virtual circuits between hosts that can provide error correction. It contains a series of protocols concerned with transportation issues between hosts. These protocols may reorder the data stream if the packets arrive out of order. Layer 4 protocols are also responsible for multiplexing incoming data for different flows to applications running on the same host.

OSI Layer 4 provides a service to the session layer, meaning that after the data is received, multiplexed, and reordered, it is given to the upper layer (session) for handling.

The most common Layer 4 protocols are TCP, UDP, and SPX. The most important features of Layer 4 protocols are error correction and flow control. Because a router can discard packets for many reasons (communication errors, network congestion, etc.) Layer 4 protocols can provide retransmission of packets that the other host didn't receive. This is called **error correction**. Also, because of bandwidth limitations, if data is sent from one device using its full physical bandwidth, network congestion will occur. Layer 4 protocols are responsible for limiting transmission speed so that the network doesn't get flooded. This is called **flow control**.

We will see later in this chapter how error connection and flow control are accomplished and what protocols provide reliable or unreliable transport.

OSI Layer 3: Network

The network layer defines end-to-end delivery of data. In order for computers to be identified, the network layer defines logical addressing (e.g. IP addresses). OSI Layer 3 also defines how routing works and how routes are learned by routers for packet delivery. Also, the network layer defines fragmentation of packets, which is the process that breaks packets into smaller units in order to accommodate media with smaller maximum transmission unit (MTU) sizes.

Usually at OSI Layer 3 we find IP and IPX. When we think about OSI Layer 3, we must think of "routing". For example, routers are Layer 3 devices that run routing protocols for path determination.

Routers make their routing decisions based on the routing tables they have. Routing tables are collections of rules that define where data should go for a specific address or network.

At the beginning of this chapter, I was talking about one very common issue these days—"Layer 3 switches". Layer 3 switches switch packets according to a Layer 3 routing table. Usually, routers have a small number of interfaces that connect to switches for connectivity with other endpoints. In IP, Layer 3 switches are transparent routers with a very high density of ports.

OSI Layer 2: Data Link

The data link layer specifications are concerned with transferring data over a particular medium. For example, IEEE 802.3, which is the protocol for Ethernet, is found at OSI Layer 2. Hubs and switches are Layer 2 devices because they forward Ethernet packets over copper wires. At the data link layer we find protocols like ATM, Frame Relay, HDLC, PPP, FDDI, etc.

What we need to understand from this is that OSI Layer 2 specifies how packets are sent to the communication link. When we think about OSI Layer 2, we can think "switching", for example.

OSI Layer 1: Physical

The physical layer contains specifications for the physical medium of transmission that the data link layer protocols use. Layer 1 specifications are about connectors, pins, electrical currents, light modulation, etc. At Layer 1, we find the 802.3 standard, which has definitions about the Ethernet pinout, cable lengths, voltages, etc. More than that, we find cabling specification standards for RJ45, RJ48, V.35, V.24, EIA/TIA-232, and so on.

When we think about Layer 1, we can think "cables and connectors".

OSI Functionality Example and Benefits

Let's think about one world-wide service that wouldn't have been possible without standardization, like email services. There are so many email client software applications out there, and all of them use the same protocols to transmit and receive data.

Let's say you are in a company LAN and you want to send an email.

Layer 7: You use an email client (like Outlook Express for example), which has SMTP and POP3 functions according to OSI Layer 7 (application).

Layer 6: You send the email, formatted in ASCII or HTML. The application then creates a data unit formatted in ASCII or HTML according to OSI Layer 6 (presentation).

Layer 5: The email message uses the operating system to open a session for inter-host communication according to OSI Layer 5 (session).

Layer 4: A TCP socket with the SMTP server is opened by the operating system. A virtual circuit is opened between your computer and the email server using TCP according to OSI Layer 4 (transport).

Layer 3: Your computer searches for the IP address of the SMTP server according to the routing table of the operating system. If it is not found in the routing table, it will forward it to the company router for path determination. The IP protocol is at OSI Layer 3 (network).

Layer 2: The IP packet is transformed to an Ethernet frame according to OSI Layer 2 (data link).

Layer 1: The Ethernet frame is converted to electrical signals that are sent throughout the CAT5 cable according to OSI Layer 1 (physical).

By creating specifications on multiple layers, the OSI model has a lot of benefits:

- Reduced complexity allows faster evolution. There are companies specialized in creating products specific for one layer, instead of rebuilding everything from the application to the physical layer.
- Interoperability is much easier due to standardization.
- Each layer uses the service of the layer immediately below it, and so it is easier to remember what the lower layer does.
- It simplifies teaching. For example, network administrators need to know the functions of the lowest four layers, while programmers need to know the upper layers.

The TCP/IP Model

The TCP/IP model was developed by the U.S. Department of Defense (DoD) and originated from the need of a network that could survive any conditions, including a nuclear war. After it was released to the public, in a few years the TCP/IP model became the most popular networking model and it is now the core of the Internet.

In a world where we have data transmitted over wires, microwaves, satellite links, and optical fiber, there is the need to transmit data reliably over any media and under any circumstances. Let's see how the TCP/IP model can do that.

First of all, the TCP/IP model consists of four layers as in the following figure:

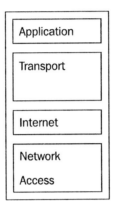

So, the layers of the TCP/IP model are: Application, Transport, Internet, and Network Access.

Even if some layers from the TCP/IP model share the same name with some layers from the OSI model, they include different functions.

The TCP/IP Application Layer

The TCP/IP application layer handles high-level protocols, representation, encoding, and dialog control. The Application layer in the TCP/IP model defines not only the application, but also how data is formatted, and how sessions are initialized and destroyed. As an analogy to the OSI model, the TCP/IP application layer handles the functions found at the three upper layers in the OSI model—application, presentation, and session. This way, all application-related issues found in the OSI model are combined into one layer.

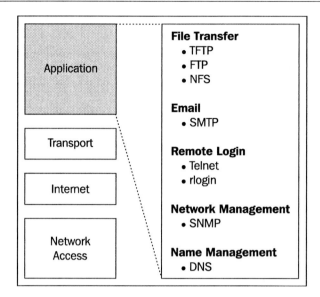

The application layer in the TCP/IP model includes protocols like FTP, SMTP, etc., with all their issues regarding data representation and dialog control. The application layer ensures that the data is properly packaged before it is passed to the transport layer.

The TCP/IP Transport Layer

The transport layer provides transport services for the application layer by creating logical connections between the source host and the destination host.

In the TCP/IP model, two protocols are found at the transport layer:

- Transmission Control Protocol (TCP)
- User Datagram Protocol (UDP)

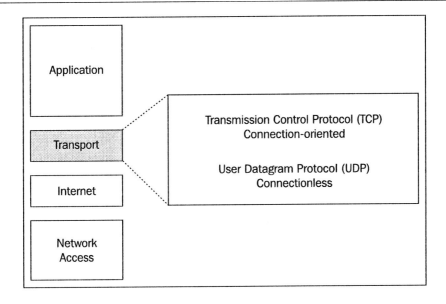

The Transmission Control Protocol (TCP)

TCP is a connection-oriented protocol and provides reliable data transfer between endpoints.

TCP breaks messages into segments, reassembles them at the destination, and sends them to the upper layer (application).

A TCP segment contains:

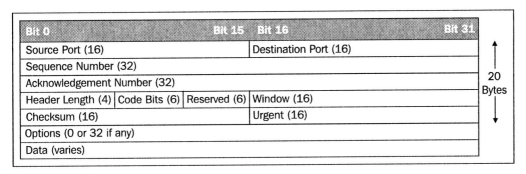

- **Source Port**: The port number used by the sending host to send data
- **Destination Port**: The port number used by the receiving host to receive data
- **Sequence Number**: The SEQ number of the segment, used to ensure the data arrives in the correct order

- **Acknowledgement Number**: The ACK number is the next expected TCP octet from the other host.

- **Header Length (HLEN)**: Number of 32-bit words in the header

- **Code Bits**: Control functions such as set up or terminate a session

- **Reserved**: Reserved bits are set to zero

- **Window**: The number of octets that the sender will accept

- **Checksum**: Calculated checksum of the header and data fields

- **Urgent**: Indicates the end of the urgent data

- **Options**: There is only one option defined, which is the maximum TCP segment size.

- **Data**: The data from the upper layer (application)

Connection-oriented means that TCP needs to establish a connection between the two hosts before it starts sending data. This is done by using a three-way handshake, which means that two hosts communicating using TCP synchronization (SYN).

First, the initiating host sends a SYN packet to the receiving host sending its sequence number (SEQ). The receiving host receives the SYN packet and sends back an acknowledgement (ACK) packet containing its own sequence number and the source's SEQ number incremented by 1. This tells the sending host that the packet was received successfully and informs it about its SEQ number. Next, the sending host sends an ACK packet to the receiving host, containing the receiving host's SEQ number incremented by one. This tells the receiving host that the sending host received its packet.

The process described above is called synchronization (the three-way handshake), and it is necessary because the network doesn't have a global clock and TCP protocols may use different mechanisms to choose initial sequence numbers.

 In a few words, synchronization is the way both hosts learn about the other host's initial SEQ number. Another important aspect that you should learn from this is that the first packet sent by a host to another is called a SYN packet.

After the synchronization is performed, TCP uses a process called **windowing** to ensure flow control and ACK packets for the reliability of the data transmission.

Windowing is a process in which the two hosts adapt the number of bytes they send by how many windows the other host receives before sending an ACK packet. For example, see the following figure:

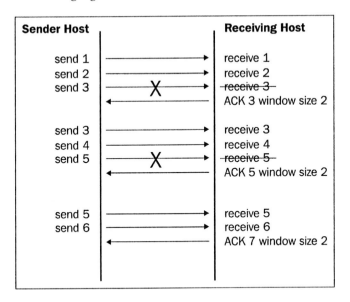

The sender host sends three packets before expecting an ACK packet, while the receiving host can only process two. The receiving host sends back an ACK packet confirming what packet the sender should send and specifies a window size of 2. The sending host sends packet 3 again but with the same window size 3. The receiver sends ACK 5, meaning that it waits for the fifth packet and specifies again the window size 2. From this point, the sender only sends two packets before waiting for an ACK packet from the receiver.

Flow control is a mechanism that keeps the data transmission in limits imposed by the physical medium. For example, a host on a network that is connected to the Internet through a router with 64 kilobits per second, without flow control would flood out 100 megabits per second to the router when sending data to another computer located at the other end of the world. With a flow control mechanism in TCP, the hosts negotiate a window size, meaning an amount of data to be transmitted by one host at once.

ACK packets are sent by the receiving host indicating the last packet has been received, and that the receiving host is waiting for the next packet after the one last received. If packets get lost along the way, this will force the sending host to resend that packet, thus ensuring a reliable communication.

Please note that TCP is a connection-oriented protocol with reliable data transmission and flow control.

Applications with the need of reliable data transmission use TCP as transport protocol. Examples of such applications are FTP, HTTP, SMTP, Telnet, SSH, etc.

The User Datagram Protocol (UDP)

UDP is a much simpler protocol than TCP is, and it's everything that TCP isn't. UDP is a transport layer protocol that doesn't need to establish a connection with the other host for sending data. This means that UDP is connectionless.

A UDP segment contains:

Bit 0	Bit 15	Bit 16	Bit 31	
Source Port (16)		Destination Port (16)		↑
Length (16)		Checksum (16)		8 Bytes
Data (if any)				↓

- **Source Port**: The port number used by the sending host to send data
- **Destination Port**: The port number used by the receiving host to receive data
- **Length**: The number of bytes in header and data
- **Checksum**: Calculated checksum of the header and data fields
- **Data**: The data from the upper layer (application)

Also, UDP doesn't have any mechanisms for flow control and doesn't retransmit data if data gets lost. This means that UDP provides unreliable delivery. However, data retransmission and error handling can be implemented at the application layer, whenever it is needed.

Now, you are probably wondering if TCP has so many great features, why use UDP?

A first answer to that question would be because there are applications that don't need to put sequences of segments together. Let's take for instance H.323, which is used for Voice over IP (VoIP). Voice over IP is a way to send real-time conversations over an IP network. If H.323 used TCP, in a conversation, when data gets lost due to network congestion, the sending host must retransmit all the lost data while encapsulating the new telephone input into new data, which would have to wait to be sent. This would be very bad for a conversation in a network with delays higher than 100 miliseconds.

A second motive for using UDP would be that a simple protocol needs less processing capacity. For example, DNS uses UDP for handling DNS requests from clients. Think about a very large network that usually has two or three DNS servers. If TCP was used to handle DNS requests, the DNS servers would have to establish TCP connections with all clients for each DNS request. This would need high processing capacity from the DNS server and would be slower than UDP is.

Another example is TFTP, which is used for file transfer, usually by routers to load their operating systems from. TFTP is much simpler than FTP, and it is far easier to code in a router's bootloader than FTP is.

 Please note that TCP and UDP are at TCP/IP Layer 3. However, when referred as networking model protocols, TCP and UDP are said to be Layer 4 protocols, because they stand at Layer 4 in the OSI model, which is the reference model for networking.

The TCP/IP Internet Layer

The Internet layer in the TCP/IP model has the functions of OSI Layer 3—network. The purpose for the Internet layer is to select a path (preferably the best path) in the network for end-to-end delivery.

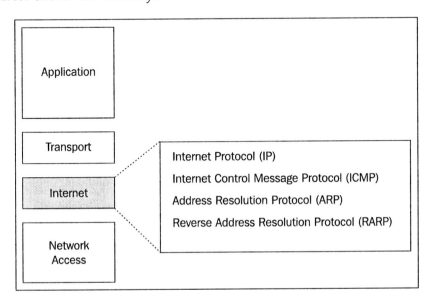

The main protocol found at the Internet layer is IP (Internet Protocol), which provides connectionless, best-effort delivery routing of packets. IP handles logical addressing, and its primary concern is to find the best path between the endpoints, without caring about the contents of the packet. IP does not perform error checking and error correction, and for this reason is called an unreliable protocol. However, these functions are handled by the transport layer (TCP) and/or the application layer.

IP encapsulates data from the transport layer in IP packets. IP packets don't use trailers when encapsulating TCP or UDP data. Let's see what an IP packet looks like:

0	4	8	16	19	24	31
VERS	HLEN	Service Type	Total Length			
Identification			Flags		Fragment Offset	
Time to Live		Protocol	Header Checksum			
Source IP Address						
Destination IP Address						
IP Options (if any)					Padding	
Data						
. . .						

The fields contained in the IP header signify:

- **Version**: Specifies the format of the IP packet header. The 4-bit version field contains the number **4** if it is an IPv4 packet, and **6** if it is an IPv6 packet. However, this field is not used to distinguish between IPv4 and IPv6 packets. The protocol type field present in the Layer 2 envelope is used for that.

- **IP header length (HLEN)**: Indicates the datagram header length in 32-bit words. This is the total length of all header information, and includes the two variable-length header fields.

- **Type of service (ToS)**: 8 bits that specify the level of importance that has been assigned by a particular upper-layer protocol.

- **Total length**: 16 bits that specify the length of the entire packet in bytes. This includes the data and header. To get the length of the data payload, subtract the HLEN from the total length.

- **Identification**: 16 bits that identify the current datagram. This is the sequence number.

- **Flags**: A 3-bit field in which the two low-order bits control fragmentation. One bit specifies if the packet can be fragmented, and the other indicates if the packet is the last fragment in a series of fragmented packets.

- **Fragment offset**: 13 bits that are used to help piece together datagram fragments. This field allows the next field to start on a 16-bit boundary.

- **Time to Live (TTL)**: A field that specifies the number of hops a packet may travel. This number is decreased by one as the packet travels through a router. When the counter reaches zero, the packet is discarded. This prevents packets from looping endlessly.

- **Protocol**: 8 bits that indicate which upper-layer protocol, such as TCP or UDP, receives incoming packets after the IP processes have been completed.

- **Header checksum**: 16 bits that help ensure IP header integrity.

- **Source address**: 32 bits that specify the IP address of the node from which the packet was sent.

- **Destination address**: 32 bits that specify the IP address of the node to which the data is sent.

- **Options**: Allows IP to support various options such as security. The length of this field varies.

- **Padding**: Extra zeros are added to this field to ensure that the IP header is always a multiple of 32 bits.

Data is not a part of the IP header. It contains upper-layer information (TCP or UDP packets) and has a variable length of up to 64 bytes.

If an IP packet needs to go out on an interface that has a MTU (Maximum Transmission Unit) size of less than the size of the IP packet, the Internet Protocol needs to fragment that packet into smaller packets matching the MTU of that interface. If the "Don't Fragment" bit in the **Flags** field of the IP packet is set to **1** and the packet is larger than the MTU of the interface, the packet will be dropped.

ICMP: Internet Control Message Protocol is a protocol that provides control and messaging capabilities to the Internet Protocol (IP). ICMP is a very important protocol because most of the troubleshooting of IP networks is done by using ICMP messages. The most important aspect of ICMP involves the types of messages that it returns and how to interpret them.

Message Returned	Description / Interpretation
Destination Unreachable	This tells the source host that there is a problem delivering a packet. The problem is that either the destination host is down or its internet connection is down.
Time Exceeded	It has taken too long for a packet to be delivered. The packet has been discarded.
Source Quench	The source is sending data faster than it can be forwarded. This message requests that the sender slow down.
Redirect	The router sending this message has received some packet for which another router, which is also directly connected to the sender, would have had a better route. The message tells the sender to use the better router.
Echo	This is used by the ping command to verify connectivity. The sender will issue an "echo request" message and will receive an "echo reply" from the other host if a path is found between the two.
Parameter Problem	This is used to identify a parameter that is incorrect.
Timestamp	This is used to measure roundtrip time to particular hosts.
Address Mask Request/Reply	This is used to inquire about and learn the correct subnet mask to be used.
Router Advertisement and Selection	This is used to allow hosts to dynamically learn the IP addresses of the routers attached to the subnet.

ARP: Address Resolution Protocol is used to determine MAC addresses for a given IP address.

RARP: Reverse Address Resolution Protocol is used to determine an IP address for a given MAC address.

The TCP/IP Network Access Layer

The network access layer in TCP/IP, also called host-to-network layer, allows IP packets to make physical links to the network media.

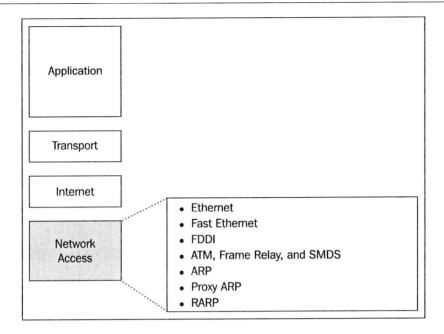

As you can notice, ARP and RARP are found at both the Internet and network access layers. Also, you can see that the TCP/IP network access layer contains LAN and WAN technologies that are found at the OSI physical and data link layers.

Network access layer protocols map IP addresses to hardware addresses and encapsulate IP packets into frames. Drivers for network interfaces, modems, and WAN interfaces also operate at the TCP/IP network access layer.

TCP/IP Protocol Suite Summary

To have an overview of the TCP/IP model, take a look at the following diagram:

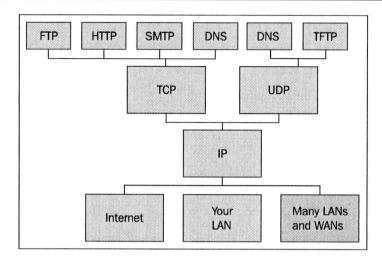

You have applications that need to reliably transfer data like FTP, HTTP, SMTP, and the zone transfers in DNS that use the TCP protocol, as well as applications that need to use a simpler protocol like TFTP and DNS requests using UDP.

Both TCP and UDP then use IP for end-to-end delivery (routing) and physical interfaces to send the data.

Let's see what the email example we gave with the OSI model looks like with TCP/IP. So, you are in a company LAN and you want to send an email:

Layer 4: You use an email client (like Outlook Express for example) that has SMTP and POP3 functions according to TCP/IP Layer 4 (application). You send the email, formatted in ASCII or HTML. The application then creates a data unit formatted in ASCII or HTML. The email client uses the operating system to open a session for inter-host communication. All those functions are performed at TCP/IP Layer 4 (application).

Layer 3: A TCP socket with the SMTP server is opened by the operating system. A virtual circuit is opened between your computer and the email server using TCP according to TCP/IP Layer 3 (transport).

Layer 2: Your computer searches for the IP address of the SMTP server according to the routing table of the operating system. If it is not found in the routing table, it will forward it to the company router for path determination. The IP protocol is at TCP/IP Layer 2 (Internet).

Layer 1: The IP Packet is transformed to an Ethernet frame. The Ethernet frame is converted to electrical signals that are sent throughout the CAT5 cable. Those functions are performed at TCP/IP Layer 1 (data link).

OSI versus TCP/IP

As it was mentioned before, the OSI model is more of a theoretical model and it is very useful in the learning process. On the other hand, the Internet was built on the TCP/IP model, and so, TCP/IP is the most popular due to its usage and its protocols.

TCP/IP Model		OSI Model	
Application	Protocols	7. Application	Application Layers
		6. Presentation	
		5. Session	
Transport		4. Transport	Data Flow Layers
Internet	Networks	3. Network	
Network Access		2. Data Link	
		1. Physical	

Some similarities between the two models are:

- Both models are layered models and have the benefits of layered communication models.
- Both models have application layers, even if they include different services.
- Both models have transport and network layers that have comparable functionality.
- Both models use packet-switching technologies instead of circuit-switching.

Some differences between the two models are:

- TCP/IP combines the three upper layers of the OSI model in a single layer, thus being more oriented towards the transmission protocols.
- The data link and physical layers from the OSI model are combined in a single layer in the TCP/IP model.

Nowadays, the OSI model doesn't have live applications as TCP/IP does, but it is the starting point of every networking model because of its benefits.

TCP/IP looks simpler because it has fewer layers than the OSI model. However, communication using TCP/IP matches all the layers in the OSI model.

Let's see an example in a TCP/IP network:

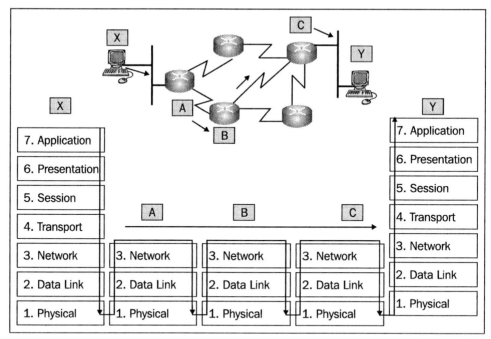

A packet originating from host X will get to host Y by traversing routers A, B, and C.

Let's say, for example, that host X is a web server replying to a request originally initiated from host Y.

The HTTPD server (X Layer 7) responds to the request by sending a HTML-formatted page (X Layer 6) to host Y. The server has many requests that it answers at that moment; so the operating system will send the data (the web page) on a session initiated when host Y made the request (X Layer 5). The data is then encapsulated in a TCP segment (X Layer 4). The TCP segment is then encapsulated in an IP packet with the source IP of host X and destination IP of host Y (X Layer 3). Host X looks for host Y in its routing table and doesn't find it; so host X should forward the IP packet to router A, which has an interface on the same subnet with the IP address of an Ethernet card on host X. The IP packet is sent to the Ethernet interface and converted to Ethernet frames (X Layer 2), which are then converted to electric currents and sent through the RJ45 socket of the Ethernet card (X Layer 1).

Router A receives some currents on the cable entering one of its Ethernet interfaces (A Layer 1) and converts these currents to Ethernet frames (A Layer 2). Ethernet frames are then converted to IP packets. The router looks at the destination IP address in the IP packet, and sees that it matches none of its IP addresses; so it knows that it should find a path to host Y. Looking at its routing table, it finds that the best path is advertised by router B and decides to send the IP packet to it (A Layer 3). If router A is connected to router B through a modem, it will convert the IP packet into PPP frames (A Layer 2), and the modem will convert the PPP frames into sounds (A Layer 1).

Routers B and C will do the same thing as router A, except that router C will find host Y directly connected to one of its interfaces (Y has an IP address in the same subnet as one if C's IP addresses), and so it will send the packet directly to Y.

Host Y receives some currents on the cable connected to its Ethernet interface (Y Layer 1), which it will convert to Ethernet frames (Y Layer 2) and then to IP packets (Y Layer 3). It will then look for the destination host in the IP packet that matches one of its IP addresses. The contents of the IP packet are then taken by the TCP protocol (Y Layer 4), which puts the received segments together. The operating system of host Y will handle the data received from TCP to send it on the session that requested this data (Y Layer 5). For example, if host Y has three web browsers opened, the operating system will give the data from TCP to the browser that requested it. The data received is HTML formatted (Y Layer 6); so it will be read by the web browser using the HTML standard. Finally, after all data is received, the web browser will display to the user the web page received (Y Layer 7).

IP Addressing, IP Subnetting, and IP Supernetting

The Internet Protocol (IP) found at OSI Layer 3 is responsible for end-to-end delivery of data between computers in an IP network (the Internet). To find a path between two computers in a large network such as the Internet, computers must be uniquely identified. To do that, the Internet Protocol defines IP Addresses, which are unique 32 bit sequences of one and zeros.

For example, 11000000101010000000000100000001 is a valid IP address. For the ease of use, IP addresses are represented in a form called the dotted decimal format. The 32 bits of the IP address are grouped in 4 bytes delimited by dots and transformed into the decimal form because it is simpler to use decimal number instead long sequences of ones and zeros. For example, the IP address shown here is:

Binary	11000000	10101000	00000001	00000001
Decimal	192	168	1	1
Dotted decimal form	192.168.1.1			

Please note that we will discuss IP version 4 (IPv4). There is also IP version 6 (IPv6), which is intended to replace IPv4 in the future. Because each byte has 8 bits, each byte in the IPv4 address can vary from minimum 0 to maximum 255. This gives us a maximum of 4,294,967,296 IP addresses. The IPv6 protocol extends the number of IP addresses by creating IP addresses 16 bytes long. Since IPv4 is most widely used protocol and it will still be for many years, we will refer to IPv4 addresses in this book.

One device connected to the Internet can have more than one IP address assigned to a single interface. In order for one interface to communicate in an IP network, it must have at least one IP address. Two hosts that have the same IP address in the same network will conflict with each other, and only one or none of them will work on the Internet.

Obtaining an IP Address

An IP address can be statically configured on a device, by assigning an interface a fixed IP address in the dotted decimal format. This way, that host has a static IP address, and will use it until the user changes it.

Servers, routers, and network printers should be assigned static IP addresses. Also, if a network is small, statically assigning IP addresses doesn't make it difficult for the administrator to keep track of computers.

A computer connecting to the Internet by using a modem usually receives an IP address from the access server that it dials into. The Point to Point Protocol (PPP) is used in such cases, and IPCP (Internet Protocol Control Protocol) is responsible for IP address negotiation and can also provide DNS and WINS addresses.

The most popular protocol for dynamic IP address configuration these days is DHCP (Dynamic Host Configuration Protocol). Configuring a DHCP involves a few simple tasks like specifying a range of IP addresses that can be assigned to clients, DNS servers, and the default gateway for the clients. This is very simple to set up when administering a large LAN, because you don't have to set up static IP addresses on each computer. The DHCP server does all the work.

The predecessor of DHCP is the Bootstrap Protocol (BOOTP). BOOTP, however, was not made to provide IP addresses dynamically; so, for every host in the network, an entry containing the IP address and MAC address of that host is added in the configuration file. You still have to provide computers static IP addresses, but, using BOOTP, instead of setting those up manually on the computers, you set them in a file on the server.

The Reverse Address Resolution Protocol (RARP) can be also used to assign IP addresses. RARP associates a known MAC address to an IP address. A RARP server must be configured with the MAC addresses of the stations using RARP and IP addresses for those stations.

 Please note that MAC addresses are Layer 2 addresses that make sense only in the local network. Routers will not forward these outside the LAN.

IP Classes

An IP address has two parts: one that specifies the network that it is in, and one that uniquely identifies it in that network. The first part is called the network part of the IP address, and the second part is called the host part of the IP address.

To identify the two parts of an IP address, devices use a network mask. Network masks have the same format as IP addresses (32 bits) and have the bits in the network part of the IP address set to 1 and the bits in the host part set to 0.

For example, if we find computers from 192.168.1.0 to 192.168.1.255 on a network, it means that all computers have the network part 192.168.1, and the rest will be the host part. The network mask in this case will be 11111111111111111111111100000000 in binary, and 255.255.255.0 in dotted decimal form.

To accommodate different sized networks, IP addresses are divided in groups called classes, identified by the leftmost bit or sequence of bits. The classes are called A, B, C, D, and E, and this process is called **classful addressing**.

Class	Leftmost bits	Start Address	End Address
A	0xxx	0.0.0.0	127.255.255.255
B	10xx	128.0.0.0	191.255.255.255
C	110x	192.0.0.0	223.255.255.255
D	1110	224.0.0.0	239.255.255.255
E	1111	240.0.0.0	255.255.255.255

Class A was designed to accommodate very large networks, with more than 16 million hosts. The first bit in a class A IP address must be 0; so the minimum value of the first byte is 0 and the maximum is 127. However, 0 and 127 are reserved; so valid class A IP addresses start with numbers between 1 and 126. The network 127.0.0.0 is used for loopback testing, and it is used by devices to communicate with themselves using TCP/IP. A loopback interface is a virtual interface that emulates the TCP/IP network access layer or OSI Layers 1 and 2.

Class B addresses accommodate medium to large networks. The first two bits in the first byte of the IP address must be 10; so the first byte is between 128 and 191 in decimal. A valid class B IP address starts with a number between 128 and 191.

Class C addresses accommodate small networks with a maximum of 254 hosts. The first three bits in the first byte of a class C IP address must be 110; so the first byte must have its decimal value between 192 and 223. A valid class C IP address starts with a number between 192 and 223.

Class D addresses were created to enable multicasting in IP networks. **Multicasting** is a process in which you define a number of IP addresses from a network that will receive a data stream from a streaming source. Multicasting is used mainly for broadcasting video and audio over an IP network. A streaming device such as a video server can multicast a data stream that will be received by some computers, not necessarily all (like broadcast) and not individually (like multicast). Class D IP addresses must have the first four bits in the first byte 1110; so a valid class D IP address may start with a value between 224 and 239 in the dotted decimal format.

Class E addresses have not been released for the public use in the Internet. They have been defined and are reserved by the Internet Engineering Task Force (IETF) for its own research. Class E IP addresses must have the first four bits 1111; so a class E IP address can start with a value between 240 and 255.

Reserved IP Addresses

An IP network has two IP addresses that can't be used by any device connected to the network. These are the first and the last IP addresses in that network.

- **The Network Address**: The first IP in the network. It identifies the network itself and is the most relevant IP address for devices outside the network. For example, for the 192.168.1.xxx class C, the first IP address is 192.168.1.0, which is the network address for that class C. Devices outside this network must first "find" the network 192.168.1.0, meaning that IP packets must be routed towards the 192.168.1.0 network, and only after that is the host part of the IP address relevant. The first IP address in the network always has all the bits in the host part of the IP address 0.

- **The Broadcast Address**: The last IP in the network. It is used to broadcast packets to all devices in that network. For example, for the 192.168.1.xxx class C, the broadcast address is 192.168.1.255. A host that sends an IP packet with the destination IP address 192.168.1.255 is sending a broadcast to the network; so all devices receive that IP packet. Broadcasts are used to make the network aware of some services on the broadcasting device or to request a service from a device without knowing its IP address. Broadcast addresses always have the bits in the host part 1.

Public and Private IP Addresses

The Internet is a public network, and therefore a device connected directly to the Internet has a public IP address. Those IP addresses must be administered by someone in such way that two devices connected to the public network don't use the same IP address or that two networks don't have the same network address. This job was done by InterNIC (Internet Network Information Center), which has been succeeded by IANA (Internet Assigned Numbers Authority). IANA makes sure to provide unique IP network addresses to Internet Service Providers (ISPs) and keeps track of their usage.

Both IPv4 and IPv6 addresses are assigned in a delegated manner. Users are assigned IP addresses by ISPs. ISPs obtain allocations of IP addresses from a local Internet registry (LIR) or national Internet registry (NIR), or from their appropriate regional Internet Registry (RIR):

- **AfriNIC** (African Network Information Centre): Africa Region, `http://www.afrinic.net`
- **APNIC** (Asia Pacific Network Information Centre): Asia/Pacific Region, `http://www.apnic.net`
- **ARIN** (American Registry for Internet Numbers): North America Region, `http://www.arin.net`
- **LACNIC** (Regional Latin-American and Caribbean IP Address Registry): Latin America and some Caribbean Islands, `http://www.lacnic.net`
- **RIPE NCC** (Réseaux IP Européens): Europe, the Middle East, and Central Asia, `http://www.ripe.net`

A local area network connected to the Internet through a router doesn't always need public IP addresses for all the devices in that network. The devices will use local IP addresses, and when going outside the network, the router can do Network Address Translation (NAT), a process that translates the local IP address of the device into one IP address that is actually routed on the Internet to that router. NAT will be explained in greater detail later in this book.

NAT must be done by using private IP addresses that are not routed anywhere on the Internet. If we didn't have private IP addresses when using NAT, devices behind NAT could access any public IP address, except those within the same subnet as the ones used for the network behind NAT.

For example, a network administrator decides to use for a local network the class C IP address 217.207.125.0, which the router will translate into its own IP address whenever a device will access the Internet. This way, everything works fine, except one thing: no devices in the local network will be able to access, for example, www.packtpub.com, which has the IP address 217.207.125.58, because they will search for that IP address in the local network. In fact, no device in the local network will be able to access any devices in the Internet that have public addresses assigned by IANA within the class C network 217.207.125.0.

To address this problem, IANA has reserved several IP classes that can't be used in the public network, meaning that they will not be routed in the Internet. These IP classes are described by RFC 1918 as private IP addresses that should be used in private networks. They are:

- 10.0.0.0 to 10.255.255.255 class A IP addresses
- 172.16.0.0 to 172.31.255.255 class B IP addresses
- 192.168.0.0 to 192.168.255.255 class C IP addresses

By using these private IP addresses for local networks (intranets) connected to the Internet, the number of public IP addresses needed for devices accessing the public network decreases a lot. If a company has two local networks connected to the Internet in geographically distanced locations without a separate connection between those two networks, it doesn't have to use public IP addresses for the devices in each network. Instead, both networks can communicate by creating a virtual connection over the Internet, thus creating a VPN (Virtual Private Network), which will be discussed later in this book.

Since private IP addresses are not routed by any ISP, a company with two geographically distanced locations that have internet connections from different providers can't access one network from the other directly. In this case, they can create a virtual connection between the two locations and add routes to the public IP addresses in those locations only on their routers. This creates the advantage that both private networks can access the Internet and each other, but other hosts from the Internet can't access them. This is called a VPN (Virtual Private Network).

IP Subnetting

Subnetting is the process in which you break a network into smaller pieces. This can be done for a variety of reasons. For example, a company having department LANs connected to different interfaces in a router or in different VLANs in a switch can't use the same network part and the same mask for devices in all departments because they would not communicate with each other.

Using different IP network addresses for devices in different LANs within the same company is not recommended because of the large number of IP addresses that might be wasted in the process.

Subnetting is done by choosing an appropriate mask, called a **subnet mask** or NetMask to define the number of hosts in that network. The network address of a subnet can be a valid IP address from the subnetted network that devices will no longer be able to use. By subnetting, you lose some usable IP addresses (two for each subnet).

The Subnet Mask

The subnet mask is a 32 bit sequence of zeros and ones, just like the IP address. The subnet mask has all the bits in the network part of the IP address set to 1, and all the bits in the host part of the IP address set to 0. The subnet mask works like the network mask (it's basically the same thing), except that the subnet mask borrows some bits from the host part to identify the subnet.

Let's say the IP address 192.168.1.130 is in the class C network 192.168.1.0-255; so, it has the mask 255.255.255.0. The company has two different departments, and they are both in the same network, but it is required that they should be on different networks. When assigning IP addresses, the network administrator used to assign IP addresses ascending, starting with 192.168.1.1 to department A and descending starting from 192.168.1.254 to department B, and so decided to divide this class C network into two subnets, each containing 128 addresses. Those subnets will be 192.168.1.0-127 and 192.168.1.128-255.

Initially, we would have:

11000000.10101000.00000001.10000010	192.168.1.130
11111111.11111111.11111111.00000000	255.255.255.0

In order to break the class C network in two subnets, we need to borrow one bit from the host part of the IP address for the network part, so we will have the subnet mask:

```
11111111.11111111.11111111.10000000=255.255.255.128
```

The first bit in the last byte of the subnet mask is called a "borrowed bit". The logic is pretty simple and it's based on Boolean logic. A device with IP capabilities does a logical AND between the subnet mask and the IP address to find out the network this IP address belongs to.

For example, for 192.168.1.130 with the subnet mask of 255.255.255.128, a device does the following operation:

```
11000000.10101000.00000001.10000010     AND
11111111.11111111.11111111.10000000      EQUALS
11000000.10101000.00000001.10000000   = 192.168.1.128
```

This way it finds out that the IP address 192.168.1.130 having the subnet mask 255.255.255.128 is in the subnet 192.168.1.128.

For 192.168.1.1 having the subnet mask 255.255.255.128, the logical AND will be:

```
11000000.10101000.00000001.00000010     AND
11111111.11111111.11111111.10000000      EQUALS
11000000.10101000.00000001.00000000   = 192.168.1.0
```

So the address is in the subnet 192.168.1.0.

By performing a logical AND of all IP addresses in the 192.168.1.0-255 class C with the subnet mask 255.255.255.128, the results can only be 192.168.1.0 or 192.168.1.128. This way, we divide the class C network in two.

Before dividing the class C network, we had the broadcast address 192.168.1.255. Now, the last IP address from every subnet becomes the broadcast address for that subnet. The first subnet will have 192.168.1.127 as a broadcast address, and the second will have 192.168.1.255 as a broadcast address. By dividing this class C in two, we lost two possible host IP addresses—192.168.1.127 (first subnet's broadcast) and 192.168.1.128 (second subnet's network).

Everything Divided in Two

If we need four subnets in that class C network, we do the same thing to the 255.255.255.128 subnet mask. This means we will borrow one bit from the host part of the IP address and add it to the subnet mask, and so we will be borrowing two bits from the class C mask:

```
11111111.11111111.11111111.11000000  =    255.255.255.192
```

By performing a logical AND with any IP address starting with 192.168.1, we will have four possible values for the last byte:

```
00000000  =     0
01000000  =     64
10000000  =     128
11000000  =     192
```

So we have created four subnets: 192.168.1.0, 192.168.1.64, 192.168.1.128, and 192.168.1.192.

We can divide those subnets in another two subnets, and so on.

The rule with the first and the last address of the subnet as being reserved still applies here; so, the first IP address in the subnet is the network address (to identify the subnet) and the last possible address in a subnet is used for broadcast. For the example we just saw, we have:

Usable IP addresses	Network Address	Broadcast Address
192.168.1.1 to 192.168.1.62	192.168.1.0	192.168.1.63
192.168.1.65 to 192.168.1.126	192.168.1.64	192.168.1.127
192.168.1.129 to 192.168.1.190	192.168.1.128	192.168.1.191
192.168.1.193 to 192.168.1.254	192.168.1.192	192.168.1.255

If the class C 192.168.1.0-255 network is subneted as in the example, the host having the IP address 192.168.1.71 and the subnet mask 255.255.255.192 will send the broadcasts to the IP address 192.168.1.127, and only the devices having IP addresses in the same subnet will receive those broadcasts.

For a subnet mask to be valid, it must have a host part, meaning it cannot borrow all the bits in the last byte. At least the last bit must be 0; so the last valid subnet mask is: 11111111.11111111.11111110 = 255.255.255.254. However, a subnet with the subnet mask 255.255.255.254 has only two possible IP addresses, and by using one for broadcast and one for network address, there are no usable IP addresses in that subnet!

For a class C network, the valid subnets are:

```
11111111.11111111.11111111.10000000 = 255.255.255.128
11111111.11111111.11111111.11000000 = 255.255.255.192
11111111.11111111.11111111.11100000 = 255.255.255.224
11111111.11111111.11111111.11110000 = 255.255.255.240
11111111.11111111.11111111.11111000 = 255.255.255.248
11111111.11111111.11111111.11111100 = 255.255.255.252
```

The smallest number of usable IP addresses in a subnet is two, given by the subnet mask 255.255.255.252, which has four IP addresses in that network (one for network, one for broadcast, and two usable IP addresses).

A Different Approach

Thinking in binary is not always that simple, but that is the process that devices using IP communication use to calculate things. A simple logic in decimal would be like this:

A class C network has 256 IP addresses (from 0 to 255). I need to create four subnets in that class C, and so, each subnet will have (256 / 4 =) 64 IP addresses (only 62 usable for devices). The last byte (in decimal) for the subnet mask will be (256 – 64 =) 192, and so, I get the subnet mask 255.255.255.192, and subnets 192.168.1.0, 192.168.1.64, 192.168.1.128, and 192.168.1.255.

The trick for subneting class C networks is to subtract the number of hosts that you want in that subnet from 256 and you get the subnet mask. Please remember that the number of hosts in that subnet must be a power of 2. For 16 addresses in a subnet, you will use the subnet mask 255.255.255.240 (256 – 16 = 240).

To subnet a class B network, if you don't want to use the binary logic, you can still use this procedure by working on the third byte of the subnet mask. For example, a full class B network has 256 * 256 IP addresses. If I want to use 16 * 256 IP addresses in a subnet, I will use for the third byte of the subnet mask the value 256 – 16 = 240, so I will have a subnet mask of 255.255.240.0.

IP Supernetting or CIDR

CIDR stands for "Classless Inter-Domain Routing". It is a new addressing scheme for the Internet, intended to replace the old classful (Class A, B, C) address scheme. CIDR allows a more efficient allocation of IP addresses and uses routing aggregation for minimizing the routing table entries, and is also called **supernetting**.

A recapitulation of classful IP addressing shows us the following:

Address Class	Number of Network Bits	Number of Hosts Bits	Decimal Address Range
Class A	8 bits	24 bits	1-126
Class B	16 bits	16 bits	128-191
Class C	24 bits	8 bits	192-223

- 126 class A networks with up to 16,777,214 hosts each
- 65,000 class B networks with up to 65,534 hosts each
- Over 2 million class C networks with 254 hosts each

If a provider needed 10,000 IP addresses for a project, then it would receive a class B network, and 55,534 IP addresses would not be used. If however, the provider had been assigned 40 class C networks for that 10,000 IP addresses, it could not match its needs (not all the IP addresses would be in the same network) and the routing tables of routers on the Internet would grow with 40 new routes.

CIDR is an addressing scheme that supports masks not only of 8, 16, or 24 bits as in classful routing but of arbitrary length. The CIDR notation is:

xxx.xxx.xxx.xxx/n

where xxx.xxx.xxx.xxx is the IP address of the network and "n" is the number of '1' bits in the mask. For example, the class C network 192.168.1.0 with the mask 255.255.255.0 is written in CIDR as 192.168.1.0/24.

The CIDR masks for classes A, B, and C respectively are /8, /16, and /24.

For the earlier example with the provider requesting 10,000 IP addresses, with CIDR the provider would be assigned a network having a mask of /18, meaning the subnet mask would be 255.255.192.0 with 16,382 usable IP addresses and only one prefix in all the routing tables in the world.

Nowadays, providers are assigned large blocks of addresses that their customers can buy instead of every customer having different IP classes. For example, the provider that was assigned a /18 network can give 64 of its customers a class C IP class (a /24). This is called aggregation, and it significantly reduces the size of the routing tables on the Internet.

Let's have a look at the CIDR prefixes down to /16 (class B):

CIDR Prefix	Subnet Mask	Number of IP Addresses
/32	255.255.255.255	/32 is used in CIDR to specify a single host or IP address. If the prefix is missing, /32 is assumed
/30	255.255.255.252	4
/29	255.255.255.248	8
/28	255.255.255.240	16
/27	255.255.255.224	32
/26	255.255.255.192	64
/25	255.255.255.128	128
/24	255.255.255.0	256
/23	255.255.254.0	512
/22	255.255.252.0	1024

CIDR Prefix	Subnet Mask	Number of IP Addresses
/21	255.255.248.0	2048
/20	255.255.240.0	4096
/19	255.255.224.0	8192
/18	255.255.192.0	16384
/17	255.255.128.0	32768
/16	255.255.0.0	65536

How the Internet Works

Large providers are assigned large IP blocks for them and for their customers. When accessing an IP address outside the provider's network, the data must travel through certain routers to get to the destination IP. The Internet Protocol is responsible for routing the packet to the destination.

Providers have some large, carrier-class routers located at the edge of their network where they interconnect to other providers. Every provider that has at least two interconnections with two different other providers must have an Autonomous System (AS) number to be identified in the exchange of routing information.

All the Internet is based on BGP (Border Gateway Protocol), which is a dynamic routing protocol used to exchange information between providers about the networks they have.

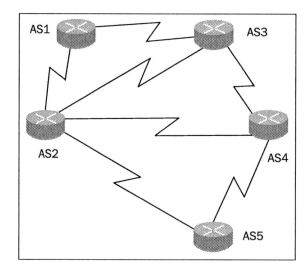

A provider having the Autonomous System number 1 (AS 1) has two interconnections: one with AS 2 and another with AS 3. Depending on the agreement between the providers, AS 1 can route to either of them only their own networks (Local Exchange or Local Peerings), or it can announce all the routes received from other peers (Full Exchange or Full BGP).

AS 3 can receive the routes to AS 1 networks directly from AS 1, and can also receive them from AS 2 and AS 4. The router finds the best path to AS 1 networks and sends packets to those networks on that path, and if that link fails, on the next best path. (e.g. AS 3 sends the packets to AS 1 directly on their interconnection. If that link fails, it will send them to AS 2, which will forward the packets to AS 1.)

Summary

In this chapter, we saw that:

- Layered models for networking communication allow interoperability, ease of use, and a faster growth of the Internet.

- The TCP/IP model is the most popular model, but the OSI model is used as a reference in network communication. For example, TCP, which is at TCP/IP Layer 3, is referred to as a Layer 4 protocol.

- TCP is a connection-oriented and reliable protocol that implements flow-control, while UDP is much simpler, and provides connectionless, unreliable delivery of packets.

- IP classes A, B, C, D, and E were defined.

- Subnetting is a process to divide an IP class into smaller pieces by borrowing bits from the host part of the IP address to the network part.

- CIDR or IP supernetting is an IP addressing scheme that allows a more efficient management of IP addresses and aggregation for reducing the size of routing tables.

- Providers exchange routing information using the Border Gateway Protocol, thus making the Internet work.

2
Security Threats

Creating firewalls may block some malicious attempts on your network, but this step is far from running an entirely secure network. As a network administrator or security consultant, to design a proper firewall for your network you need to know what you defend your network from. We cannot fully discuss this topic, even in 1000 pages, but we want to explain some principles that you should consider in running a safe network.

As hard as it may seem to protect your network from the outside world, the most dangerous threats always come from inside your network. Whether it is a user with malicious intentions or a hacker who broke into a less important part of your network, the inner threat is the worse.

Besides outside and inside attacks on your network, there is one more attack type, called MIM (Man In the Middle) attack. This involves two trusted parts of your network that transit one or many routers that you don't control.

For instance, we might have a network in one building and another network in a distant building and we ask our ISP to connect both of the networks, but due to the ISP's distribution network, the packets pass through one of its routers. If we don't make an encrypted VPN connection between the sites, the Man In the Middle (our provider) can easily sniff the traffic going from one network to the other, discovering passwords, servers' IP addresses, remote control ports, etc.

If the provider has bad intentions, he or she can assume trusted IP addresses from one of the sites to log in into protected servers on the other site after sniffing out users and passwords. Of course, a serious provider would never do that, but still you might consider that behind everything there are people that can have malicious intentions, or that there is a small chance that some hacker that wants your data may hack your provider's systems.

Well, we've now established that a security threat may come from inside, outside, or from transit points of the network. This means you are exposed to everywhere, and so a good practice would be to close some doors. Closing doors means eliminating transit points (create encrypted VPNs), identifying weak parts of your network, and treating them as outside network. If you can do this with your network, you will have only outside attacks to care about.

Even if the Internet runs on the TCP/IP protocol suite, we explained in Chapter 1 that the reference model for networking is the OSI layered model. Network security should be addressed at each OSI layer for different vulnerabilities and types of attacks. You will find out that every layer has its own security challenges.

Layer 1 Security Threats

OSI Layer 1 defines physical links. There are quite a few types of attacks that can be found at Layer 1, including:

- Cable / Fiber cuts
- High voltage applied on copper lines
- Wireless links jamming
- Electromagnetic field sources brought near copper cables, etc.

Securing the physical layer is beyond the scope of this book and must be done by field or transmission engineers.

However, it is important for network administrators to know how the physical links are built, and to have backup routes for the most important ones as well as for the most exposed ones.

Layer 2 Security Threats

Layer 2 of the OSI model defines the data link layer. The data link layer can be a very weak link in terms of security, and the worst thing is that it can affect the upper layers by causing service disruptions or security breaches.

At Layer 2 we can find ATM, frame relay, PPP, Ethernet, Wireless LAN (802.11a/b/g), etc. Since the most popular Layer 2 protocol is Ethernet, we will discuss its security in more detail.

MAC Attacks

MAC addresses used in Ethernet, 802.11x Wireless networks, Bluetooth, FDDI, Fiber Channel, and Token Ring are unique identifiers attached to the networking equipment. MAC addresses are 48 bits long, should be unique, and are usually shown in hexadecimal format (e.g. "00-13-F7-18-A1-AC"). The first 24-bit part of a MAC address is the manufacturer code assigned by IEEE, and the second 24 bits are assigned by the manufacturer to this interface.

By convention, the MAC address FF-FF-FF-FF-FF-FF is used for broadcast.

A security issue found at Layer 2 is **CAM table overflow**, which affects switches in the network. CAM is a physical part of a switch; it stands for Content Addressable Memory, and it stores information about MAC addresses available on each physical port and their associated VLAN parameters.

Physically, a CAM is a normal memory limited in size. In 1999, Ian Vitek created a tool called macof, later integrated in dsniff, which floods switches with invalid source MAC addresses (up to 155,000/minute). This tool quickly fills up the CAM table of the switch to which the computer running the tool is connected, and also the adjacent switches. The result of this attack is an abnormal behavior of the switch by flooding incoming traffic out on all ports (like a simple old Hub), thus making possible a Man-In-the-Middle (MIM) attack — the attacker can start sniffing network traffic.

Unfortunately, Linux can't protect you against this type of attack. Only managed switches with port security options can do that. However, the attacker can only sniff packets within his or her VLAN; so it is important to determine where these attacks may come from, and make sure that no important traffic passes through that VLAN.

Another security issue with this subject is **MAC address spoofing**, which is used by attackers to replace a CAM table entry of a known MAC address on another port. This will cause the switch to send the traffic destined for the port of the attacked computer to the port at which the attacker is connected. This attack causes service disruption and can be used as an MIM attack with the attacker sniffing the packets destined to the attacked computer.

MAC address spoofing attacks can be blocked only in the switches, if the switches have facilities for that.

DHCP Attacks

DHCP (Dynamic Host Configuration Protocol) described by RFC 2131 (http://www.ietf.org/rfc/rfc2131.txt) is a protocol used by devices in a network to obtain the network configuration settings like IP Address, subnet mask, default router, and DNS servers' IP addresses from a server in the network running DHCP Server software.

DHCP servers are configured to assign clients (devices in the network) IP addresses from defined ranges. The basic DHCP operation is described in the following figure:

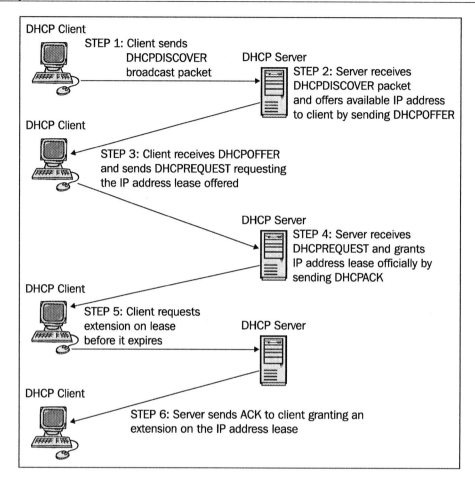

The DHCP server gives the IP address to a requesting device on a lease basis, meaning that the IP address is "leased" for a limited amount of time. During this time, the DHCP server will not lease that IP address to any other clients. Before the lease time expires, the DHCP client must request an extension of the lease time from the DHCP server. The DHCP lease time is configurable from 120 seconds to whatever the administrator chooses.

DHCP starvation attack consists of consuming the IP address space allocated by a DHCP server. This can easily be accomplished by an attacker by broadcasting a large number of DHCP requests using spoofed MAC addresses. The DHCP server will lease its IP addresses one by one to the attacker until it runs out of available IPs for new, normal clients. This leads to Denial of Service for those clients in the network requesting IP addresses from the DHCP server.

At this point, the attacker can set up a **rogue DHCP server** serving clients with false details, for example giving them its own IP address as default router. This will result in all the traffic passing through the attacker's computer, thus making it really easy for him or her to sniff all the network traffic from the clients.

The rogue DHCP server can be set up even without performing the DHCP starvation attack, as clients accept the first DHCPOFFER they receive.

Both these attacks can be easily accomplished using gobbler, a simple tool that can be found on the Internet. Unfortunately, only switches can protect users against these attacks. DHCP starvation attack can be prevented by using port security features that don't allow more than X MAC addresses on one port (the same method of prevention as for CAM attacks).

However, the rogue DHCP server attack is more difficult to prevent, but hopefully it will be in the future with the implementation of "Authentication for DHCP Messages" described by RFC 3118. For now some smart and expensive switches have a "DHCP snooping" function, which filters DHCP messages from non-trusted hosts.

ARP Attacks

ARP stands for **Address Resolution Protocol**, and it's the protocol used to map IP addresses into MAC addresses.

Within the same broadcast domain (network segment), computers exchange ARP messages to find each other's MAC address based on the IP address they have. ARP is essential to TCP/IP communications, and is a very simple protocol with almost zero security features.

ARP spoofing is a simple way to conduct ARP attacks by sending broadcasts with spoofed MAC or IP addresses causing either Denial-of-Service or Man-In-the-Middle attacks.

Adding IP/MAC pairs manually in the ARP tables of the computers in the network can solve some of the ARP spoofing attack scenarios, but it's far from being a solution to this type of attack.

The very popular dsniff package (`http://www.monkey.org/~dugsong/dsniff/`) contains ARP spoofing tools among other network attack/audit tools.

STP and VLAN-Related Attacks

Virtual LANs (VLANs) are logically independent networks physically connected in a larger network. The idea behind VLANs is to create multiple broadcast domains within a single network and to separate different traffic types from each other.

Multiple VLANS can exist in a single switch, and VLAN information can be carried between switches using trunks. Trunks are interconnections between switches that carry data between them using tags to identify to which VLAN the data belongs to. The dominant tagging protocol is IEEE 802.1Q.

Creating VLANS is a very good security measure at Layer 2 because of separation of different types of traffic. However, misconfigured switches can allow a certain type of attack called **VLAN hopping**.

VLAN hopping is an attack in which an attacker tries to send data to hosts that belong to other VLANs by tagging the data with a different VLAN ID than the one it belongs to. As 802.1Q implementations are available for Linux and other OSes, and some vendors' (e.g. Cisco) switches have the default mode for a port as trunking, an attacker can easily create a trunk link between the switch and itself, thus being able to communicate to hosts in all VLANs configured on that switch.

Another type of attack that probably everyone knows about is creating **network loops**. A network loop appears when two ports belonging to the same VLAN have a link to each other, or when there are two or more paths between two switches. Malicious users can physically create network loops, and the easiest way to do that is connecting a cross-connect cable to two ports that belong to the same switch and the same VLAN (the same broadcast domain). When a loop appears in a network, broadcasts travel infinitely within that VLAN, flooding every port that belongs to that VLAN for every switch in the network, thus bringing the network down.

STP **Spanning Tree Protocol** (IEEE 802.1D) was designed to prevent network loops. STP works by deactivating links that can form a network loop, raising the possibility of deploying redundant links in the network that, without STP, would create network loops.

STP manipulation is a type of threat in which an attacker broadcasts STP configuration or topology change BPDUs (Bridge Protocol Data Units), forcing STP recalculations and expecting that the attacker becomes the root bridge. As root bridge, the attacker can sniff Ethernet frames belonging to other VLANs. 802.1D STP takes about 30 to 45 seconds to re-elect a root bridge if the old root bridge fails, thus resulting in a DoS attack.

Layer 3 Security Threats

At the network layer of OSI model, we find the Internet Protocol (IP) with ICMP being a part of the Internet Protocol. Layer 3 is vulnerable to multiple DoS attacks and privacy disclosure attacks.

Packet Sniffing

We discussed packet sniffing earlier in this chapter and how attackers in a switched network can sniff packets that don't belong to them. If the network is not switched (e.g. a Hub is used) packet sniffing becomes a lot easier.

Sniffing packets means capturing IP traffic using tools like dsniff, tcpdump, ethereal, etc. Because data from upper layers is encapsulated into IP packets, all the information from those layers can be disclosed when analyzing (decapsulating) IP packets.

Protocols like POP3, SMTP, SNMP, etc., transmit passwords in clear text, and so, decoding captured IP packets may result in disclosing such sensitive data. Packet sniffers like dsniff have very nice tools to decode those packets and store this information in a file in clear text.

Securing Layer 2 with managed switches can drastically reduce the success of packet sniffers in the network. Also, creating encrypted VPNs using IPSec or other encryption means will decrease the possibility of the data being sniffed almost to zero.

IP Spoofing

An attacker might spoof a trusted IP address when communicating to a host in order to gain unauthorized access on that host. There are a variety of tools that can be found on the Internet to do IP spoofing.

Using IP spoofing, attackers can also initiate Denial of Service by sending data with the source IP spoofed to the attacked IP address. The receiver then sends back replies that can contain large amounts of data to the attacked IP address resulting in a flood attack to that address. Sending data using the spoofed IP address to many hosts will result in a **Distributed Denial-of-Service** attack.

To protect against IP spoofing, the Linux kernel has an option named "rp_filter", which can be modified at run time using:

```
root@router:~# echo 0 > /proc/sys/net/ipv4/conf/all/rp_filter
```

This command disables rp_filter on all interfaces. To disable on one interface, eth0 for example, we can use:

```
root@router:~# echo 0 > /proc/sys/net/ipv4/conf/eth0/rp_filter
```

Setting rp_filter to:

- 1 enables IP spoofing protection
- 0 disables IP spoofing protection

IP packets coming from one host enter the Linux box on one interface. The replies to those IP packets must be on the same interface if `rp_filter` is set to `0`.

Routing Protocols Attacks

Misconfigured dynamic routing protocols such as RIP, BGP, and OSPF may allow attackers to inject routes into the routing tables of the machines running instances of those protocols. This may allow attackers to conduct Denial-of-Service attacks by injecting wrong routes or IP sniffing by configuring its computer to act like a router from the network.

We will discuss later in this book how to set up, configure, and secure BGP on Linux.

ICMP Attacks

ICMP is a very important part of the IP protocol enabling hosts and routers to exchange control messages.

Using spoofed IP addresses, an attacker might disrupt communications between two hosts by sending "Time Exceeded" or "Destination Unreachable" messages to both hosts, resulting in a DoS attack.

By sending ICMP "redirect" messages, an attacker might force a router to forward packets destined to one host to the attacker's IP address.

With Linux, we can force the kernel not to accept redirect messages for one or all interfaces:

```
root@router:~# echo 0 > /proc/sys/net/ipv4/conf/eth0/
accept_redirects
```

ICMP Flooding is one of the easiest ways to attack a host. `ping` is one of the most commonly used tools to verify connectivity, but it can also be used as a DoS attack tool.

For example, using Linux, one can flood a host using `ping -f`. The following command floods the host 10.10.10.12 with 1000 packets:

```
root@router:~# ping -f 10.10.10.12 -c 1000
PING 10.10.10.12 (10.10.10.12) 56(84) bytes of data.
```

This type of attack can be stopped by limiting the number of ICMP `echo-request` messages with iptables:

```
root@router:~# iptables -A FORWARD -p icmp --icmp-type
echo-request -m limit --limit 10/s -j ACCEPT
```

```
root@router:~# iptables -A FORWARD -p icmp --icmp-type
echo-request -j DROP
```

 We will learn in the following chapters more on the iptables syntax. For now, we are just presenting the ways to stop some DoS attacks using iptables. You can always come back to these commands after learning more on the iptables syntax from the next chapters.

Old ICMP implementations had some other vulnerabilities; for example, the **Ping of Death**. The ping of death crashed machines by sending ICMP "echo request" messages in IP packets larger than the maximum legal length of 65535 octets, causing a buffer overflow to crash the victim's device (computer, printer, etc.). A Linux patch for the ping of death was out in 2 hours, 35 minutes, and 10 seconds, and shortly after, patches for other OSes were available from vendors.

However, the ping of death problem generated a trend of filtering ICMP packets, which, as you will see later in this book, is not a good practice.

Teardrop Attacks

Teardrop, targa, NewTear, Nestea Bonk, Boink, TearDrop2, Syndrop, and many others are all tools to crash machines that have a vulnerability in the IP stack.

Those tools exploit a fragmentation bug in the IP stack implementation of some old Linux kernels (2.0), Windows NT, and Windows 95. Teardrop sent fragmented IP packets that could not be assembled properly by the attacked machine, by manipulating the offset values of the packets. The effect was a kernel panic in Linux or a blue screen in Windows. A reboot solved the problem until the next attack.

Layer 4 Security Threats

TCP and UDP are the transport protocols found at OSI Layer 4—transport. We've learned about them in more detail in Chapter 1, with TCP being more complex than UDP because it's a connection-oriented protocol that has a flow-control mechanism (windowing), while UDP is simple and connectionless, and with no flow-control implemented in the protocol.

TCP Attacks

Being a connection-oriented protocol, a TCP connection is established using a three-way handshake as described in Chapter 1. An attacker can exploit this property of the protocol by sending a very large number of SYN packets without regarding the SYNACK the attacked host sends back. This type of attack is called **TCP SYN attack** or **SYN flooding**.

SYN flooding can be successful as the attacked computer keeps track of partially opened connections for minimum 75 seconds in a "listen queue". The queue is limited on various TCP implementations; therefore a SYN flood can fill it up, causing the machine to reboot or to crash.

In Linux, the TCP listen queue differs from one kernel version to another. For 2.2 and older kernels, the default listen queue is 1024 for TCP connections in SYN_RECV state; for 2.0 kernels, there was a backlog keeping track of opened and partially opened TCP connections. The listen queue can be seen and modified using `sysctl` parameter `tcp_max_syn_backlog`:

```
root@router:~# cat /proc/sys/net/ipv4/tcp_max_syn_backlog
1024
root@router:~# echo 2048 > /proc/sys/net/ipv4/tcp_max_syn_backlog
```

The first command shows the backlog size of 1024, and the second command sets it to 2048.

The default Linux Kernel behavior is to discard new SYN packets if the queue is full. This can be modified by another `sysctl` parameter `tcp_syncookies`, which can be used only if the Linux kernel is compiled with syncookies support (`CONFIG_SYN_COOKIES="Y"`).

```
root@router:~# echo 1 > /proc/sys/net/ipv4/tcp_syncookies
```

This command sets `tcp_syncookies` to 1 and the Linux kernel will ignore the `tcp_max_syn_backlog` size. However, the use of `tcp_syncookies` can have unwanted side-effects. For example, a web server that partially handles 1024 TCP connections normally will discard a new SYN packet when overloaded. This may lead new clients to another, less loaded web server that can process their request faster. With syncookies enabled, new clients may wait for a very long time for a reply from the overloaded server.

We can use iptables to protect against SYN flooding by limiting the number of SYN packets in a defined amount of time, as we did for ICMP `echo-requests`:

```
root@router:~# iptables -A INPUT -p tcp --syn  -m limit --limit
10/s -j ACCEPT
root@router:~# iptables -A INPUT -p tcp --syn  -j DROP
```

Another TCP-related type of attack is the **Land attack**. The Land attack is very simple and was very devastating at the same time, as not only a large number of Unix versions and all Windows versions were affected, but also Cisco routers. The Land attack is conducted using a small program written in C (land.c) that sends a SYN packet to a host on an opened TCP port with the source IP address spoofed to the destination IP address (e.g. 192.168.1.1 port 139 to 192.168.1.1 port 139).

Another popular TCP-related attack is a Man-In-the-Middle attack called **TCP Connection Hijacking**. An attacker standing in the path of two computers communicating via TCP can seize control of the TCP connection during the three-way handshake, or afterwards, when the connection is in established, by creating a **desynchronized state**, which means that the TCP connection is established, no data is sent, and the SEQ number of one host differs from the ACK number of the other host and the other way around (A_SEQ <> B_ACK and B_SEQ <> A_ACK). During a desynchronized state, the hosts discard packets from one another (DoS), but the attacker can create a sequence of correct numbers, injecting commands into the communication.

UDP Attacks

Since UDP is a simple protocol with no connection establishment procedures, the only way UDP can be affected is by sending a large number of UDP packets to random ports at the attacked machine. This type of attack is called **UDP flooding**. The attacked machine will try to determine the application that the packet is destined for. If no application listens on that UDP port, the packet will be discarded. By flooding the victim with these types of packets, the victim computer might overload, resulting in system a crash.

TCP and UDP Port Scan Attacks

Port scanning is probably the first thing an attacker does when trying to hack a victim. Using a tool from a variety of programs found on the Internet (e.g. Nmap), an attacker can discover which TCP and UDP ports a host has opened in order to identify running services for further exploitation of vulnerabilities.

Layer 5, 6, and 7 Security Threats

We have grouped Layers 5, 6, and 7 of the OSI model corresponding to the TCP/IP Layer 4 — application. There are a lot of applications that are known from the past to be vulnerable to exploits. Most of these applications had problems at all of the three upper layers of the OSI model. We will present a few of these applications, known to contain a large number of vulnerabilities, and that are very popular.

BIND Domain Name System (DNS)

BIND (Berkley Internet Name Domain) is the most used DNS server on the Internet. Nowadays, every Linux distribution has a BIND package for DNS services.

The problem with BIND and any DNS server is that in order to be able to translate names into IP addresses it has to communicate with a whole lot of other DNS servers, and so, filtering DNS packets is not possible.

DNS services are vital for internet connection; so in order to disrupt services to victims, attackers have a great interest in bringing down DNS servers. Although BIND is well known for its security issues, there are many vulnerable BIND servers out there, and so you have to be really careful running BIND. A DNS server survey at `http://mydns.bboy.net/survey` shows the popularity of BIND, and that there are still quite a lot of vulnerable versions out there.

Here is some of my advice on what would provide a more secure BIND:

- Don't use the BIND package that comes with your distribution of Linux; download the latest from BIND website (`http://www.isc.org`).
- Place BIND in a chroot jail. This is the best thing to do to protect against remotely exploitable vulnerabilities in BIND that allow attackers to get a shell on the server running BIND. If you don't chroot your version of BIND and such a vulnerability is discovered, your Linux server and all data on it may be compromised before you have the time to upgrade.
- Always apply patches and upgrade BIND whenever a bug is discovered or a new version comes out.
- Secure zone transfers between primary and secondary DNS servers using DNS Transaction Signatures (TSIG).
- Disable recursion and glue fetching to defend against DNS cache poisoning.

Although BIND is more popular and easier to configure, consider using TinyDNS, as it has proven to be more secure over the years.

Apache Web Server

The most popular web server is Apache, found at `http://www.apache.org`, which had some security issues in the past, whether they were Apache bugs or add-on modules' vulnerabilities. Here is some of my advice on what would provide a more secure Apache server:

- Patch your server and try to keep it as up to date as possible.
- Remove all sample scripts of add-on modules (`mod_php`, `mod_cgi`, `mod_perl`, etc.).

- If running PHP, CGI, and other script languages, consider using suEXEC, a wrapper program called by Apache to allow it to call scripts from a different user ID than the one it uses for Apache.

- Don't allow uploads of any scripts into your web server by untrusted parties.

- Read about all vulnerabilities of any open-source projects that you install, such as PHPBB forums, for example.

- Don't run the web server as root. Create a user with minimal rights to run the web server.

- Modify the response token for your web server. It's harder for an attacker to bring it down when he or she doesn't know what web server you are running.

Version Control Systems

Version control systems provide tools for software developers to concurrently work on the same set of files and manage different versions of source code.

In Linux systems, the most popular version control system is CVS (Concurrent Versions System), used by many open-source software projects that allow anonymous access to their CVS repositories via the pserver protocol that runs on TCP port 2401 by default. A CVS server with remote access has the following vulnerabilities:

- A heap-based buffer overflow that can be triggered by specially crafted entry lines. Exploit code for CVS servers was published on security lists, and allows attackers to execute arbitrary code on the CVS server.

- There are some vulnerabilities in the implementation of other commands and functions that may be exploited by an authenticated user to cause Denial of Service or execute arbitrary code on the CVS server. Some of these may be exploited by anonymous users.

To protect against these vulnerabilities, consider the following steps:

- Update CVS to the latest stable release. CVS can be found at `http://www.cvshome.org`.

- Run the CVS server in a chroot jail.

- Configure CVS to use the SSH protocol instead of the pserver protocol (which sends the passwords in plaintext).

- If you don't allow anonymous access to your CVS server, try filtering port 2401 to allow only trusted hosts to connect to it.

- Host the CVS server for anonymous read-only access on a stand-alone system.

- Run the published exploits against your CVS servers.

Another version control system that gained popularity on Linux is subversion. A subversion repository can be remotely accessed via the svn protocol. The svn server runs on the TCP port 3690 by default and contains the following vulnerabilities:

- A heap-based buffer overflow that can be exploited by unauthenticated attackers to execute arbitrary code on the subversion server.

- A stack-based buffer overflow that can be triggered by a specially crafted `get-date-rev` svn command. In this way too an unauthenticated attacker can execute arbitrary code. For this vulnerability, multiple exploits were published on security lists.

To protect your subversion server against those vulnerabilities, consider the following steps:

1. Update your subversion software to the latest stable version from `http://subversion.tigris.org/`.

2. Configure subversion to use webDAV instead of the svn protocol.

3. If you don't allow anonymous access to your subversion server, try filtering the TCP port 3690 to allow only trusted hosts.

4. Run the published exploits against your subversion server.

5. Host the subversion server for anonymous read-only access on a stand-alone system.

Mail Transport Agents (MTA)

Email is one of the most popular services on the Internet and for a company it is a vital service in almost every department. SMTP (Send Mail Transport Protocol) is one of the oldest protocols on the Internet and it is used by MTAs to send email from the sender to the recipients. SMTP listens on the TCP port 25 by default, and if it is used to receive email from any email address on the Internet, it must not be filtered.

The most popular MTA for Linux is Sendmail, which had a lot of security issues including buffer overruns that could be remotely exploited to compromise the MTA server. Popular alternatives to Sendmail are Postfix, Qmail, Exim, and Courier-MTA.

MTAs' most popular problems are the following:

- Vulnerabilities such as buffer overruns, heap overflows, etc., which can be used by remote or local attackers to compromise the server running the MTA.

- Missconfiguration of the MTA allowing everyone to use it for sending mail. This is called open relay. Missconfigured MTAs as open relays immediately fall in the hands of spammers, which may cause big damages to your company by having your email server in one of the many email servers blacklists, plus the fact that all the spam consumes your bandwidth. You can check your mail server to see if it is an open relay at `http://www.abuse.net/relay.html`, which runs a set of tests to see if there's any way for a spammer to use your email server to send mail to other people.

- User-account database disclosure vulnerabilities.

Simple Network Management Protocol (SNMP)

These days, most network devices use SNMP for remote monitoring and configuration. SNMP is a simple protocol used usually to create monitoring software that can retrieve information such as network traffic, CPU load, disk load, etc., and also to modify configuration of devices such as wireless equipment, broadband routers, etc.

Most SNMP implementations on those kinds of network devices use version 1 or version 2, which have a very weak authentication method. SNMP version 1 contains a set of bugs in the way SNMP traps and requests messages are handled and decoded that can be exploited in many ways, from denial of service to rewriting the configuration.

SNMP versions 1 and 2 use community strings for authentication. These are sent on UDP port 161 unencrypted; so it is very easy for a man in the middle to sniff the community strings. When you set up SNMP on a device (including a Linux box), you must set up two community strings: one that has read-only access and the default is "public", and one that has read-write access and the default is "private". If you don't change the communities to SNMP-enabled devices, it is very easy in the absence of a firewall to view their configuration and change it.

This is very dangerous for the devices and the network; so here's what you should try to do:

- Try not to use SNMP, unless you have to.
- Whenever possible, use SNMP version 3, which has user mode authentication and can do encryption.
- In any case, if you use SNMP, change the default communities.
- Create a proper firewall on the device or on a device in front of it, allowing only trusted hosts to connect using SNMP.

For instance, a Cisco router running SNMP with the community string "public" reveals its entire running configuration, including usernames and passwords as well as the enable secret and password. If the router has the SNMP community "private" for write access, you can modify absolutely everything in the configuration. More than that, most Cisco routers have SNMP enabled by default with the default communities and without filters.

Open Secure Sockets Layer (OpenSSL)

The OpenSSL library is the most popular choice for applications that need cryptographic support in network communications. Such applications are Apache (HTTP secure connections), Sendmail, OpenLDAP, OpenSSH, etc.

Vulnerabilities in one version of the OpenSSL libraries affect all applications that use them and can be exploited through those. Depending on the functions used by the application, vulnerabilities in OpenSSL can be exploited through the application to execute arbitrary code on the server or even to get root privileges.

OpenSSL had some vulnerabilities in the past that did a lot of damage to servers running applications compiled with OpenSSL support, especially Apache, Sendmail and OpenSSH. In the Sendmail case, an exploit that gave the attacker root privileges was published on security mailing lists.

To stay protected, consider the following:

- Identify the OpenSSL version on each of the servers that has the libraries installed. Check to see if you have the latest version and if your version of OpenSSL has remotely exploitable vulnerabilities.

- Upgrade your OpenSSL library to the latest version from the OpenSSL website at `http://www.openssl.org`.

- Identify applications that use the OpenSSL library, and if they require recompilation because of the upgrade, recompile them to use the new libraries.

If applications using OpenSSL don't require connections from everyone, create a proper firewall to allow connections only from trusted sites.

Protect Running Services—General Discussion

A network administrator's job is to keep the network running and safe. There are services that don't depend on him or her; for example a web server could be administered by a webmaster. The steps outlined here would make you feel more secure. We will follow this up by actually testing out these steps on a Linux box so that you get a better idea.

1. Identify services that run on every system. Most importantly, identify open ports and the services that opened them.

2. Verify every running service's current version. Update to the latest software version. Search for vulnerabilities for the service at its homepage and at `http://nvd.nist.gov/`.

3. Verify the configurations and, when you can, create software-based access lists to allow only trusted hosts to use that service. Try changing default usernames and passwords every time. If you can run the software in a chroot jail, do it.

4. If the service doesn't require access from everywhere, create a firewall to limit the access only to trusted hosts.

5. Audit your network! Try to hack into your network. Connect to your network as an outsider and test all running services against known exploits. Search for hacker tools and use them against your own network to see what happens.

6. Create logs for authentication requests. Also try to run a network intrusion detection system such as Snort, available at `http://www.snort.org`, which produces really good log files.

Not all the steps are required for every service that runs in your network; for example, there are some services for which you allow connections only from localhost and that's it.

Let's take a look at one of the Linux boxes in my network. For security reasons, I will interchange the IP addresses from the real world with reserved IP addresses.

1. First I will identify the opened TCP ports on the server:

```
root@router:~# netstat -an
Active Internet connections (servers and established)
Proto Recv-Q Send-Q Local Address      Foreign Address     State
tcp       0      0 0.0.0.0:2601        0.0.0.0:*           LISTEN
tcp       0      0 0.0.0.0:2605        0.0.0.0:*           LISTEN
tcp       0      0 0.0.0.0:179         0.0.0.0:*           LISTEN
```

So, we have TCP ports 179, 2601, and 2605 listening. For me, those are very well-known ports, but if I forget them, we need to see what services opened those ports:

```
root@router:~# fuser -n tcp 2601 2605 179
2601/tcp:              1520
2605/tcp:              1521
179/tcp:               1521
root@router:~# ps ax | grep -E "(1520|1521)"
```

```
1520 ?          Ss      1:03 /usr/local/sbin/zebra
1521 ?          Ss      1:00 /usr/local/sbin/bgpd
```

This means that the TCP port 2601 was opened by the process zebra, and the TCP ports 179 and 2605 were opened by the process bgpd.

> Zebra is Linux routing software that knows routing protocols such as BGP, OSPF, RIPv1, and RIPv2. In this case, I use zebra for BGP connections. The bgpd process is for making BGP connections, and the zebra process is responsible for adding routes received from neighbors in the Linux kernel.

2. Let's identify the versions:

```
root@router:~# zebra -v
zebra version 0.95 ()
Copyright 1996-2001, Kunihiro Ishiguro
root@router:~# bgpd -v
bgpd version 0.95 ()
Copyright 1996-2001, Kunihiro Ishiguro
```

The latest vulnerabilities for Zebra were in version 0.93b; so no known vulnerabilities here.

3. The next step is to configure the software. For Zebra, port 2601 is for its command line interface, which is very similar to a Cisco router. The same with the BGP for port 2605.

The /etc/services file reveals (on some Linux distributions) the CLI ports used by the Zebra protocols:

```
zebrasrv        2600/tcp                 # zebra service
zebra           2601/tcp                 # zebra vty
ripd            2602/tcp                 # ripd vty (zebra)
ripngd          2603/tcp                 # ripngd vty (zebra)
ospfd           2604/tcp                 # ospfd vty (zebra)
bgpd            2605/tcp                 # bgpd vty (zebra)
ospf6d          2606/tcp                 # ospf6d vty (zebra)
ospfapi         2607/tcp                 # OSPF-API
isisd           2608/tcp                 # ISISd vty (zebra)
```

For zebra and bgpd, we create software-based access lists to allow VTY access only from localhost. This is done using the CLI, as follows:

```
root@router:~# telnet 127.0.0.1 2601
```

```
Trying 127.0.0.1...
Connected to 127.0.0.1.
Escape character is '^]'.

Hello, this is zebra (version 0.95).
Copyright 1996-2004 Kunihiro Ishiguro.
User Access Verification

Password:
Router> ena
Password:
Router# conf t
Router(config)# access-list 1 permit host 127.0.0.1
Router(config)# access-list 1 deny any
Router(config)# line vty
Router(config-line)# access-class 1
Router(config-line)# exit
Router(config)# exit
Router# write memory
Configuration saved to /usr/local/etc/zebra.conf
Router# exit
Connection closed by foreign host.
```

This was for `zebra`; now we will do the same thing for `bgpd`:

```
root@router:~# telnet 127.0.0.1 2605
Trying 127.0.0.1...
Connected to 127.0.0.1.
Escape character is '^]'.

Hello, this is zebra (version 0.95).
Copyright 1996-2004 Kunihiro Ishiguro.


User Access Verification

Password:
Router> ena
Password:
Router# conf t
Router(config)# access-list 1 permit host 127.0.0.1
Router(config)# access-list 1 deny any
Router(config)# line vty
Router(config-line)# access-class 1
Router(config-line)# exit
```

```
Router(config)# exit
Router# write memory
Configuration saved to /usr/local/etc/bgpd.conf
Router# exit
Connection closed by foreign host.
```

We have changed the default passwords, and created software access lists to deny access for everyone except localhost. Now, if I try to connect to this server on 2601 or on 2605, I get the following:

```
router-2:~# telnet 10.10.10.22 2601
Trying 10.10.10.22...
Connected to 10.10.10.22.
Escape character is '^]'.
Connection closed by foreign host.
router-2:~#
```

Now, no one from outside can try to guess the password.

4. The router has BGP connections with 10.10.10.1, 10.10.11.13, and with 10.10.15.1. What we want to do is deny access on the TCP port 179, which is used for BGP connections, to anyone except those IP addresses. Also, we want to double the protection we created with the software-based access lists for zebra and bgpd, and allow only localhost to connect to the Zebra and its routing protocol's VTYs. We create a firewall script like this:

```
#!/bin/bash


I=/sbin/iptables

#flush all rules
$I -F

#allow packets on the loopback interface
$I -A INPUT -i lo -j ACCEPT

#reject all zebra vtys
$I -A INPUT -p tcp --dport 2601:2608 -i eth+ -j REJECT

#allow the bgp neighbors to connect to tcp port 179
$I -A INPUT -p tcp --dport 179 -s 10.10.10.1 -j ACCEPT
$I -A INPUT -p tcp --dport 179 -s 10.10.11.13 -j ACCEPT
$I -A INPUT -p tcp --dport 179 -s 10.10.15.1 -j ACCEPT

#reject the rest of the world for the tcp port 179
$I -A INPUT -p tcp --dport 179 -j REJECT
```

5. Since we don't have software known for vulnerabilities, what we can do is to test and see if our firewall works:

```
root@router:~# telnet 127.0.0.1 2601
Trying 127.0.0.1...
Connected to 127.0.0.1.
Escape character is '^]'.

Hello, this is zebra (version 0.95).
Copyright 1996-2004 Kunihiro Ishiguro.


User Access Verification

Password:

root@router:~# telnet 127.0.0.1 2605
Trying 127.0.0.1...
Connected to 127.0.0.1.
Escape character is '^]'.

Hello, this is zebra (version 0.95).
Copyright 1996-2004 Kunihiro Ishiguro.


User Access Verification

Password:
```

As you can see, we can connect to zebra and bgpd CLI from localhost; let's see if we can do this from other locations:

```
router-2:~# telnet 10.10.10.22 2601
Trying 10.10.10.22...
telnet: Unable to connect to remote host: Connection refused
router-2:~# telnet 10.10.10.22 2605
Trying 10.10.10.22...
telnet: Unable to connect to remote host: Connection refused
```

Good! We can't connect from anywhere except localhost on the CLI of zebra and bgpd. Now, we should try to connect on TCP port 179 from one of the BGP neighbors:

```
router-2:~# telnet 10.10.10.22 179
Trying 10.10.10.22...
Connected to 10.10.10.22.
Escape character is '^]'.
```

It worked, which means the BGP connections should stay up. We can verify this in the `bgpd` CLI with `show ip bgp summary`. Now, let's see if we can connect from a computer that is not a BGP peer for our router:

```
srv-x:~# telnet 10.10.10.22 179
Trying 10.10.10.22...
telnet: Unable to connect to remote host: Connection refused
```

Well, everything looks OK; so at this point what we need to do is to periodically check to see if vulnerabilities for Zebra 0.95 will be found.

Summary

Throughout this chapter, we discussed security threats found at each of the OSI layers and saw how we can protect running services with a practical example.

- Layer 1 attacks (mostly cable cuts) cannot be addressed with Linux.

- Layer 2 attacks can be very disruptive as they can affect upper layer information.

- Layer 3 attacks include packet sniffing, IP spoofing, and ICMP attacks.

- Layer 4 attacks derived from TCP and UDP vulnerabilities include TCP SYN flooding, Land attacks, TCP connection hijacking, UDP floods, and Port scan attacks.

- Layer 5, 6, and 7 attacks consist of attacks against different applications. We saw some advice on how to safely run DNS, CVS, Apache web server, Mail, OpenSSL, and SNMP services.

- We gave an example on how to protect running services.

3
Prerequisites: netfilter and iproute2

The two things needed to build firewalls and Quality of Service (QoS) with Linux are two packages named netfilter and iproute. While netfilter is a packet filtering framework included in the Linux kernels 2.4 and 2.6, iproute is a package containing a few utilities that allow Linux users to do advanced routing and traffic shaping.

This chapter is intended to introduce the tools we will use throughout this book. However, netfilter and iproute are very large subjects; so what I'll try to do in this chapter is to introduce readers who are not familiar with the subject, along with building a nice overview for readers who already know the subject.

There are two websites with a lot of documentation on both projects — for netfilter, http://www.netfilter.org, and for iproute, http://www.lartc.org.

netfilter/iptables

netfilter is a very important part of the Linux kernel in terms of security, packet mangling, and manipulation. The front end for netfilter is iptables, which "tells" the kernel what the user wants to do with the IP packets arriving into, passing through, or leaving the Linux box.

The most used features of netfilter are packet filtering and network address translation, but there are a lot of other things that we can do with netfilter, such as packet mangling Layer 7 filtering.

A rough explanation on how netfilter works is like this:

- The user instructs the kernel about what it needs to do with the IP packets that flow through the Linux box using the iptables tool.
- The Linux box then analyzes the IP headers on all packets flowing through it.
- If, when looking at the IP headers, the kernel finds matching rules, then the packet is manipulated according to the matching rule.

It might look very simple at the beginning, but actually is a lot more complicated process. netfilter has a few **tables**, each containing a default set of rules, which are called chains. The default table loaded into the kernel is the filter table, which contains three chains:

- **INPUT**: Contains rules for packets destined to the Linux machine itself.
- **FORWARD**: Contains rules for packets that the Linux machine routes to another IP address.
- **OUTPUT**: Contains rules for packets generated by the Linux machine.

By loading the NAT and mangle modules of netfilter, nat and mangle tables are automatically loaded. The nat and mangle tables, and their predefined chains, are detailed in Chapter 4.

Here's an overview of how packets travel through the tables and their chains:

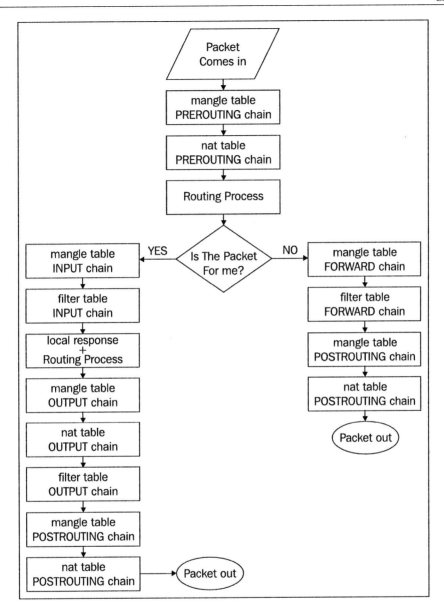

This diagram shows how packets travel the tables and their chains when the NAT and mangle modules are loaded into the kernel. Immediately after a packet arrives at our Linux box, the mangle table PREROUTING chain is analyzed. At this point we can do all sorts of modifications on the IP packets supported by the mangle table (e.g. TOS byte modifications, marking packets, and so on) before the routing process takes place.

Next, the packets flow through the pre-routing chain of the nat table, where we can do DNAT, port redirection, etc.

It is only logical to be able to perform destination network address translation before the routing process occurs. As you will see in Chapter 4, where we discuss DNAT in more detail, DNAT is the process of translating one (usually public) IP address into another (usually private). This is done by modifying the destination IP address in the IP packet's header. netfilter must do that before the kernel makes a routing decision so that the kernel will look for the new destination IP address in the IP packet.

After passing through the two chains, the Linux kernel makes a routing decision. This is not the netfilter's job. By analyzing the destination IP address from the IP packet header, the Linux box knows if the packet needs to be routed elsewhere or it was destined for it.

If the Linux box is the destination for the IP packet, the packet goes through the mangle table's INPUT chain for packet mangling. Afterwards, the packet is passed to the filter table INPUT chain, where it can be accepted, rejected, or dropped. If the packet is accepted (e.g. a request to a web server running on our Linux box), the Linux box generates a response to that packet, which goes through the mangle table OUPUT chain first.

Next, the packet is passed through the nat table OUTPUT chain and the filter table OUTPUT chain. At this point, the mangle table POSTROUTING chain and the nat table POSTROUTING chain are analyzed and the packet is ready to be sent out on the corresponding interface.

The chains presented here are the predefined chains of each table (filter, nat, and mangle). However, users can set up custom chains with custom names, and pass packets to those chains from the corresponding predefined chain. For example, if we want to create some rules for SSH access into the Linux box, we can create a custom chain named SSH, and insert one rule in the INPUT chain that instructs the kernel to analyze the SSH chain for incoming packets on port 22/TCP.

The predefined chains cannot be deleted or renamed.

This packet flow diagram is one basic thing to have in mind for all people who work with netfilter/iptables on a daily basis. It's recommended to memorize it or at least keep it handy if you are just starting out.

Iptables — Operations

iptables has a syntax somewhat similar to the old ipchains (netfilter for 2.2 kernels). However, the concepts of netfilter for 2.4+ kernels are totally different from netfilters' concepts for 2.2 kernels.

The operations iptables can do with chains are:

- List the rules in a chain (`iptables -L CHAIN`).
- Change the policy of a chain (`iptables -P CHAIN ACCEPT`).
- Create a new chain (`iptables -N CHAIN`).
- Flush a chain; delete all rules (`iptables -F CHAIN`).
- Delete a chain (`iptables -D CHAIN`), only if the chain is empty.
- Zero counters in a chain (`iptables -Z CHAIN`). Every rule in every chain keeps a counter of the number of packets and bytes it matched. This command resets those counters.

For the `-L`, `-F`, `-D`, and `-Z` operations, if the chain name is not specified, the operation is applied to the entire table, which if not specified is by default the filter table.

To specify the table on which we do operations, we must use the `-t` switch like so `iptables -t filter …`

Operations that iptables can execute on rules are:

- Append rules to a chain (`iptables -A`)
- Insert rules in a chain (`iptables -I`)
- Replace a rule from a chain (`iptables -R`)
- Delete a rule from a chain (`iptables -D`)

The most used switches are `-A` and `-D` (append and delete rules). Usually, when designing firewalls, the rules are appended to chains.

During run time, users use `-I` more than `-A` because often they need to insert temporary rules in the chain.

`iptables -A` places the rule at the end of the chain, while `iptables -I` places the rule on the top of the other rules in the chain. However, you can insert a rule anywhere in the chain by specifying the position where you want the rule to be in the chain with the `-I` switch: `iptables -I CHAIN 4` will insert a rule at the fourth position of the specified chain.

`iptables -D` can be used by specifying the position of the rule you want to delete or by specifying the entire rule.

The syntax for adding a rule to a chain is:

```
iptables -A <CHAIN_NAME> ...<filtering specifications>... -j <TARGET>
```

Filtering specifications is a part of an iptables rule that is used by the kernel to identify IP packets for which the kernel does the action specified by TARGET.

Filtering Specifications

IP packets can be identified in a large number of ways by specifying interfaces, protocols, ports, etc., to iptables rules. The beauty of it is that we can mix any of those specifications, having a high flexibility and a wide range of selectors. I'm not planning to cover all those selectors in depth, but keep in mind that if you think about something logical about IP packets, you have every chance to identify those packets using iptables rules.

Filtering specifications for Layer2: Interfaces can be specified as selectors with `-i` and `-o` switches.

`-i` stands for "`--in-interface`", and `-o` for "`--out-interface`". `+` can be used to specify only the beginning string of the interface—for example `-i eth+` will match all interfaces beginning with the string `eth`; so we've specified all Ethernet interfaces as input interfaces for one rule.

Short version switches (e.g `-i`) and long version switches (e.g. "`--in-interface`") have absolutely the same effect. Some people prefer using short switches for command lines and long switches for scripts as they can offer better readability, but we will use only short switches in this book even in the scripts to get used to the command lines better.

The exclamation mark "!" represents a negation and can be used to specify on which interface(s) not to apply this filter (e.g. `-i ! eth1` will *not* match packets coming in on eth1).

Packets analyzed in the OUTPUT and POSTROUTING chains don't have input interfaces, and so it is not allowed to use the `-i` switch on those chains.

Also, INPUT and PREROUTING chains don't have output interfaces, and so you can't use the `-o` switch for rules in those chains.

Layer 3: Source IP address(es) can be specified using -s, --src, or --source, and destination IP address(es) with -d,--dst, or --destination. Sources or destinations can be IP addresses, subnets, or canonical names (e.g, "-s 217.207.125.58", "-s www.packtpub.com", or "-s 217.207.125.58/32" have the same effect). Specifying canonical names for hosts that have multiple IP addresses will result in adding the same number of rules as the number of IP addresses the DNS server resolves for that host at the time the rules are added.

 Don't use canonical names on rules with high risk. For example, don't allow SSH access from ahost. anotherisp.com, as this will easily allow a man-in-the-middle attack.

Layer 4: Protocol can be specified using the -p switch, which stands for "--protocol". Protocols can be specified by their corresponding numbers or by their names—tcp, udp, or icmp (case insensitive).

For the ICMP protocol, you can specify ICMP message types using "--icmp-type". The list of ICMP messages can be found by using the command "iptables -p icmp --help".

For the UDP protocol, you can specify source or destination ports with "--source-port" or "--sport" and "--destination-port" and "--dport".

TCP, being the most complete Layer 4 protocol, has more options. You can specify, besides source or destination ports as for the UDP protocol, "--tcp-flags", "--syn" and "--tcp-option". TCP flags can be "SYN ACK FIN RST URG PSH ALL NONE". "--syn" is used to identify the initiating connections and is equivalent to "--tcp-flags SYN,RST,ACK SYN". "--tcp-option" followed by a number matches TCP packets with the option set to that number.

 Filtering specifications can combine all of the features just mentioned; so we can have a combination of Layers 2, 3, and 4 specifications in the same rule.

Another beautiful thing about netfilter/iptables is that matching extensions can be developed separately and added later. On the netfilter site, there is a large repository of matching extensions called "patch-o-matic", at http://www.netfilter.org/ projects/patch-o-matic/index.html.

A new and "daring" extension to iptables plans to extend its capabilities from the lower layers to the upper layer of the OSI model, Layer 7—application. The project is called l7-filter and it will be explained later in this book, in Chapter 6.

Target Specifications

For the filter table, the most used targets for firewall rules are DROP and ACCEPT. If a rule matches the filtering specifications and has a DROP target, the packet will simply be discarded. If a packet matches a rule with a DROP target, the Linux kernel will drop the packet without consulting other rules in the firewall. If the target is ACCEPT, then the packet is accepted without further consultation of other firewall rules.

An alternative to DROP is the REJECT target, which drops the packet but sends an ICMP packet to the source IP of the packet. By default, the REJECT target will send an ICMP 'port unreachable' message to the sender, but that can be overwritten using the "`--reject-with`" switch.

The target in an iptables rule can also be used to pass a packet to a user-defined chain. For example, if we create a new chain like "`iptables –N SSH`", we need to tell the kernel to look for this chain for all incoming TCP connections on port 22 like this:

```
iptables -A INPUT -p tcp --dport 22 -j SSH
```

Another useful target is LOG, which can be used to log packets matching a filtering specification in the kernel log, which can be read with dmesg or syslogd. LOG target options are:

- `--log-level` level: The level of logging can be a name or a number. The valid names are debug, info, notice, warning, err, crit, alert, and emerg with corresponding numbers from 7 to 0.

- `--log-prefix` prefix: Log prefix is followed by a string of up to 29 characters, placed at the beginning of the log message.

- `--log-tcp-sequence`: Logs TCP sequence numbers.

- `--log-tcp-options`: Logs the option field of TCP packet headers.

- `--log-ip-options`: Logs the option field of the IP packet headers.

- `--log-uid`: Logs the user ID of the process that generated the packet.

The LOG target is not a terminating target like ACCEPT, DROP, and REJECT. This means that if a packet matches a rule that has the LOG target, the kernel looks up the rules that follow to also match this packet. A limit match for rules with LOG targets would be a good idea to prevent flooding the log files.

As an example, earlier we created the SSH chain and passed packets coming in on port 22/TCP. Now, we want to accept incoming SSH connections from 192.168.0.0/27 and 10.10.15.0/24, for example, and log all other attempts, but we will limit logging to 5/s, because in the case of a SYN flood on port 22/TCP, the logs would fill quickly.

First, we will append the rules to the SSH chain to allow connections from the trusted hosts:

```
iptables -A SSH -s  192.168.0.0/27 -j ACCEPT
iptables -A SSH -s  10.10.15.0/24 -j ACCEPT
```

Next, we will add the logging rule:

```
iptables -A SSH  -m limit --limit 5/s -j LOG
```

And then DROP all other connections:

```
iptables -A SSH -j DROP
```

We need to verify the configuration, and we will use `iptables -L -n` for that. We will see in the INPUT chain:

```
root@router:~/lucix# iptables -L -n
Chain INPUT (policy ACCEPT)
target       prot opt source           destination
SSH          tcp  --  0.0.0.0/0        0.0.0.0/0        tcp dpt:22
```

And we will see the SSH chain:

```
Chain SSH (1 references)
target       prot opt source              destination
ACCEPT       all  --  192.168.0.0/27      0.0.0.0/0
ACCEPT       all  --  10.10.15.0/24       0.0.0.0/0
LOG          all  --  0.0.0.0/0           0.0.0.0/0
limit: avg 5/sec burst 5 LOG flags 0 level 4
DROP         all  --  0.0.0.0/0           0.0.0.0/0
```

To test the SSH chain we will try to telnet port 22 from an unauthorized host. Using `iptables -L -n -v`, we will see that the packet matched the LOG and DROP rules:

```
Chain SSH (1 references)
 pkts bytes target     prot opt in    out    source            destination
    0     0 ACCEPT     all  --  *     *      192.168.0.0/27    0.0.0.0/0
    0     0 ACCEPT     all  --  *     *      10.10.15.0/24     0.0.0.0/0
    1    48 LOG        all  --  *     *      0.0.0.0/0         0.0.0.0/0
limit: avg 5/sec burst 5 LOG flags 0 level 4
    1    48 DROP       all  --  *     *      0.0.0.0/0         0.0.0.0/0
```

Now, if you look at the logs using `dmesg` command, you will see:

```
IN=eth0 OUT= MAC=00:d0:b7:a7:6f:74:00:04:23:cf:14:e6:08:00
SRC=192.168.168.168 DST=192.168.0.1 LEN=48 TOS=0x00 PREC=0x00
TTL=109 ID=54250 DF PROTO=TCP SPT=27276 DPT=22 WINDOW=16384
RES=0x00 SYN URGP=0
```

which tells us that 192.168.168.168 tried to connect on port 22 TCP.

For the nat and mangle tables, we will discuss the targets in the following chapter.

 The targets presented here are the most commonly used targets of iptables. There are a lot of add-ons published on patch-o-matic, which can provide new targets for iptables.

A Basic Firewall Script—Linux as a Workstation

So far, we've learned mostly about the usage of iptables filtering options. I will now build up a small firewall script that I think should be default when installing any Linux distribution.

By default, all Linux distributions have the default policy ACCEPT on all filter chains. Also, on a default installation, most Linux distributions leave a lot of services running. If you install an old Linux distribution and decide to go for lunch after you have just booted up without any firewall and with a public IP address, good chances are that by the time you've eaten your soup, a rootkit is already installed on your computer.

Let's take a look at the following simple script:

```
#!/bin/bash

#assign variable $IPT with the iptables command
IPT=/sbin/iptables

#set policies on each chain
$IPT -P INPUT DROP

$IPT -P FORWARD DROP

$IPT -P OUTPUT ACCEPT #default, but set it anyway
#flush all rules in the filter table
$IPT -F

#allow traffic on the loopback interface
```

```
$IPT -A INPUT -i lo -j ACCEPT

#allow icmp traffic
$IPT -A INPUT -p icmp -j ACCEPT

#allow incoming DNS traffic
$IPT -A INPUT -p udp --sport 53 -j ACCEPT

#allow established TCP connections
$IPT -A INPUT -p tcp ! --syn -j ACCEPT
```

So, what we did here was to set the INPUT and FORWARD chains policy to DROP. The OUTPUT chain policy is set to ACCEPT, which is the default policy for this chain.

We will not append any rules in the FORWARD chain because this is a personal computer and not a router, and so the forwarding will be off. We will also not append any rules in the OUTPUT chain—anything we originate is OK.

Next, we flush all existing rules out from the filter table. At this point, nothing really works. Some applications use TCP/IP connections on the loopback interface; so it's safe to allow packets that come in on the interface "lo".

We learned about ICMP attacks in Chapter 2. However, it is my opinion that ICMP should be allowed. Filtering ICMP will not allow you to test your internet connection using ping, traceroute, mtr, etc., and also path MTU discovery will not work, which is a very important protocol in many cases.

DNS responses use the UDP protocol and source port 53. Keep in mind that the line:

```
$IPT -A INPUT -p udp --sport 53 -j ACCEPT
```

is a potential security breach. We left it like this because we earlier stated that this is what we think the default firewall should look like. However, if you're not running a DNS server (which is not recommended for a personal computer), accept incoming UDP connections with source port 53 only from your provider's DNS servers (the ones you have in /etc/resolv.conf). For example, if the provider's DNS servers are 1.1.1.1 and 1.1.2.1, replace the earlier line with:

```
$IPT -A INPUT -s 1.1.1.1 -p udp --sport 53 -j ACCEPT
$IPT -A INPUT -s 1.1.2.1 -p udp --sport 53 -j ACCEPT
```

This way, you will be safer.

The last thing we need for our internet connection to work is to allow incoming TCP traffic for already established TCP connections. Better phrased, deny any incoming TCP traffic that doesn't belong to a TCP connection that this computer initiated (deny TCP SYN packets).

 This rough introduction on netfilter/iptables covers only some basic parts of the subject. The intention of this book is not to teach the reader the complete syntax of iptables. For that, there is a manpage at `http://www.netfilter.org/documentation/HOWTO/packet-filtering-HOWTO.html`.

iproute2 and Traffic Control

iproute2 is a software package that provides various tools for advanced routing, tunnels, and traffic control.

iproute2 was originally designed by Alexey Kuznetsov, and is well known for implementing QoS in Linux kernels and is now maintained by Stephen Hemminger. The primary site for iproute2 is `http://linux-net.osdl.org/index.php/Iproute2` and its main documentation site is `http://www.lartc.org`.

The most important tools that iproute2 provides are `ip` and `tc`.

Network Configuration: "ip" Tool

The `ip` tool provides most of the networking configuration a Linux box needs. You can configure interfaces, ARP, policy routing, tunnels, etc.

Now, with IPv4 and IPv6, `ip` can do pretty much anything (including a lot that we don't need in our particular situations). The syntax of `ip` is not difficult, and there is a lot of documentation on this subject. However, the most important thing is knowing what we need and when we need it.

First of all, `ip` is the main tool we need for dynamic routing protocols (BGP, OSPF, and RIP) on Linux provided by Zebra, which will be discussed later in this book.

Let's have a look at the `ip` command help to see what `ip` knows:

```
root@router:~# ip help
Usage: ip [ OPTIONS ] OBJECT { COMMAND | help }
where  OBJECT := { link | addr | route | rule | neigh | tunnel |
                   maddr | mroute | monitor | xfrm }
```

```
        OPTIONS := { -V[ersion] | -s[tatistics] | -r[esolve] |
                     -f[amily] { inet | inet6 | ipx | dnet | link } |
   -o[neline] }
   root@router:~#
```

The `ip link` command shows the network device's configurations that can be changed with `ip link set`. This command is used to modify the device's proprieties and not the IP address.

The IP addresses can be configured using the `ip addr` command. This command can be used to add a primary or secondary (alias) IP address to a network device (`ip addr add`), to display the IP addresses for each network device (`ip addr show`), or to delete IP addresses from interfaces (`ip addr del`). IP addresses can also be flushed using different criteria, e.g. `ip addr flush dynamic` will flush all routes added to the kernel by a dynamic routing protocol.

Neighbor/Arp table management is done using `ip neighbor`, which has a few commands expressively named `add`, `change`, `replace`, `delete`, and `flush`.

`ip tunnel` is used to manage tunneled connections. Tunnels can be `gre`, `ipip`, and `sit`. We will include an example later in the book on how to build IP tunnels.

The `ip` tool offers a way for monitoring routes, addresses, and the states of devices in real-time. This can be accomplished using `ip monitor`, `rtmon`, and `rtacct` commands included in the iproute2 package.

One very important and probably the most used object of the `ip` tool is `ip route`, which can do any operations on the kernel routing table. It has commands to add, change, replace, delete, show, flush, and get routes.

One of the things iproute2 introduced to Linux that ensured its popularity was policy routing. This can be done using `ip rule` and `ip route` in a few simple steps.

Traffic Control: tc

The `tc` command allows administrators to build different QoS policies in their networks using Linux instead of very expensive dedicated QoS machines. Using Linux, you can implement QoS in all the ways any dedicated QoS machine can and even more. Also, one can make a bridge using a good PC running Linux that can be transformed into a very powerful and very cheap dedicated QoS machine.

For that, QoS support must be configured in the Linux kernel (`CONFIG_NET_QOS="Y"` and `CONFIG_NET_SCHED="Y"`).

Queuing Packets

First of all, queuing is used to determine the way data is sent; so with queuing, we can control how much data is sent, and with what priority we send data that matches some criteria.

Please keep in mind that there is no way to queue incoming data. When we talk about limiting upload and download speeds for some IP address, for example, we talk about limiting the data our Linux router sends to that IP address on the interface that IP address is connected to (download) and the data our Linux router sends over the Internet from that IP address (upload), as in the following figure:

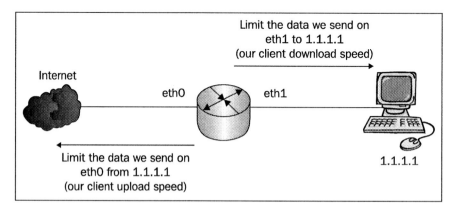

This is quite satisfying because TCP has flow control, which actually negotiates the speed of the packet flow between two communicating hosts depending on the capabilities of each host. UDP doesn't have flow control, but most of the applications that use UDP as transport protocol implement flow control within themselves.

Well, things look pretty good, but this is how things work in the "perfect world", where there aren't people with bad intentions (or stupid people without bad intentions) that generate flood attacks because we can't limit the incoming data.

So, what's the problem? Well, put 99 computers near the 1.1.1.1 computer in the earlier figure! Let's say there are 100 users on a FastEthernet connection (with more switches, as the router has one Ethernet cable in one switch). We can limit each computer to 1Mbps upload / 1Mbps download; so we're using 100 Mbps when everyone is on the top of their limits. Now, if 1.1.1.1 wants to disrupt service to the other users, it's very simple. Because there is no way of limiting incoming traffic, if 1.1.1.1 floods one or many random hosts on the Internet with a 100Mbps data stream, the router limits the outgoing data from 1.1.1.1 to 1Mbps, but it still receives 100Mbps on its eth1 interface. This results in denial of service, and there isn't really much to do about it. If the switches are unmanaged, the only thing you can do about it is to plug out the cable from the port in which 1.1.1.1 is connected.

Now, to get back to the subject, queuing disciplines are of two kinds: classless and classful.

Classless Queuing Disciplines (Classless qdiscs)

Classless qdiscs are the simplest ones because they only accept, drop, delay or reschedule data. They can be attached to one interface and can only shape the entire interface.

There are several qdisc implementations on Linux, most of them included in the Linux kernel.

- **FIFO (pfifo and bfifo)**: The simplest qdisc, which functions by the First In, First Out rule. FIFO algorithms have a queue size limit (buffer size), which can be defined in packets for pfifo or in bytes for bfifo.

- **pfifo_fast**: The default qdisc on all Linux interfaces. It's important to know how pfifo_fast works; so we'll explain it soon.

- **Token Bucket Filter (tbf)**: A simple qdisc that is perfect for slowing down an interface to a specified rate. It can allow short bursts over the specified rate and is very processor friendly.

- **Stochastic Fair Queuing (SFQ)**: One of the most widely used qdiscs. SFQ tries to fairly distribute the transmitting data among a number of flows.

- **Enhanced Stochastic Fair Queuing (ESFQ)**: Not included in the Linux kernel, it works in the same manner as SFQ with the exception that the user can control more of the algorithm's parameters such as depth (flows) limit, hash table size options (hardcoded in original SFQ) and hash types.

- **Random Early Detection and Generic Random Early Detection** (RED and GRED): qdiscs suitable for backbone data queuing, with data rates over 100 Mbps.

There are more qdiscs than the ones I have stated here. However, from my experience, SFQ and ESFQ do a great job, and are the qdiscs that I have got the best results with.

As I said earlier, the default qdisc on Linux for all interfaces is pfifo_fast. Normally, one would think that this is just like pfifo, meaning there is a buffer and packets pass through the buffer using the First In First Out rule. Actually, it's not quite true. pfifo_fast has 3 bands—0, 1, and 2—in which packets are placed according to their TOS byte. Packets are sent out from those bands as follows:

- Packets in the 0 band have the highest priority

- Packets in the 1 band are sent out only if there aren't any packets in the 0 band

- Packets in the 2 band have the lowest priority and are sent out only if there aren't any packets in the 0 and 1 bands.

It's important to know this because this can be a way to optimize how packets travel through the network interfaces of our Linux routers. The TOS byte looks like this:

0	1	2	3	4	5	6	7
PRECEDENCE			Type of Service — TOS				MBZ

The TOS bits are defined as follows:

- 0000   Normal Service
- 0001   Minimize Monetary Cost (MMC)
- 0010   Maximize Reliability (MR)
- 0100   Maximize throughput (MT)
- 1000   Minimize Delay (MD)

Based on the TOS byte, the packets are placed in one of the three bands as follows:

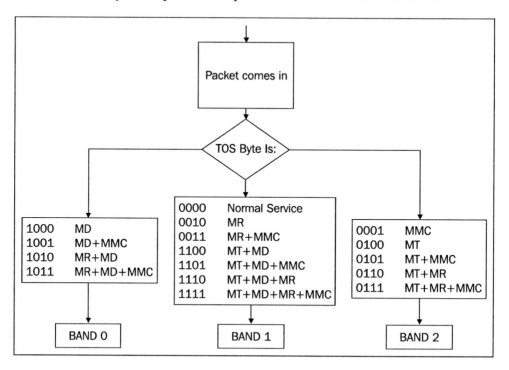

This means that, by default, Linux is smart enough to prioritize traffic according to the TOS bytes. Usually, applications like Telnet, FTP, SMTP modify the TOS byte to work in an optimal way. We will see later in this book how to optimize the traffic ourselves.

Classful Queuing Disciplines

These qdiscs are used for shaping different types of data. The commonly used classful qdiscs are CBQ (Class Based Queuing) and HTB (Hierarchical Token Bucket).

First of all, we need to learn how classful queuing disciplines work. The whole process is not difficult; so I'll try to explain it as simply as possible.

Everything is based on a hierarchy. First, every interface has one root qdisc that talks to the kernel. Second, there is a child class attached to the root qdisc. The child class further has child classes that have qdiscs attached to schedule the data and leaf classes, which are child classes of the child classes.

All confused? Have a look at the following image, which will explain away the confusion:

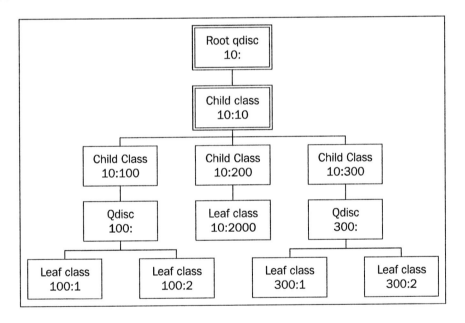

So, basically CBQ or HTB qdiscs allow us to create child CBQ or HTB classes, which we can set up to shape some kind of data. For each child class, we can attach a qdisc for scheduling packets within that child class. Next, we can create leaf classes, which are child classes of the qdiscs we attached to the child classes, or we can create leaf classes as child classes' child classes attached to the root qdisc.

tc qdisc, tc class, and tc filter

To build the tree configuration in the earlier figure, we need to use the tc command:

- tc qdisc manipulates queuing disciplines.
- tc class manipulates classes.
- tc filter manipulates filters used to identify data.

Both CBQ and HTB have a few parameters that can be adjusted to optimize their performance. Throughout this book we will use different values to suit the applications we are building. There is a lot of tuning to be done with these parameters, and I'm not going to explain all of them as there are some that you will probably never need.

CBQ qdiscs and classes have the following parameters:

```
root@router:~# tc qdisc add cbq help
Usage: ... cbq bandwidth BPS avpkt BYTES [ mpu BYTES ]
                [ cell BYTES ] [ ewma LOG ]
root@router:~# tc class add cbq help
Usage: ... cbq bandwidth BPS rate BPS maxburst PKTS [ avpkt BYTES ]
                [ minburst PKTS ] [ bounded ] [ isolated ]
                [ allot BYTES ] [ mpu BYTES ] [ weight RATE ]
                [ prio NUMBER ] [ cell BYTES ] [ ewma LOG ]
                [ estimator INTERVAL TIME_CONSTANT ]
                [ split CLASSID ] [ defmap MASK/CHANGE ]
```

and HTB qdiscs and classes' parameters are:

```
root@router:~# tc class add htb help
Usage: ... qdisc add ... htb [default N] [r2q N]
 default   minor id of class to which unclassified packets are sent {0}
 r2q       DRR quantums are computed as rate in Bps/r2q {10}
 debug     string of 16 numbers each 0-3 {0}

 ... class add ... htb rate R1 [burst B1] [mpu B] [overhead O]
                        [prio P] [slot S] [pslot PS]
                        [ceil R2] [cburst B2] [mtu MTU] [quantum Q]
 rate      rate allocated to this class (class can still borrow)
 burst     max bytes burst which can be accumulated during idle
period {computed}
 mpu       minimum packet size used in rate computations
 overhead per-packet size overhead used in rate computations
 ceil      definite upper class rate (no borrows) {rate}
 cburst    burst but for ceil {computed}
 mtu       max packet size we create rate map for {1600}
```

```
    prio      priority of leaf; lower are served first {0}
    quantum   how much bytes to serve from leaf at once {use r2q}

TC HTB version 3.3
```

I will try to explain a few of these parameters while using them in the actual example that follows.

Filters are used to identify the data we need to shape. We can identify the data based on the way the firewall marked it using the `fw` classifier, based on fields of the IP header using the `u32` classifier, based on the kernel's routing decision using the `route` classifier, or based on RSVP using `rsvp` or `rsvp6` classifiers.

The `tc filter` command has the following parameters:

```
root@router:~# tc filter help
Usage: tc filter [ add | del | change | get ] dev STRING
        [ pref PRIO ] [ protocol PROTO ]
        [ estimator INTERVAL TIME_CONSTANT ]
        [ root | classid CLASSID ] [ handle FILTERID ]
        [ [ FILTER_TYPE ] [ help | OPTIONS ] ]

        tc filter show [ dev STRING ] [ root | parent CLASSID ]
Where:
FILTER_TYPE := { rsvp | u32 | fw | route | etc. }
FILTERID := ... format depends on classifier, see there
OPTIONS := ... try tc filter add <desired FILTER_KIND> help
```

The most used classifier is `u32`, because most people desire to identify data by IP addresses, source or destination ports, etc. However, we will use the fw classifier along with u32 throughout the book. The u32 parameters are:

```
root@router:~# tc filter add u32 help
Usage: ... u32 [ match SELECTOR ... ] [ link HTID ] [ classid CLASSID
]
                [ police POLICE_SPEC ] [ offset OFFSET_SPEC ]
                [ ht HTID ] [ hashkey HASHKEY_SPEC ]
                [ sample SAMPLE ]
or              u32 divisor DIVISOR

Where: SELECTOR := SAMPLE SAMPLE ...
    SAMPLE := { ip | ip6 | udp | tcp | icmp | u{32|16|8} } SAMPLE_ARGS
    FILTERID := X:Y:Z
```

And for the fw classifier:

```
root@router:~# tc filter add fw help
Usage:  ... fw [ classid CLASSID ] [ police POLICE_SPEC ]
        POLICE_SPEC := ... look at TBF
        CLASSID := X:Y
```

A Real Example

In the following example we will try to divide a 10Mbps bandwidth between three entities: a home-user, an office, and another ISP, as shown in the following figure:

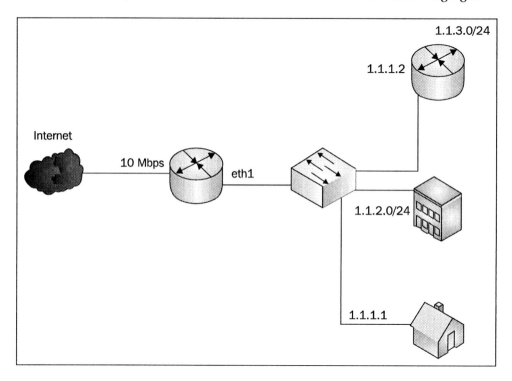

Let's assume we want to give the home user 1Mbps of our bandwidth, the office 4Mbps, and the ISP 5Mbps.

First, let's see how this looks using CBQ. First, we need to add the root qdisc to the eth1 interface on which the clients are connected:

```
tc qdisc add dev eth1 root handle 10: cbq bandwidth 100Mbit avpkt 1000
```

So, the command used is `tc qdisc add` with the `dev` parameter set to `eth1` to define the interface we will attach the qdisc to. The `root` parameter specifies that this is the root qdisc. We will assign `handle 10` for the root qdisc. After specifying the handle, we specified cbq as the type of the qdisc, followed by the parameters for cbq. bandwidth is set to 100Mbit, which is the physical bandwidth of the device, and avpkt, which specifies the average packet size is set to 1000.

Next, we need to create a child class that will be the parent of all classes. This class will have the bandwidth parameter equal to that of the root qdisc, equal to the physical bandwidth of the interface:

```
tc class add dev eth1 parent 10:0 classid 10:10 cbq bandwidth 100Mbit
rate \
    100Mbit allot 1514 weight 10Mbit prio 5 maxburst 20 avpkt 1000
bounded
```

For the child classes, we need to specify the parent class, which in this case is 10:0 — the root class. classid specifies the ID of the class, and bandwidth is the physical bandwidth of the interface (100Mbit). The speed limit is specified with the rate parameter, followed by the rate in bits (in this case, 100Mbit). The allot parameter is the base unit for how much data the class can send in one round. weight is a parameter used by CBQ with allot to calculate how much data is sent in one round. Actually, from our experience and tests, weight pretty much specifies the rate in bytes for the class.

> We will be using in this book parameters that gave the best results in our tests. Except bandwidth, rate, and weight, we don't recommend learning about all the other parameters. However, there is a more detailed explanation at: http://www.lartc.org/howto/lartc.qdisc.classful.html#AEN939.

For each client, we will create leaf classes, qdiscs, and filters. Let's start with the home user:

```
tc class add dev eth1 parent 10:10 classid 10:100 cbq bandwidth
100Mbit rate \
    1Mbit allot 1514 weight 128Kbit prio 5 maxburst 20 avpkt 1000
bounded

tc qdisc add dev eth1 parent 10:100 sfq quantum 1514b perturb 15

tc filter add dev eth1 parent 10:0 protocol ip prio 5 u32 match ip dst
1.1.1.1 flowid 10:100
```

So we created the 10:100 class with a rate of 1Mbit and 128Kbit weight. Next, we attached an sfq qdisc and a u32 filter to match all traffic with the destination IP address 1.1.1.1. The bounded argument of the tc class add cbq command means that the class isn't allowed to borrow bytes from other classes, meaning that there is no way that data for this class will go over 1Mbps.

A lot of documentation explains that `weight` should be `rate/10`. In our case, weight would be 100Kbit and the user wouldn't get data with speed above 100KB/s which is not 1Mbps. We've been always using `weight` as `rate/8` because this seems more fair to me.

Now, the other classes, qdiscs, and filters look like this:

```
#the office
tc class add dev eth1 parent 10:10 classid 10:200 cbq bandwidth
100Mbit rate \
   4Mbit allot 1514 weight 512Kbit prio 5 maxburst 20 avpkt 1000
bounded

tc qdisc add dev eth1 parent 10:200 sfq quantum 1514b perturb 15

tc filter add dev eth1 parent 10:0 protocol ip prio 5 u32 match ip dst
1.1.2.0/24 flowid 10:200

#the ISP
tc class add dev eth1 parent 10:10 classid 10:300 cbq bandwidth
100Mbit rate \
   5Mbit allot 1514 weight 640Kbit prio 5 maxburst 20 avpkt 1000
bounded

tc qdisc add dev eth1 parent 10:300 sfq quantum 1514b perturb 15

tc filter add dev eth1 parent 10:0 protocol ip prio 5 u32 match ip dst
1.1.1.2 flowid 10:300
tc filter add dev eth1 parent 10:0 protocol ip prio 5 u32 match ip dst
1.1.3.0/24 flowid 10:300
```

As you can see in the ISP case, we can add as many filters as we want to a class.

To verify the configuration, we can use `tc class show dev eth1` and see the classes:

```
root@router:~# tc class show dev eth1
class cbq 10: root rate 100000Kbit (bounded,isolated) prio no-transmit
class cbq 10:100 parent 10:10 leaf 806e: rate 1000Kbit (bounded) prio 5
class cbq 10:10 parent 10: rate 100000Kbit (bounded) prio 5
class cbq 10:200 parent 10:10 leaf 806f: rate 4000Kbit (bounded) prio 5
class cbq 10:300 parent 10:10 leaf 8070: rate 5000Kbit (bounded) prio 5
```

Now, to see that a class is actually shaping packets, we send three `ping` packets to 1.1.1.1, and check to see if the CBQ class matched those packets using `tc -s class show dev eth1`:

```
root@router:~# tc -s class show dev eth1 | fgrep -A 2 10:100
class cbq 10:100 parent 10:10 leaf 806e: rate 1000Kbit (bounded) prio 5
 Sent 294 bytes 3 pkts (dropped 0, overlimits 0)
  borrowed 0 overactions 0 avgidle 184151 undertime 0
```

Now everything looks OK; so let's move on to HTB. Before we do that, we need to delete the CBQ root qdisc using:

```
root@router:~# tc qdisc del root dev eth1
```

Using HTB looks a bit simpler than CBQ. First, the root qdisc looks like this:

```
tc qdisc add dev eth1 root handle 10: htb
```

Next, we will create the child class:

```
tc class add dev eth1 parent 10:0 classid 10:10 htb rate 100Mbit
```

Now, the qdiscs and filters within the client classes are the same as in the CBQ example. The only thing that differs is how the classes are built. Let's see the home-user class, qdisc, and filter:

```
tc class add dev eth1 parent 10:10 classid 10:100 htb rate 1Mbit

tc qdisc add dev eth1 parent 10:100 sfq quantum 1514b perturb 15

tc filter add dev eth1 protocol ip parent 10:0 prio 5 u32 match ip dst
1.1.1.1 flowid 10:100
```

So much simple, isn't it? Let's create the other two entities' classes, qdiscs, and filters:

```
#the office
tc class add dev eth1 parent 10:10 classid 10:200 htb rate 4Mbit

tc qdisc add dev eth1 parent 10:200 sfq quantum 1514b perturb 15

tc filter add dev eth1 parent 10:0 protocol ip prio 5 u32 match ip dst
1.1.2.0/24 flowid 10:200


#the ISP
tc class add dev eth1 parent 10:10 classid 10:300 htb rate 5Mbit

tc qdisc add dev eth1 parent 10:300 sfq quantum 1514b perturb 15

tc filter add dev eth1 parent 10:0 protocol ip prio 5 u32 match ip dst
```

```
1.1.1.2 flowid 10:300
tc filter add dev eth1 parent 10:0 protocol ip prio 5 u32 match ip dst
1.1.3.0/24 flowid 10:300
```

Now it's time to verify the configuration using `tc class show dev eth1`:

```
root@router:~# tc class show dev eth1
class htb 10:10 root rate 100000Kbit ceil 100000Kbit burst 126575b
cburst 126575b
class htb 10:100 parent 10:10 leaf 8072: prio 0 rate 1000Kbit ceil
1000Kbit burst 2849b cburst 2849b
class htb 10:200 parent 10:10 leaf 8073: prio 0 rate 4000Kbit ceil
4000Kbit burst 6599b cburst 6599b
class htb 10:300 parent 10:10 leaf 8074: prio 0 rate 5000Kbit ceil
5000Kbit burst 7849b cburst 7849b
```

and after sending three `ping` packets to 1.1.1.1, we should see them on the 10:100 class:

```
root@router:~# tc -s class show dev eth1 | fgrep -A 4 10:100
class htb 10:100 parent 10:10 leaf 8072: prio 0 rate 1000Kbit ceil
1000Kbit burst 2849b cburst 2849b
 Sent 294 bytes 3 pkts (dropped 0, overlimits 0)
 rate 24bit
 lended: 3 borrowed: 0 giants: 0
 tokens: 18048 ctokens: 18048
```

 There is no catch in all of this—HTB looks simpler and it really is. CBQ has more parameters that can be adjusted by the user, while HTB does much of the adjustments internally.

Summary

This chapter introduced netfilter/iptables and iproute2. A very important thing for anyone building firewalls is to know how and where packets are analyzed. For that, we introduced a diagram of how packets traverse the chains in the filter, nat, and mangle tables for netfilter.

For beginners, a first look the iptables syntax might seem a bit difficult. An iptables rule contains the table on which we make an operation (filter table being default), a command (`append`, `insert`, `delete`, `list`), some filtering specifications to match the packets we want, and a target (DROP, ACCEPT, REJECT, LOG) that specifies what we want to do with the packet.

The iproute2 package introduces two complex tools. One is `ip`, which can be used to set up Layer 3 communication like IP addresses and routing. `tc` stands for *traffic control*, and it is used to implement QoS.

Before digging into `tc` commands, we learned a bit of theory on classless and classful queuing disciplines. The best and most popular classful qdiscs are CBQ and HTB, which we will use throughout this book.

We saw that HTB is simpler to use than CBQ because the command lines for CBQ must contain a lot of parameters. On the other hand, CBQ can be tuned for more advanced configurations, but the needs for these tunings are very rare.

We made a lot of tests with CBQ, and we will use in this book the parameters that produced the best results for us.

4

NAT and Packet Mangling with iptables

In the first part of this chapter we will learn how to perform Network Address Translation (NAT) and Port Address Translation (PAT), also referred to as Network Address and Port Translation (NAPT), with iptables. After that, we will learn what packet mangling is and how to mangle packets.

A Short Introduction to NAT and PAT (NAPT)

According to the way TCP/IP works, in order for hosts to communicate on the Internet, each must have a unique IP address.

However, due to the shortage of public IP addresses available, it is necessary to use one IP address for many hosts using NAT.

Network Address Translation is a way to translate one IP address into another. This implies a NAT router (Linux in our case) that rewrites the source or destination IP of a device behind the NAT router.

There are many small boxes called SOHO routers or NAT routers that can be used to perform NAT for a small private LAN. They are cheap and usually you can just plug them in and everything works. If you have already used one, you will see that there are many things you can do with Linux.

To explain NAT in more detail, let's take a look at the following diagram:

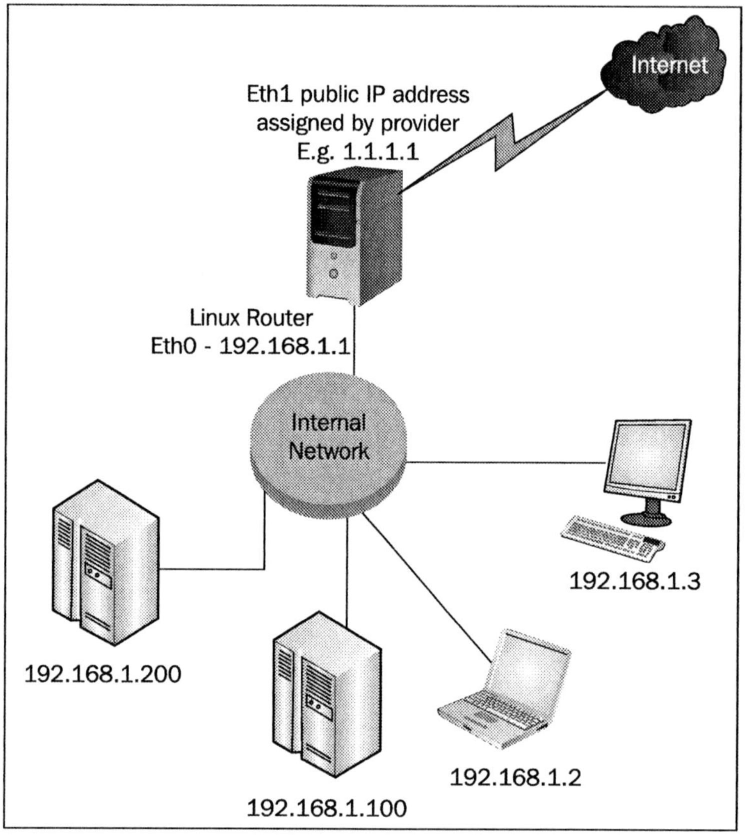

We have a Linux router with one Internet connection and a public IP address—1.1.1.1. We can use whatever IP addresses we want from the private IP segments we presented in Chapter 1; so we choose for this network 192.168.1.0/24 as a subnet for our private network. The private IP segments are described in RFC 1918, and are:

- 10.0.0.0 - 10.255.255.255 (10/8 prefix)
- 172.16.0.0 - 172.31.255.255 (172.16/12 prefix)
- 192.168.0.0 - 192.168.255.255 (192.168/16 prefix)

Now, since 192.168.1.0/24 is a private network, those IP addresses are not routed anywhere in the Internet, meaning that no host on the Internet can access the devices in our network (so, using private IP addresses also offers some protection, doesn't it?).

In order for the hosts using private IP addresses to communicate with other hosts on the Internet, the NAT router rewrites their private IP addresses into its own public IP address. This way, hosts on the Internet exchange data with the public IP address of the Linux router.

The router needs to "know" which packets are for itself, and which packets are for which hosts with private IP addresses. The router accomplishes this by keeping track of all TCP/IP connections that pass through it. This process is called connection tracking.

Connection tracking gives Linux the ability to hold state information about TCP and UDP connections in memory tables. Information about every connection is stored in /proc/net/ip_conntrack and includes IP addresses, port numbers, protocol types, connection state, and timeouts. Here are some example entries in /proc/net/ip_conntrack:

```
tcp      6 262872 ESTABLISHED src=2.2.2.2 dst=1.1.1.1 sport=80
dport=65000 [UNREPLIED] src=192.168.1.2 dst=2.2.2.2 sport=65000
dport=80 use=1

udp      17 174 src=1.1.1.1 dst=1.1.1.11 sport=40997 dport=161
src=1.1.1.11 dst=1.1.1.1 sport=161 dport=40997 [ASSURED] use=1
```

Using connection tracking, the router is aware that when a packet arrives to 1.1.1.1 as a result of a request originated from 192.168.1.2, the packet must be forwarded to the laptop computer, and so it rewrites the destination IP address in the IP packet header from 1.1.1.1 to 192.168.1.2.

Firewalls that do connection tracking are known as "stateful firewalls".

NAT can be performed in different scenarios:

- **One-to-one** (1:1): We translate one private IP address into one public IP address, for example, in the previous diagram if we perform NAT only for the laptop computer, then we would be performing one-to-one NAT.
- **One-to-many** (1:Many): One private IP address is translated into many public IP addresses. This means that for each connection the private device initiates with a host on the Internet, the NAT router chooses a public IP address from a range to translate the private IP address into it. For example, if we performed NAT only for the laptop computer and we have more than one public IP address in the diagram, we would have one-to-many NAT.
- **Many-to-one** (Many:1) This is just like in the previous diagram, where many private IP addresses are translated into one public IP address (if the public IP address belongs to the router, this is also known as **masquerading**).
- **Many-to-many** (Many:Many): Many private IP addresses are translated using a range of public IP addresses. If we had more than one public IP address and we were to NAT all the computers in the earlier diagram using multiple public IP addresses, then we would perform many-to-many NAT.

SNAT and Masquerade

SNAT is an alias for Source Network Address Translation. It is called so because only the source IP address gets translated. The NAT box will overwrite the source address in IP headers of all packets sent by a box behind NAT to one or many IP addresses.

One or many hosts can be translated into one or many public IP addresses only when accessing the Internet, but when a request from the Internet is made to the public IP address(es), the request will not reach any of the hosts (if the translated address is the router's, it will reach the router; otherwise packets will be dropped). This is a good protection for local networks and saves a lot of public IP addresses.

If one or many hosts behind NAT are translated into only one public IP address, the process is called **static SNAT**. If they are translated into several public IP addresses (usually a range of IP addresses), the process is called **dynamic SNAT**. In the case of dynamic SNAT, the NAT router chooses an IP address from a range; so one computer accessing the Internet is very likely to be translated into different IP addresses for each connection it initiates. For dynamic SNAT, iptables chooses the least used IP address from the specified range. If many IP addresses from the range are not used at all, iptables randomly chooses one of those.

Masquerade or MASQ works exactly like static SNAT does, except that you cannot specify the public IP address to be used. It will automatically use the IP address of the outgoing interface of the NAT router.

SNAT was introduced with iptables, and did not exist in netfilter for kernels lower than 2.4. However, Masquerade was kept in iptables simply because with interfaces like PPP adapters that receive a dynamically assigned IP address, it is simpler to do a MASQ rather than find the dynamically assigned IP address and do SNAT.

In order to do SNAT or Masquerade, the router needs to use connection tracking so that it "knows" where to send flows of data belonging to connections initiated by hosts behind NAT.

The following diagram presents an example of how SNAT or Masquerade works:

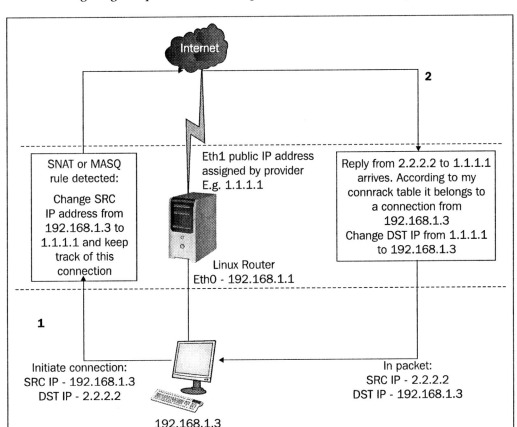

In this diagram, the computer with the IP address 192.168.1.3 tries to initiate a connection to 2.2.2.2. The packet is passed to the Linux router with the source IP address 192.168.1.3 and destination IP address 2.2.2.2.

If the computer is SNATed or Masqueraded, the Linux router will change the source IP address in the packet header from 192.168.1.3 to 1.1.1.1 and will pass the packet towards 2.2.2.2 according to the routing process. Information about this connection is stored in /proc/net/ip_conntrack.

When 2.2.2.2 replies, the IP packet that arrives in the Linux router will have source IP address 2.2.2.2 and destination IP address 1.1.1.1. Linux searches for information about this packet in /proc/net/ip_conntrack, and finds a match against information stored at the previous step. At this point, Linux will change the destination IP address in the packet header to 192.168.1.3 and will pass the IP packet towards the NATed computer according to the routing process.

> Using SNAT or Masquerade, 192.168.1.3 can initiate a connection to 2.2.2.2, but 2.2.2.2 can't initiate a connection to 192.168.1.3, because this is a private IP address.

DNAT

DNAT or Destination Network Address Translations maps a public IP address to a private IP address. DNAT is the reverse of SNAT; so, if you SNAT to translate a private IP address into a public IP address and DNAT to translate the same public IP address into the same private IP address, the result will be **full NAT**.

DNAT is usually used when you have servers behind NAT, so the same public IP address is mapped to different private IP addresses depending on ports or protocols. This process is also called **port forwarding**.

Let's take a look at the following diagram:

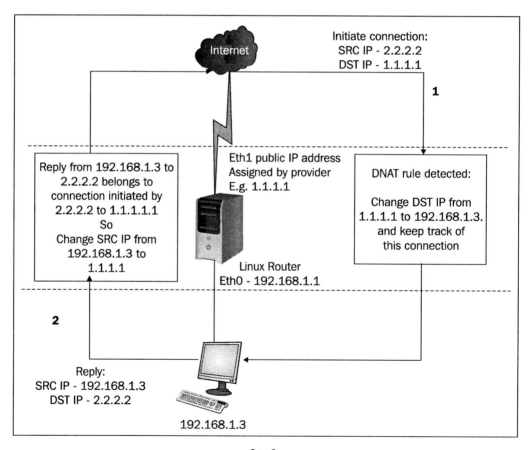

Normally, 2.2.2.2 cannot initiate a communication to 192.168.1.3 because this is a private IP address and is not routed on the Internet.

2.2.2.2 tries to initiate a connection with 1.1.1.1. If a DNAT rule is matched for this packet, the Linux router will change the destination IP address in the IP packet header from 1.1.1.1 to 192.168.1.3, pass the packet towards 192.168.1.3, and keep a track of this connection.

When 192.168.1.3 replies, the packet is found in the `conntrack` table of the Linux router so it "knows" that the packet belongs to the connection initiated by 2.2.2.2 to 1.1.1.1. The Linux router will change the source IP address in the IP packet header from 192.168.1.3 to 1.1.1.1.

 If DNAT is configured, but SNAT is not, 2.2.2.2 will be able to establish connections to 192.168.1.3 using 1.1.1.1 as destination IP address, but 192.168.1.3 will not be able to initiate connections to 2.2.2.2.

To get a little off-topic here, there are quite a lot of SOHO routers calling their DNAT functions DMZ. Actually, most of the SOHO routers call DNAT DMZ, which is not entirely correct. DMZ, acronym for Demilitarized Zone is a place in your network where you don't filter anything. DMZ is basically a set of public IP addresses that are allowed to do anything (all incoming and outgoing traffic to and from these IP addresses is allowed to pass without exceptions).

Due to the fact that most SOHO routers are programmed to Masquerade for a LAN, they call a process in which one private IP address receives all (unfiltered) traffic destined to the public IP of the router's WAN interface DMZ.

Full NAT (aka Full Cone NAT)

Full NAT is a way to fully map one IP address to another. With full NAT, one device behind the NAT box which has a private IP address (e.g. 192.168.1.3) will be seen on the Internet as another IP address routed to the NAT box by the provider (e.g. 1.1.1.1).

This means that when a request is sent by 192.168.1.3 to any device on the Internet, the receiving device will "see" that it received a packet from 1.1.1.1 (so far, this is simple source NAT). More than that, for any packet from the Internet with the destination IP address 1.1.1.1, the NAT box will rewrite the destination address in the IP header to 192.168.1.3 and will forward that packet to 192.168.1.3, even if the connection was not initiated by 192.168.1.3 (this is simple destination NAT).

In other words, full NAT is SNAT and DNAT as presented earlier.

This is the function that SOHO routers call "DMZ", as explained earlier. The reason they call this function "DMZ" is that IP packets that don't belong to a connection initiated by any host from the private network 192.168.1.0/24 will be forwarded to 192.168.1.3, and so this host doesn't have the protection provided by the fact that it has a private IP address.

> In the case just presented, 1.1.1.1 can be the NAT router IP address or it can just be routed to it. If it's the router's public IP address (as in the earlier diagrams), the NAT router can't be accessed from the Internet (e.g. you can't SSH into it) because it will forward all packets to 192.168.1.3.

PAT or NAPT

PAT stands for Port Address Translation and it is also called NAPT, which stands for Network Address and Port Translation. The idea behind PAT is to translate not only the IP address, but also the port number for specific hosts and ports.

The company's web server is behind NAT and it has the IP address 192.168.1.100. Having only one public IP address, `http://www.<ourcompanyname>.com` is configured to respond to 1.1.1.1. For the web server to be accessed from the Internet, we have to rewrite the address 1.1.1.1 to 192.168.1.100 whenever a request comes into our NAT router with the destination port 80.

More than this, we have a company intranet server with the IP address 192.168.1.200, running a web server on port 80. When being in the office, the employees have to type `http://192.168.1.200` in their web browser and they can log in the intranet web server.

If we want to allow users to log on to the intranet server when they are outside the office, PAT is the answer. With PAT, we can choose a port that's not opened on the NAT router (e.g. 2143), and whenever a request comes from the Internet with the destination IP address 217.156.123.3 and the destination port 2143, the NAT router rewrites the destination IP address to 192.168.1.200 and the destination port from 2143 to 80.

This way, from the Internet when a user types:

- `http://www.<ourcompanyname>.com/` the request is forwarded to 192.168.1.100 on port 80 and the company's web page is displayed

- `http://www.<ourcompanyname>.com:2143/` the request is forwarded to 192.168.1.200 on port 80 and the company's intranet web page is displayed

We don't have to rewrite the port when a packet has the source IP address 192.168.1.200; we just have to set up SNAT or Masquerade so that the intranet server accesses the Internet using 1.1.1.1.

NAT Using iptables

So far, we discussed general NAT principles, NAT types, and what every sort of NAT does.

netfilter/iptables can be used to perform NAT in any of the ways that we discussed. Actually, there are many things that you can do with iptables in this area and we will try to cover as much as possible in this chapter. Before we get there, let's see what we need to be able to successfully perform NAT on Linux.

Setting Up the Kernel

Usually, every Linux distribution comes with a kernel compiled with netfilter support, iptables tool, and all the modules needed for performing Network Address Translation.

A very good HowTo on compiling Linux 2.4 and 2.6 kernels is written by Kwan Lowe and can be found at `http://www.digitalhermit.com/linux/Kernel-Build-HOWTO.html`

When compiling a new kernel or recompiling the kernel that you have, you must set `NETFILTER=y` in order to use iptables. In the 2.6 kernels, this option is usually found under **Device Drivers | Networking support | Networking support (NET [=y]) | Networking options**, but it really depends on the kernel version.

For example, in kernel 2.6.14, this option is found under **Networking | Networking Options**.

If you use `make menuconfig` or `make xconfig` to configure your kernel for recompiling, select **Networking | Networking options | Network packet filtering (replaces ipchains) | IP: Netfilter Configuration**:

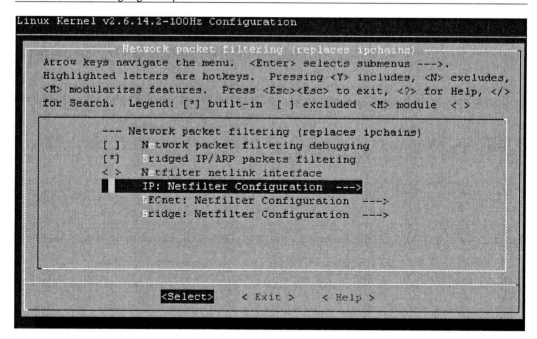

In the **IP: Netfilter Configuration** section you will find the options needed for NAT as follows:

- IP_NF_CONNTRACK or **Connection tracking (required for masq/NAT)** keeps a record of the IP packets that passed through the machine in order to pass them correctly to the NATed endpoints when requests made from those are answered. This is vital for NAT. If you say **No** here, you will not be able to perform NAT.

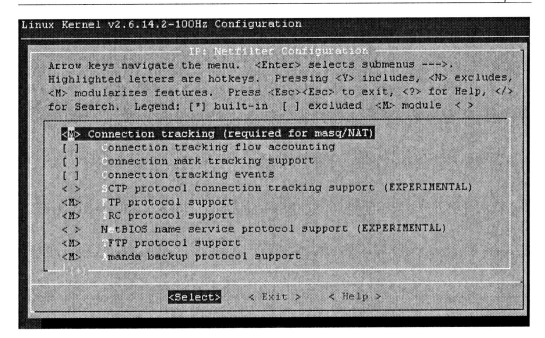

```
Linux Kernel v2.6.14.2-100Hz Configuration
┌──────────────────── IP: Netfilter Configuration ─────────────────────┐
│ Arrow keys navigate the menu. <Enter> selects submenus --->.          │
│ Highlighted letters are hotkeys.  Pressing <Y> includes, <N> excludes,│
│ <M> modularizes features.  Press <Esc><Esc> to exit, <?> for Help, </>│
│ for Search.  Legend: [*] built-in  [ ] excluded  <M> module  < >      │
│ ┌───────────────────────────────────────────────────────────────────┐ │
│ │<M> Connection tracking (required for masq/NAT)                    │ │
│ │[ ]     Connection tracking flow accounting                        │ │
│ │[ ]     Connection mark tracking support                           │ │
│ │[ ]     Connection tracking events                                 │ │
│ │< >     SCTP protocol connection tracking support (EXPERIMENTAL)   │ │
│ │<M>     FTP protocol support                                       │ │
│ │<M>     IRC protocol support                                       │ │
│ │< >     NetBIOS name service protocol support (EXPERIMENTAL)       │ │
│ │<M>     TFTP protocol support                                      │ │
│ │<M>     Amanda backup protocol support                             │ │
│ └───────────────────────────────────────────────────────────────────┘ │
│           <Select>    < Exit >    < Help >                            │
└───────────────────────────────────────────────────────────────────────┘
```

> It is highly recommended that you select *M* for conntrack,
> meaning that you compile the connection tracking option
> of netfilter as a module. In time, you might want to use
> your Linux box to do routing without NAT, and conntrack
> would slow things down in that case.

- IP_NF_NAT or **Full NAT** allows you to do SNAT, DNAT, MASQ, and redirects. You must select this module for NAT.

- IP_NF_TARGET_MASQUERADE or **MASQUERADE target support** is needed for MASQ. If you will need MASQ, select this module.

- IP_NF_TARGET_REDIRECT or **REDIRECT target support** is needed to do redirection of packets to the local machine instead of letting them pass through. We will need this if we want to set up a transparent proxy, for example.

- IP_NF_TARGET_NETMAP or **NETMAP target support** is an implementation of static 1:1 NAT mapping of a network address.

- IP_NF_TARGET_SAME or **SAME target support** is exactly like SNAT, except that when using a range of public IP addresses for a network, SAME tries to allocate clients the same IP address for all outgoing connections.

- IP_NF_FTP (FTP protocol support), IP_NF_IRC (IRC protocol support), IP_NF_TFTP (TFTP protocol support), IP_NF_AMANDA (Amanda backup protocol support), and IP_NF_CT_PROTO_SCTP (SCTP protocol connection tracking support) are connection tracking helpers for the protocols they describe. If we need to allow the NATed endpoints to one of these protocols, we need to compile that module and load it when starting our firewall.

The netfilter nat Table

The nat table contains three chains—PREROUTING, POSTROUTING, and OUTPUT. Each chain may contain rules that are examined sequentially until one of the rules matches a packet, the same as for the chains in the netfilter table. These chains can be viewed by issuing the command iptables -t nat -L.

```
router:~# iptables -t nat -L
Chain PREROUTING (policy ACCEPT)
target     prot opt source                destination

Chain POSTROUTING (policy ACCEPT)
target     prot opt source                destination

Chain OUTPUT (policy ACCEPT)
target     prot opt source                destination
```

If the kernel modules are properly built, the Linux box will automatically load the modules iptable_nat and ip_conntrack when issuing any commands with iptables -t nat; so there is no need to use Linux utilities insmod or modprobe for NAT to work.

The OUTPUT chain is not fully supported, so we will have to ignore that for now.

The PREROUTING and POSTROUTING chains have meaningful names. The PREROUTING chain is analyzed by the kernel before any routing decision is made. Therefore, what we should do in the PREROUTING chain is to change the address of the destination IP and then leave it to the routing process to find the destination that we just changed (DNAT).

The POSTROUTING chain contains rules that the kernel analyzes after a routing decision is made. This means that we have a path to the destination, and so we can change the source IP address if that path is outside our network (SNAT).

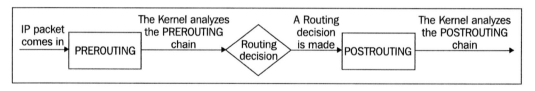

Let's have a look at this diagram to visualize how DNAT and SNAT work.

DNAT means that we rewrite the destination IP address; so the kernel must do that before looking up its routing table to check where to send the packet (this is the PREROUTING chain). For instance, if we perform DNAT for a host in a private network that is directly connected to the NAT router (e.g. 192.168.1.3), the IP packet comes in, the destination IP address is rewritten with 192.168.1.3, and the kernel looks it up in its routing table:

```
router:~# route -n
Kernel IP routing table
Destination    Gateway      Genmask          Flags Metric Ref    Use Iface
192.168.1.0    0.0.0.0      255.255.255.0    U      0      0        0 eth1
```

The kernel sees the 192.168.1.0/24 network directly connected on the device Eth1, and so it will forward the packet to the host 192.168.1.3.

SNAT on the other hand means that the source IP address gets rewritten. To be able to understand the process better, we will think about Masquerading. A packet originating from 192.168.1.3 must access a host on the Internet. The kernel looks up its routing table, and if it has a route to the destination host on one interface, the source IP address is rewritten to the IP address of that interface in the router. If a route to the destination host is not found, then the NAT router will match the default route, and the source IP packet is rewritten with the IP address of the interface on which the default route resides.

To append, insert, or delete rules in the nat table, the syntax of iptables is basically the same as in packet filtering.

- Append: `iptables -t nat -A <chain> <rule>`
- Insert: `iptables -t nat -I <chain> <rule>`
- Delete: `iptables -t nat -D <chain> <rule>`
- Delete all: `iptables -t nat -F`

where `<chain>` can be PREROUTING, POSTROUTING, or OUTPUT, and `<rule>` is the actual rule.

 Please note that the command `iptables -F` flushes all rules in the INPUT, FORWARD, and OUTPUT chains of the netfilter table, and doesn't flush the rules in the nat table.

SNAT with iptables

SNAT is one of the most commonly used types of NAT with iptables because of the topology used.

Let's see, for example, the following scenario:

Network 192.168.1.0/24 is in our office. We have an Ethernet connection from our provider, which assigned us the IP address 1.2.3.1/30 and the default gateway 1.2.3.2.

All the computers in the 192.168.1.0/24 network have the default gateway set to 192.168.1.1.

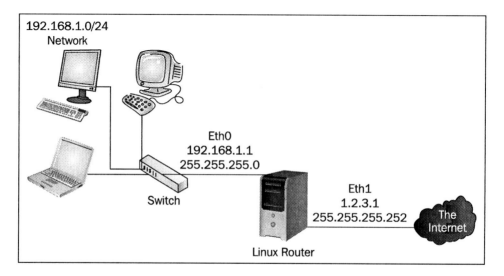

Our Linux router has two Ethernet interfaces:

- Eth0, with the IP address 192.168.1.1 and netmask 255.255.255.0, is connected to a switch that connects other devices in the 192.168.1.0/24 network.
- Eth1, with the IP address 1.2.3.1 and netmask 255.255.255.252, is connected to the provider's CPE (Customer Premises Equipment), which can be a DSL modem, cable modem, media converter, etc.

We can set up SNAT so that all devices in the 192.168.1.0/24 network access the Internet with only one rule:

```
iptables -t nat -A POSTROUTING -s 192.168.1.0/24 -j SNAT --to 1.2.3.1
```

This command has the same effect as the following command, which we would use if the IP address of Eth1 were dynamically assigned, or if we used a dial-up modem instead of an Ethernet card:

```
iptables -t nat -A POSTROUTING -s 192.168.1.0/24 -j MASQUERADE
```

Let's say our provider filters out all ports higher than 1024. In this case, we will need to change the source port as well, and not only the source IP address. This can be done by:

```
iptables -t nat -A POSTROUTING -s 192.168.1.0/24 -j SNAT --to
1.2.3.1:1-1024
```

The laptop user seen in the previous figure is an IRC fan and he gives us a call saying he can't connect to any IRC networks. This means that the ip_conntrack module needs a little help, and we can give it to him by inserting the ip_conntrack_irc module in the kernel. Also, we might want to let users make successful FTP connections, and so we want to add the ip_conntrack_ftp module as well.

```
modprobe ip_conntrack_irc   #or   insmod ip_conntrack_irc
modprobe ip_conntrack_ftp   #or   insmod ip_conntrack_ftp
```

After a few weeks, the laptop user has convinced other users in the 192.168.1.0/24 network of how wonderful the IRC is; so we have about 20-30 users connecting to the same IRC network. Now, they have started to complain about how difficult it is to get connected on the IRC network, because the IRC network only allows a few connections from the same IP address. We figure that 32 IP addresses are enough for them, so we call the provider to assign us a /27 public IP subnet. For a few dollars extra, they assign us 1.2.4.0/27. We have to change the initial rule to:

```
iptables -t nat -A POSTROUTING -s 192.168.1.0/24 -j SNAT --to 1.2.4.0-
1.2.4.32
```

They stop complaining, but we realize that we don't use the public IP address of our Linux router for NAT anymore. Let's add that too; so we give them an extra IP address:

```
iptables -t nat -A POSTROUTING -s 192.168.1.0/24 -j SNAT --to 1.2.4.0-
1.2.4.32 --to 1.2.3.1
```

One of our users gets into an argument on IRC, and gets flooded while SNAT mapps his IP address to 1.2.4.15. Our provider's flood-detection system automatically filters that IP address and sends us an email informing us about it. We need to stop SNAT to map any internal addresses to that IP address, so we do the following:

```
iptables -t nat -A POSTROUTING -s 192.168.1.0/24 -j SNAT --to 1.2.4.0-
1.2.4.14 --to 1.2.4.16-1.2.4.32  --to 1.2.3.1
```

One guy from accounting with the IP address 192.168.1.19 complains that he can't access any computers with IP addresses over 192.168.1.32. It is possible that he has changed his netmask to 255.255.255.227, and so all IP packets from his computer to computers in 192.168.1.0/24 that are not in 192.168.1.0/27 pass through the Linux router and get SNATed. To solve this problem, we have two alternatives.

The first would be not to SNAT 192.168.1.0/24 when the destination is another computer in 192.168.1.0/24:

```
iptables -t nat -A POSTROUTING -s 192.168.1.0/24 -d ! 192.168.1.0/24
-j SNAT --to 1.2.4.0-1.2.4.32 --to 1.2.3.1
```

The second choice we have is to SNAT only the packets that go out on Eth1:

```
iptables -t nat -A POSTROUTING -s 192.168.1.0/24 -o eth1 -j SNAT --to
1.2.4.0-1.2.4.32 --to 1.2.3.1
```

Our provider connected another location of our company to the same equipment, and since we are in the same VLAN, we don't have to build a tunnel between the routers at each location, but just route the networks through the Linux router at that location. On the other site, we have the network 192.168.2.0/24. We need to let computers in our network access computers in the 192.168.2.0/24 network without SNATing them:

```
iptables -t nat -I POSTROUTING -s 192.168.1.0/24 -d 192.168.2.0/24 -j
ACCEPT
```

This command will insert the rule before the NAT rule; so if any packet from 192.168.1.0/24 is destined to any IP in the 192.168.2.0/24 network, this rule will match and the chain will not be analyzed further, so SNAT will not take place.

Jane, our secretary, is famous for her good coffee, but since she got the IRC fever, she's not doing anything anymore. The manager is angry about this but she doesn't want to fire Jane because she's addicted to her famous coffee; so she comes to ask us to do something about it. There are many things we can do in this matter, for instance drop packets from Jane (192.168.1.31) when trying to access ports 6666 to 6669 in the POSTROUTING chain:

```
iptables -t nat -I POSTROUTING -s 192.168.1.31 -p tcp --dport
6666:6669 -j DROP
```

We might want to ask the manager what Jane is allowed to do. For instance, if the manager wants to allow Jane only web access, we can do the following:

```
iptables -t nat -I POSTROUTING -s 192.168.1.31 -p tcp --dport ! 80 -j
DROP
```

This rule will not SNAT Jane's IP address when trying to access something other than port 80 TCP, but it will SNAT her IP address when accessing any UDP services because UDP packets will not match this rule; so she will be able to access any DNS server outside our network.

DNAT with iptables

We will continue with the previous scenario for DNAT as well. One day, the manager calls us telling she needs to access her computer from home. Of course she can't do that because of her private IP address 192.168.1.50. We decide to allocate one of the public IP addresses that we have for her office computer, but if we were to create an alias on Eth0 for that, we would not only lose some IP addresses, but she also won't be in the same network as the others. The best solution is to *map* a public IP address (let's say 1.2.4.1) to her office computer's private IP address (192.168.1.50). This is, of course, DNAT:

```
iptables -t nat -A PREROUTING -d 1.2.4.1 -j DNAT --to 192.168.1.50
```

So the next thing to do is to call her and tell him that whenever she tries to connect to her office computer from home, she must connect to 1.2.4.1.

Our intranet server has the IP address 192.168.1.100. One guy from the financial department has a broadband connection and asks us if he can access the intranet server from home. He gives us his public IP address as 1.2.5.17. We tell him that from his home he should try the IP address 1.2.4.2 in his web browser, and we execute:

```
iptables -t nat -A PREROUTING -s 1.2.5.17 -d 1.2.4.2 -p tcp --dport 80
-j DNAT --to 192.168.1.100
```

We think we might want to SSH to the intranet server from anywhere. It would not be a very wise idea to map one IP address to the intranet server as it is vital for our company, and if an SSH bug is discovered, we don't want that server to be hacked. A good idea would be to map a high-number port to the SSH port on the intranet server (this is PAT or NAPT).

```
iptables -t nat -A PREROUTING -d 1.2.4.2 -p tcp --dport 65521 -j DNAT
--to 192.168.1.100:22
```

This way, when we are not at the office and we want to SSH into the intranet server, we open an SSH connection to 1.2.4.2 port 65521.

After a while, suppose we installed a web server with the IP address 192.168.1.200. The web server is www.mycompany.whatever and points in DNS to 1.2.4.5. To be accessible to the outside world, we perform the following:

```
iptables -t nat -A PREROUTING -d 1.2.4.5 -p tcp --dport 80 -j DNAT --
to 192.168.1.200
```

Transparent Proxy

Transparent proxy is a way to force users to use a proxy server, even if their browsers are configured not to. You probably know about the benefits of using a proxy server—

bandwidth saving for cached pages and access control implementation (e.g. deny downloads of files that have dangerous extensions).

We can perform transparent proxy for all or some users to prevent them from bypassing the proxy whenever they want. This is especially good for children's computers to deny them access to sexually explicit sites, for example.

On our Linux router, we installed a Squid proxy server to cache some content from the Web. Also, we want to deny access to sex sites or malicious downloads for users. The users are not very pleased about using our proxy server, and they usually remove it from their browser configuration. We can force them to use the proxy server anyway. If the proxy server listens on port 3128 we will do the following:

```
iptables -t nat -A PREROUTING -s 192.168.1.0/24 -p tcp --dport 80 -j
REDIRECT --to-port 3128
```

If we want to allow the manager (who has the IP address 192.168.1.50) to bypass the proxy server, we do so like this:

```
iptables -t nat -I PREROUTING -s 192.168.1.50 -p tcp --dport 80 -j
ACCEPT
```

So this rule will be matched in the PREROUTING chain, and she will be SNATed in the POSTROUTING chain.

Setting Up the Script

This is a commonly used configuration, but there are many other things we can do with the NAT support for netfilter. We will discuss more NAT issues and configurations in the third section of this book in the small networks case studies. For now, let's see how we should set up the script for this example scenario.

The NAT part of the firewall should be included in the same script as the rest of the firewall rules as described earlier. So, we have:

```
#!/bin/bash

IP=/sbin/iptables

#... some packet filtering rules

### NAT SECTION

#first of all, we want to flush the NAT table

$IP -t nat -F
```

```
############ SNAT PART


#Jane's special rule.
#Don't SNAT any TCP connections from her computer except www and all
#udp connections except DNS

$IP -t nat -A POSTROUTING -s 192.168.1.31 -p tcp --dport ! 80 -j DROP
$IP -t nat -A POSTROUTING -s 192.168.1.31 -p udp --dport ! 53 -j DROP


#Don't SNAT anything from 192.168.1.0/24 to 192.168.2.0/24

$IP -t nat -A POSTROUTING -s 192.168.1.0/24 -d 192.168.2.0/24 -j ACCEPT

#The boss needs DNAT but we should also SNAT her IP address to 1.2.4.1

$IP -t nat -A POSTROUTING -s 192.168.1.50 -j SNAT --to 1.2.4.1

#Snat Everyone

$IP -t nat -A POSTROUTING -s 192.168.1.0/24 -o eth1 -j SNAT --to
1.2.4.0-1.2.4.32 --to 1.2.3.1
############ DNAT PART

#Dnat the boss so she can access her PC from home

$IP -t nat -A PREROUTING -d 1.2.4.1 -j DNAT --to 192.168.1.50

#DNAT the intranet server for the guy in the financial department

$IP -t nat -A PREROUTING -s 1.2.5.17 -d 1.2.4.2 -p tcp --dport 80 -j
DNAT --to 192.168.1.100

#DNAT for us to ssh into the intranet server

$IP -t nat -A PREROUTING -d 1.2.4.2 -p tcp --dport 65521 -j DNAT --to
192.168.1.100:22

#DNAT the web server

$IP -t nat -A PREROUTING -d 1.2.4.5 -p tcp --dport 80 -j DNAT --to
192.168.1.200
############ Transparent Proxy

#Allow the boss to bypass the proxy server
```

```
$IP -t nat -A PREROUTING -s 192.168.1.50 -p tcp --dport 80 -j ACCEPT

#Do transparent proxy for the rest of the people

$IP -t nat -A PREROUTING -s 192.168.1.0/24 -p tcp --dport 80 -j
REDIRECT --to-port 3128

### End of NAT section
```

Verifying the Configuration

To verify the configuration, we need to see the chains of the nat table.

```
root@router:~# iptables -t nat -L -n
Chain PREROUTING (policy ACCEPT)
target      prot opt source            destination
DNAT        all  --  0.0.0.0/0         1.2.4.1     to:192.168.1.50
DNAT        tcp  --  1.2.5.17          1.2.4.2     tcp dpt:80
                                                   to:192.168.1.100
DNAT        tcp  --  0.0.0.0/0         1.2.4.2     tcp dpt:65521
                                                   to:192.168.1.100:22
DNAT        tcp  --  0.0.0.0/0         1.2.4.5     tcp dpt:80
                                                   to:192.168.1.200
ACCEPT      tcp  --  192.168.1.50      0.0.0.0/0   tcp dpt:80
REDIRECT    tcp  --  192.168.1.0/24    0.0.0.0/0   tcp dpt:80 redir
                                                   ports 3128

Chain POSTROUTING (policy ACCEPT)
target      prot opt source            destination
DROP        tcp  --  192.168.1.31      0.0.0.0/0       tcp dpt:!80
DROP        udp  --  192.168.1.31      0.0.0.0/0       tcp dpt:!53
ACCEPT      all  --  192.168.1.0/24    192.168.2.0/24
SNAT        all  --  192.168.1.50      0.0.0.0/0       to:1.2.4.1
SNAT        all  --  192.168.1.0/24    0.0.0.0/0       to:1.2.4.0-1.2.
                                                       4.32 1.2.3.1

Chain OUTPUT (policy ACCEPT)
target      prot opt source                destination
root@router:~#
```

We can see here that all the lines we wrote in the script have been successfully entered in the nat table.

After building a script like this, the only way to test its correct functionality is to send test packets for each line and track them with a network analyzer like TCPdump, ethereal, etc.

For example, if we capture packets on our Linux router and try to initiate a connection from the Internet to 1.2.4.1 on a random port and TCPdump shows a sequence of packets like:

1. In on Eth0 from 2.2.2.2 to 1.2.4.1

2. Out on Eth0 from 1.2.3.1 — destination host unreachable

and nothing on Eth1, then we will know from the start that the DNAT rule was not matched.

If the packet flow from the analyzer looks OK, then we should see the packets matching the rules using the `-v` when listing the rules (in this case `iptables -L -n -v`).

A Less Normal Situation: Double NAT

Our company opened a remote office in a third-world country that didn't have an internet connection. The administrator hired in that location configured the local network with IP addresses in the private class C network 192.168.1.0/24.

After a while, they were able to install a permanent internet connection with a static assigned IP address 1.2.8.1. The database server on their location has the same IP address as the database server in our location — 192.168.1.60.

The configuration is the same as in the following figure:

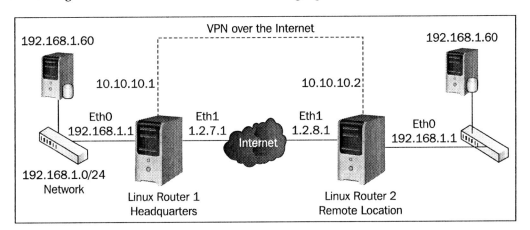

In the headquarter's location, we have:

*   HQ local network: 192.168.1.0/24

*   HQ database server: 192.168.1.60

- Linux Router 1 with two Ethernet interfaces: Eth0, which connects to the local network and has the IP address 192.168.1.1, and Eth1, which connects to the Internet with the IP address 1.2.7.1

In the remote location, we have:

- Remote local network: 192.168.1.0/24

- Remote database server in the remote location: 192.168.1.60

- Linux Router 2 with two Ethernet interfaces: Eth0, which connects to the local network and has the IP address 192.168.1.1, and Eth1, which connects to the Internet with the IP address 1.2.8.1

The next step is to create a VPN between these locations. On Linux Router 1 at the headquarters, we perform the following:

```
iptunnel add vpn1 mode gre remote 1.2.8.1 local 1.2.7.1 key 8132912

ifconfig vpn1 10.10.10.1 pointopoint 10.10.10.2 netmask
255.255.255.252
```

On Linux Router 2 at the remote location, what we do is:

```
iptunnel add vpn1 mode gre remote 1.2.7.1 local 1.2.8.1 key 8132912

ifconfig vpn1 10.10.10.2 pointopoint 10.10.10.1 netmask
255.255.255.252
```

In a normal situation, we would have a network at the headquarters and another network at the remote location, and we would route them on the vpn1 interface and don't perform SNAT. As the heading says, this is not a normal situation. On Linux Router 1 we can route on the Linux Router 1 network 192.168.1.0/24 through 10.10.10.2 (Linux Router 2), but it would have absolutely no effect, because the Linux kernel prefers directly connected routes (and it is normal for it to be this way).

In order for a computer from headquarters to communicate with a computer from the remote location, we have to "fake" the fact that we have different networks on each side. So, we will tell the headquarters' computers that the computers in the remote location are in the network 192.168.20.0/24. We will also tell the remote computers that the computers in the headquarters location are in the network 192.168.10.0/24.

In the following example, we will show how the database servers can communicate, for example, for data replication. So, we will teach you how to map one IP, and you can do the same for the other 252 IP addresses (i.e. from 254, excluding the database server and the gateway).

From their point of view, the database server in the headquarters location is communicating with the database server in the remote location that has the IP address 192.168.20.60, and the database server in the remote location is communicating with the database server in the headquarters location that has the IP address 192.168.10.60. In fact, they both have the IP address 192.168.1.60.

Let's configure Linux Router 1 (at the headquarters).

Step 1

```
ifconfig eth1:0 192.168.10.1 netmask 255.255.255.0
```

This is an optional step. IP packets with destination IP addresses in 192.168.10.0/24 will arrive at this router, and if we have no rules in the PREROUTING chain, we don't want to forward them on the default route.

Step 2

```
route add -net 192.168.20.0 netmask 255.255.255.0 gw 10.10.10.2
```

This will add a route to network 192.168.20.0/24 via 10.10.10.2 on the vpn1 interface.

Step 3

```
iptables -t nat -A POSTROUTING -s 192.168.1.60 -d 192.168.20.60 -j
SNAT --to 192.168.10.60
```

This will create a SNAT rule on Linux Router 1 that will map the IP address 192.168.1.60 to 192.168.10.60 if the destination IP address is 192.168.20.60.

Step 4

```
iptables -t nat -A PREROUTING -d 192.168.10.60 -j DNAT --to
192.168.1.60
```

This will create an DNAT rule for all packets arriving at Linux Router 1 having the destination IP address 192.168.10.60 to send the packets to 192.168.1.60.

This is all we need on Linux Router 1.

On Linux router 2, we do basically the same thing.

Step 1

```
ifconfig eth1:0 192.168.20.1 netmask 255.255.255.0
```

Step 2

```
route add -net 192.168.10.0 netmask 255.255.255.0 gw 10.10.10.1
```

This will add a route to network 192.168.10.0/24 via 10.10.10.1 on the vpn1 interface.

Step 3

```
iptables -t nat -A POSTROUTING -s 192.168.1.60 -d 192.168.10.60 -j
SNAT --to 192.168.20.60
```

This will create an SNAT rule on Linux Router 2 that will map the IP address 192.168.1.60 to 192.168.20.60 if the destination IP address is 192.168.10.60.

Step 4

```
iptables -t nat -A PREROUTING -d 192.168.20.60 -j DNAT --to
192.168.1.60
```

This will create a DNAT rule for all packets arriving at Linux Router 2 with the destination IP address 192.168.20.60 to send the packets to 192.168.1.60.

This is the end of the configuration we need to make. Let's see if it works both ways:

The database server in the headquarters location sends a packet to the database server in the remote location, which it thinks is 192.168.20.60. Since 192.168.20.60 is not directly connected to 192.168.1.60, it will forward the packet to the default gateway, Linux Router 1. Linux Router 1 checks out the PREROUTING chain and finds no rule to match this packet, and so it looks up the routing table for 192.168.20.60 and finds the best route through 10.10.10.2 on interface vpn1. Now, Linux Router 1 checks out the POSTROUTING chain and matches the rule that states that for every packet from 192.168.1.60 to 192.168.20.60, it should change the source IP address to 192.168.10.60. Linux Router 1 does that, and due to ip_conntrack it keeps a record of this connection. The packet with the changed source IP address is forwarded according to the routing table to 10.10.10.2 on interface vpn1.

Now, the packet arrives at Linux Router 2 at the remote location having the source IP address 192.168.10.60 and destination 192.168.20.60. Linux Router 2 looks in its PREROUTING chain and matches the rule that says to change the destination IP address to 192.168.1.60 if the packet is destined for 192.168.20.60. Linux Router 2 does this and then looks up 192.168.1.60 in its routing table and sees that 192.168.1.60 is directly connected with itself on Eth0. After analyzing the POSTROUTING chain and seeing that no rule matches this packet, Linux Router 2 forwards the packet to 192.168.1.60 as being from 192.168.10.60.

Packets traveling the other way around follow the exact same steps; so we can say "Mission Accomplished!"

Packet Mangling with iptables

The term "mangling" might mislead people to conceive it as malicious — packet mangling is nothing like that at all. Packet mangling refers to the process of intentionally altering data in IP packet headers before or after the routing process.

Well, not all fields of the IP packet header can be modified in the mangle table, but that is not necessary.

Let's recall what an IP packet header looks like:

0		4		8		16		19	24		31
VERS		HLEN		Service Type		Total Length					
Identification						Flags			Fragment Offset		
Time to Live				Protocol		Header Checksum					
Source IP Address											
Destination IP Address									Padding		
IP Options (if any)											
Data											
...											

We have already discussed NAT, where we saw that we can "mangle" a packet by modifying the **Source IP address** and **Destination IP address** fields of the IP header. This mangling of packets is done only with NAT and is a part of the NAT process.

So, using the mangle table of netfilter we can modify the following two fields:

- **TOS**: the 8 bit Type Of Service field
- **TTL**: the 8 bit Time To Live field

iptables can also set a mark to IP packets that can be used internal by iproute2 for source routing and/or QoS with `tc`. This internal mark, called **nfmark** (netfilter mark), doesn't alter any of the IP packet headers' fields. Nfmarks can be set using the MARK target in iptables, which has three options that we can see using `--help` in conjunction with the MARK target:

```
root@router:~# iptables -j MARK --help
... some lines missing ...
MARK target v1.3.1 options:
  --set-mark value          Set nfmark value
  --and-mark value          Binary AND the nfmark with value
  --or-mark  value          Binary OR  the nfmark with value
```

Example: mark packets to 192.168.1.100 with nfmark 6:

```
iptables -t mangle -A POSTROUTING -d 192.168.1.100 -j MARK --set-mark 6
```

The TOS field is 8 bits long and was discussed in the previous chapter. Alteration of the TOS field is very useful for QoS. For this, iptables uses the TOS target, which has the `--set-tos` option. We can see TOS target options using `--help` in the command line:

```
root@router:~# iptables -j TOS --help
... some lines missing...
TOS target v1.3.5 options:
  --set-tos value              Set Type of Service field to one of the
                               following numeric or descriptive values:
                                       Minimize-Delay 16 (0x10)
                                       Maximize-Throughput 8 (0x08)
                                       Maximize-Reliability 4 (0x04)
                                       Minimize-Cost 2 (0x02)
                                       Normal-Service 0 (0x00)
```

Example: set TOS to `Maximize-Throughput` for outgoing FTP data:

```
iptables -t mangle -A POSTROUTING -p tcp --sport 20 -j TOS --set-tos 8
```

There are only five TOS values we can set; so the TOS target doesn't modify the whole TOS byte. However, this can be done with DSCP (Differentiated Services Field Codepoints). The DSCP bits are the first six bits in the TOS byte, as shown in the following figure:

DSCP Differentiated Service Code Point Bits						Diffserv Flow control	
0	1	2	3	4	5	6	7
PRECEDENCE			Type Of Service - TOS				MBZ

iptables has the DSCP target that can be used to alter the DSCP bits. The options can be found using `--help` with the DSCP target.

```
root@router:~# iptables -j DSCP --help
... some lines missing...
DSCP target options
  --set-dscp value     Set DSCP field in packet header to value
```

```
                         This value can be in decimal (ex: 32)
                         or in hex (ex: 0x20)

    --set-dscp-class class          Set the DSCP field in packet header
                         to the value represented by the DiffServ class
                         value.
                         This class may be EF,BE or any of the CSxx
                         or AFxx classes.
                         These two options are mutually exclusive !
```

Example: set DSCP 32 to packets arriving on interface Eth0:

```
iptables -t mangle -A PREROUTING -i eth0 -j DSCP --set-dscp 32
```

DSCP is explained in more detail in RFC2474, which can be found at
`http://www.rfc-editor.org/rfc/rfc2474.txt`.

The TTL field of the IP packet header is the Time To Live for that IP packet, and can be altered using the TTL target of iptables.

```
root@router:~# iptables -j TTL --help
… some lines missing…
TTL target v1.3.1 options
   --ttl-set value                  Set TTL to <value 0-255>
   --ttl-dec value                  Decrement TTL by <value 1-255>
   --ttl-inc value                  Increment TTL by <value 1-255>
```

Altering TTL can be useful, for example, if you want a client not to distribute the Internet to others. If you set the TTL value to 1 for packets going to a certain IP address, then only the device having that IP address receives the IP packets. If the packet is destined to a host behind that IP address, the TTL will be decremented and the IP packet will be dropped.

Example: set TTL to 1 for packets going out interface ppp0:

```
iptables -t mangle -I POSTROUTING -o ppp0 -j TTL --ttl-set 1
```

The netfilter mangle Table

The `mangle` table has five chains, named PREROUTING, INPUT, FORWARD, OUTPUT, and POSTROUTING. Let's look again at the packet flow diagram again:

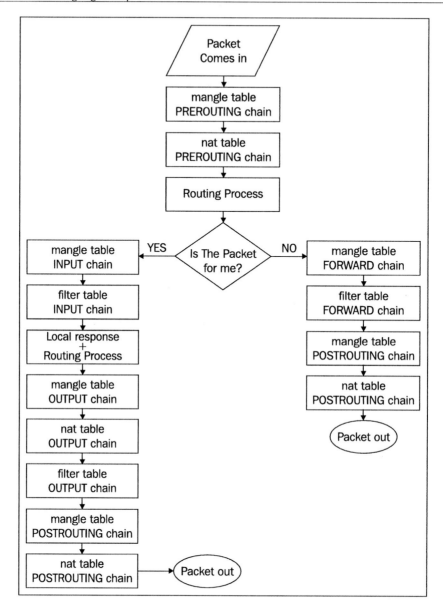

The rules in the PREROUTING chain of the mangle table are analyzed by the kernel when a packet comes in, before the routing process takes place.

If the packet is not for the router (is destined to a host behind it), the kernel looks up the rules in the mangle table FORWARD chain and afterwards the mangle table POSTROUTING chain.

If the packet is destined to the router, then the `mangle` table `INPUT` chain is analyzed. When the response is generated, the kernel looks up the rules in the `OUTPUT` chain of the `mangle` table first, and then in the `POSTROUTING` chain of the `mangle` table.

On those chains, all iptables operations are possible.

 It is not recommended to perform packet filtering in the `mangle` table. Even if you are not restricted to drop packets in the `mangle` table, it should be only for rules that `mangle` IP packets.

A particularity of the `mangle` table is that, unlike the `filter` or `nat` tables, all rules are analyzed, even if a packet is matched against one rule. This functionality of the `mangle` table was needed, because you might want to alter the same IP packet in several ways (set DSCP, nfmark, and TTL at the same time), and so, unlike the other tables, if a match is found against one rule in a chain, the kernel doesn't stop there, and tries to match the packet against all the other rules in that chain.

This is one of the major reasons for which packet filtering in the `mangle` table is strongly discouraged.

Summary

This chapter showed you how to perform Network Address Translation and IP packet mangling using netfilter/iptables.

We saw:

- What Network Address Translation is
- Types of NAT: SNAT or Masquerading, DNAT, full cone NAT
- Requirements for performing NAT with netfilter/iptables
- How to SNAT with iptables
- How to DNAT with iptables
- How to perform transparent proxy with iptables
- How to perform double NAT with iptables
- What packet mangling is
- What fields of the IP packet header can be modified using iptables
- How packets are matched against the chains of rules in the netflter `mangle` table

5

Layer 7 Filtering

In Chapter 1 of this book, we presented the OSI and TCP/IP networking models. As we saw there, even if the TCP/IP model has the widest usage, the reference model is OSI.

Let's have a look at the TCP/IP and OSI models again:

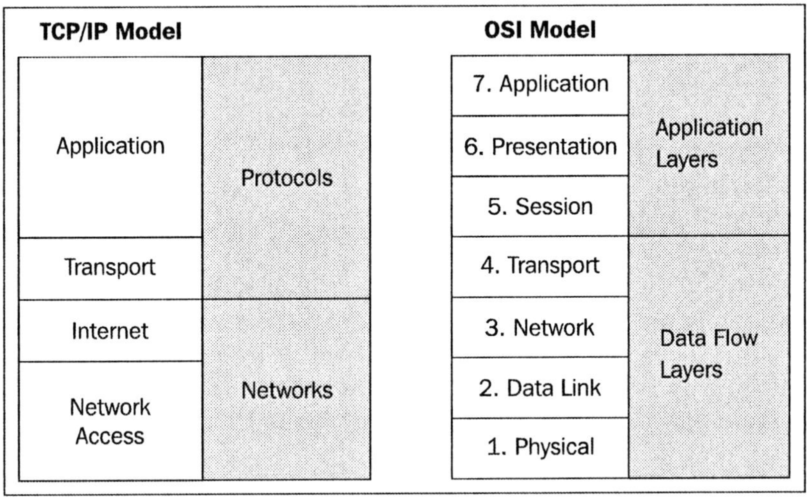

TCP/IP Model		OSI Model	
Application	Protocols	7. Application	Application Layers
		6. Presentation	
		5. Session	
Transport		4. Transport	Data Flow Layers
Internet	Networks	3. Network	
Network Access		2. Data Link	
		1. Physical	

At Layer 7 of the OSI model, we find Application (HTTP, FTP, SSH, etc.). As you can see from the picture above, TCP/IP compacted OSI Layers 7, 6, and 5 into one Layer, TCP/IP Layer 4 (Application), which has the same name, but different functionality.

Filtering and prioritizing traffic from some applications can be very easy and very hard at the same time. Normally, we would filter/prioritize web traffic by matching TCP packets with source or destination port 80, which is the standard HTTP port. However, web servers can be configured to use any port; so our filters/prioritizations won't work for that particular traffic.

Another big problem network administrators have is filtering traffic belonging to P2P (peer to peer) applications like Kazaa, DC++, Emule, etc., as those applications don't use standard ports and, even worse, they can be configured to use other applications' standard ports for communication (e.g. TCP port 80).

At one point, some people decided to do something about it and they did a pretty good job by starting the project named "Layer 7 Filtering" at `http://l7-filter.sourceforge.net`.

As you probably guessed, "Layer 7 Filtering" is a method to filter Layer 7 data. That means filtering network traffic generated by an application regardless of the protocol or port it uses at Layer 4.

L7-filter is a packet classifier for the Linux kernel that doesn't look up port numbers or Layer 4 protocols, but instead looks up the data in an IP packet and does a regular expression match on it to determine what kind of data it is, mainly what application protocol is being used.

Another project we will talk about is IP2P; it is an alternative to L7-filter, but has been designed for filtering only P2P applications while L7-filter takes into consideration a wider range of applications.

When to Use L7-filter

L7-filter is a great solution for matching application data in a network, but, as with almost every good thing, there are downsides to it too. As we will go deeper into how L7-filter works, you will see that it has to actually analyze data contained in IP packets, so it is quite obvious that this can eat up a lot of CPU power. So, using L7-filter on a Linux router with high traffic is not quite recommended, as L7-filter is CPU-consuming and can thus introduce latency and packet loss in the network. However, it really depends on the type of traffic passing through that router rather than the amount of traffic. For example, if you have 20 Mbps average of WWW data, L7-filter can work pretty well, but for 2 Mbps of VoIP traffic, the router's performance would dramatically drop.

Normally, we would consider using L7-filter for SOHO environments. In this case, L7-filter is very good for filtering viruses, limiting the bandwidth consumed by children when downloading music, etc.

Another situation when L7-filter is recommended would be for small-to-medium-sized companies that want to shape and prioritize traffic consumed by applications that are not vital or productive to the company. For example, in a company that has a 10 Mbps internet connection, an employee using P2P software can fill up the bandwidth and other traffic like Web, SSH, database replication, and so on would suffer because of that.

Another downside to using L7-filter is that it needs the connection tracking module to function. We have already discussed in the previous chapter about connection tracking (`ip_conntrack`) and we saw that it is not suitable for very high traffic conditions. So, when using L7-filter, you must also consider the disadvantage of using connection tracking.

Anyway, to draw a conclusion on this topic, L7-filter is a great tool but it also is CPU-consuming and can be used only with `ip_conntrack`; so it's quite difficult to make exact statements about when to use and when not to use L7-filter, and with what machines. I'd recommend not to use L7-filter on machines with rates over 5000 pps (packets per second), but, at the end of the day, if the machine can handle it, use it.

How Does L7-filter Work?

What L7-filter does is provides a way for iptables to match packets based on the application they belong to.

The TCP/IP model contains four layers and, before the L7-filter project, netfilter could match data by the first three layers:

- Network access layer: `iptables -A CHAIN -m mac --mac-source ...`"
- Internet: `iptables -A CHAIN -s IP_ADDRESS ...`"
- Transport: `iptables -A CHAIN -p tcp --dport 80 ...`

At the network access layer, netfilter uses `-m mac` to match packets from or to a MAC address in the network. At the layer above, the Internet layer, we have the IP protocol; netfilter matches packets from or to an IP address, regardless of the transport protocol, port number, or application the packet uses. At the transport layer, we have TCP or UDP, and netfilter can match packets by protocol, and more specifically, by port number within the protocol.

Any combination of the three lower layers is permitted; for instance:

```
iptables –A FORWARD –s 192.168.0.2 –p tcp --dport 80 –m mac --mac-
source 00:01:BC:2D:EF:2A –j DROP"
```

will drop all packets from the IP address 192.168.0.2 if the source MAC address is 00:01:BC:2D:EF:2A and the packets use the TCP protocol and have the destination TCP port 80.

L7-filter adds a new feature to netfilter by matching packets that belong to an application that is found at the TCP/IP Layer 4. A very important thing is that L7-filter is just another match option for iptables, and so all the rules of the other match options apply in this case. Therefore, you can do all the iptables operations with the packets matched by L7-filter.

The short and easy version of L7-filter is that after installing it you have `-m layer7 --l7proto [http|ftp|...]`. This is the match option we were talking about.

In order to match Layer 7 data, netfilter looks deeper into an IP packet than just at its header. However, the actual data contained in the packet doesn't just say "I'm a P2P packet; filter me!"; so the data is matched against a set of regular expressions that are common to different applications. This set of regular expressions is probably the most important part of this project, and is called "protocol definitions".

The L7-filter project contains three important parts:

- A kernel patch, which provides a way for the kernel to look into the IP packets
- An iptables patch, which provides the match option for iptables
- A collection of pattern files that contain the regular expressions for supported protocols (protocol definitions)

Installing L7-filter

To install the L7-filter project, we need to patch our kernel with the patch provided by the source found at `http://l7-filter.sourceforge.net`. To do that, we need the kernel source. The next operation would be to apply the iptables patch, recompile iptables, and install the protocol definitions files. Let's go deeper into the process.

Applying the Kernel Patch

The first step is to download the kernel source we want from `http://www.kernel.org`. Next, we need to download L7-filter from `http://l7-filter.sourceforge.net`.

For this chapter, we used kernel source 2.6.12.5 and L7-filter version 2.0 beta. After downloading what you need to the `/usr/src` folder, unzip the L7-filter TAR archive as follows:

```
router:/usr/src# tar xfvz netfilter-layer7-v2.0-beta.tar.gz
netfilter-layer7-v2.0-beta/
netfilter-layer7-v2.0-beta/stray_code
netfilter-layer7-v2.0-beta/for_older_kernels/
netfilter-layer7-v2.0-beta/for_older_kernels/
                    kernel-2.6.9-2.6.10-layer7-1.2.patch
netfilter-layer7-v2.0-beta/for_older_kernels/
                    kernel-2.6.0-2.6.8.1-layer7-0.9.2.patch
netfilter-layer7-v2.0-beta/for_older_kernels/
                    kernel-2.6.11-2.6.12-layer7-1.4.patch
netfilter-layer7-v2.0-beta/CHANGELOG
```

```
netfilter-layer7-v2.0-beta/README
netfilter-layer7-v2.0-beta/iptables-layer7-2.0.patch
netfilter-layer7-v2.0-beta/kernel-2.6.13-layer7-2.0.patch
netfilter-layer7-v2.0-beta/kernel-2.4-layer7-2.0.patch
router:/usr/src#
```

Next, go to the kernel source root and patch the kernel using the appropriate patch:

```
router:/usr/src/linux-2.6.12.5# patch -p1 < ../netfilter-layer7-v2.
        0-beta/for_older_kernels/kernel-2.6.11-2.6.12-layer7-1.4.patch
patching file include/linux/netfilter_ipv4/ip_conntrack.h
patching file include/linux/netfilter_ipv4/ipt_layer7.h
patching file net/ipv4/netfilter/Kconfig
patching file net/ipv4/netfilter/Makefile
patching file net/ipv4/netfilter/ip_conntrack_core.c
patching file net/ipv4/netfilter/ip_conntrack_standalone.c
Hunk #1 succeeded at 189 with fuzz 2 (offset 37 lines).
patching file net/ipv4/netfilter/ipt_layer7.c
patching file net/ipv4/netfilter/regexp/regexp.c
patching file net/ipv4/netfilter/regexp/regexp.h
patching file net/ipv4/netfilter/regexp/regmagic.h
patching file net/ipv4/netfilter/regexp/regsub.c
router:/usr/src/linux-2.6.12.5#
```

Next, run make config, make menuconfig, or make Xconfig. You need to enable the following options:

- **Code maturity level options | Prompt for development and/or incomplete code/drivers**
- **Netfilter (Device Drivers | Networking support | Networking Options | Network packet filtering)**
- **Connection tracking (Network packet filtering | IP: Netfilter Configuration | Connection tracking)**
- **Connection tracking flow accounting and IP tables support (on the same screen)**
- **Layer 7 match support**

Next, compile the kernel, install it as usual, and reboot your machine with the new kernel.

When compiling, you might see a warning, depending on the compiler version:

```
   CC [M]  net/ipv4/netfilter/ipt_layer7.o
net/ipv4/netfilter/ipt_layer7.c:457: warning: initialization from
incompatible pointer type
```

Just ignore the warning and go on.

Applying the iptables Patch

To apply the iptables patch, we need the iptables sources from
`http://www.netfilter.org`. Go to the iptables source root and patch it with
the patch provided by the L7-filter project.

```
router:/usr/src/iptables-1.3.4# patch -p1 < ../
               netfilter-layer7-v2.0-beta/iptables-layer7-2.0.patch
patching file extensions/.layer7-test
patching file extensions/libipt_layer7.c
```

```
patching file extensions/libipt_layer7.man
router:/usr/src/iptables-1.3.4#
```

Because file permissions can't be included in a patch, you need to set execute permission for the file extensions/.layer7-test.

```
router:/usr/src/iptables-1.3.4# chmod +x extensions/.layer7-test
```

Next, we will compile iptables using make and specifying the path to our patched kernel. In our case:

```
router:/usr/src/iptables-1.3.4# make KERNEL_DIR=/usr/src/
          linux-2.6.12.5
Making dependencies: please wait...
Extensions found: IPv4:CLUSTERIP IPv4:layer7 IPv4:recent IPv6:ah IPv6:
esp IPv6:frag IPv6:ipv6header IPv6:hbh IPv6:dst IPv6:rt
...
```

Now we will install iptables using the make install command and also specifying the path to the patched kernel. In our case:

```
router:/usr/src/iptables-1.3.4# make install KERNEL_DIR=/usr/src/
          linux-2.6.12.5
cp iptables /usr/local/sbin/iptables
cp iptables.8 /usr/local/man/man8/iptables.8
...
```

Now, we're almost done. Please note that the new iptables tool might be in a different folder than the original. For example, we can see that the make install command installed iptables in /usr/local/sbin/iptables because we didn't specify the BINDIR option when compiling iptables. We also need to make sure that we're using the right tool when issuing commands. We can verify that using iptables -V and comparing the versions we have:

```
router:~# iptables -V
iptables v1.2.11
router:~# type iptables
iptables is hashed (/sbin/iptables)
router:~# /usr/local/sbin/iptables -V
iptables v1.3.4
```

Protocol Definitions

First, we need to download the protocol definitions archive from the L7-filter project page at sourceforge, http://prdownloads.sourceforge.net/l7-filter/ l7-protocols-2006-06-03.tar.gz?download. Next, we need to copy the pattern files (.pat) from the archive to the /etc/l7-protocols folder.

```
router:/usr/src/l7-protocols-YYYY-MM-DD# mkdir /etc/l7-protocols
router:/usr/src/l7-protocols-YYYY-MM-DD# cp protocols/* /etc/
                                                        l7-protocols
```

The `/etc/l7-protocols` folder is the default folder for pattern files, and iptables will look into it and its subfolders, but not recursively. This means that iptables will search for pattern files in `/etc/l7-protocols` and in any `/etc/l7-protocols/subdir`, but not in `/etc/l7-protocols/subdir/subsubdir`.

If you don't wish to set up the `/etc/l7-protocols` folder, you can specify the pattern files folder by doing:

```
iptables [...] -m layer7 --l7dir /path-to/patterns --l7proto [...]
```

Please note that you *have to* specify the patterns folder before the protocol.

Testing the Installation

First, we might want to see if our module is in place. We can do that using the `modinfo` command:

```
router:~# modinfo ipt_layer7
filename:         /lib/modules/2.6.12.5-home.made/kernel/net/ipv4/
                    netfilter/ipt_layer7.ko
author:           Matthew Strait <quadong@users.sf.net>,
                    Ethan Sommer <sommere@users.sf.net>
license:          GPL
description:      iptables application layer match module
vermagic:         2.6.12.5-home.made preempt PENTIUMIII gcc-3.3
depends:          ip_tables
```

The output shows that we have a module called `ipt_layer7` and some information about it, such as filename, author, license, description, version, and other module dependencies.

Next, we will try to load the module using the `modprobe` command:

```
router:~# modprobe ipt_layer7
router:~# lsmod
Module                    Size  Used by
ipt_layer7                12364  0
```

The `modprobe` command didn't produce any errors. By using the `lsmod` command, we can see the module loaded into the kernel, its size, and the number of processes it is used by (in our case 0), because we didn't used it yet.

Next, we might want to test it and see if it works. We will do that by using Apache web server, placing some files in the web folder and downloading them.

When downloading the files, we should see that all packets are matched. First, we will use the command iptables -Z to zero the counters of all the rules in all chains, and then we will insert an accounting rule in the OUTPUT chain to match all the outgoing HTTP traffic.

```
router:~# iptables -Z
router:~# iptables -A OUTPUT -m layer7 --l7proto http
router:~# iptables -L OUTPUT -n -v
Chain OUTPUT (policy ACCEPT 10168 packets, 3433K bytes)
 pkts bytes target    prot opt in    out   source          destination
    0     0           all  -- *     *     0.0.0.0/0          0.0.0.0/0
                                                    LAYER7 l7proto http
```

Next, we download the file whale.qt (for example) from this server; and look in the apache access.log:

```
"GET /whale.qt HTTP/1.1" 200 11727970 "-"
```

So we must have 11 Mb matched on the accounting rule in the OUTPUT chain.

```
router:~# iptables -L OUTPUT -n -v
Chain OUTPUT (policy ACCEPT 172K packets, 65M bytes)
 pkts bytes target    prot opt in    out   source          destination
    0     0           all  --  *     *     0.0.0.0/0          0.0.0.0/0
                                                    LAYER7 l7proto http

router:~#
```

Oops! No packet was matched. Did we do something wrong or is L7-filter not good at all? Well, in most cases, the first option is valid, so when looking again at the ipt_layer7 module, we can see that it depends only on the ip_tables module. We now quickly verify what modules are loaded in the kernel, but we don't see the ip_conntrack module. Normally, ipt_layer7 should have had ip_conntrack in the dependencies, but it doesn't. That is why we neither got any errors while loading the module nor did we get any result.

We know that L7-filter uses the ip_conntrack module; so we need to load it. Let's see what happens now.

```
router:~# modprobe ip_conntrack
router:~# iptables -L OUTPUT -n -v
Chain OUTPUT (policy ACCEPT 457K packets, 159M bytes)
 pkts bytes target    prot opt in    out   source          destination
    0     0           all  --  *     *     0.0.0.0/0          0.0.0.0/0
                                                    LAYER7 l7proto http
router:~# wget http://127.0.0.1/whale.qt
--00:37:21--  http://127.0.0.1/whale.qt
           => `whale.qt'
Connecting to 127.0.0.1:80... connected.
```

```
HTTP request sent, awaiting response... 200 OK
Length: 11,727,970 [video/quicktime]

100%[=================================================================
==================>] 11,727,970    12.74M/s

00:37:22 (12.71 MB/s) - `whale.qt' saved [11727970/11727970]

router:~# iptables -L OUTPUT -n -v
Chain OUTPUT (policy ACCEPT 467K packets, 175M bytes)
 pkts bytes target     prot opt in   out   source          destination
 1433  12M             all  --  *    *     0.0.0.0/0        0.0.0.0/0
                                                           LAYER7 l7proto http
```

Well, as you can see, it worked. Now we have a Linux router with application layer filtering capabilities.

L7-filter Applications

We can use L7-filter with any iptables option; after all, L7-filter provides just another match option. However, not all the things we can do with our new match option are recommended, because L7-filter might match packets belonging to other applications than the one you want.

Filtering Application Data

Blocking application data that passes through your router is one of the non-recommended things that you can do with L7-filter.

Traffic from different applications might look similar; so you might experience problems when dropping data based on the L7-filter match. For example, if you drop packets that belong to eDonkey, there might be some other protocols that will experience problems. The eDonkey pattern matches about 1% of other streams with random data.

If you still want to use L7-filter for blocking several applications passing through your Linux router, it can be done as follows:

```
router:~# iptables -A FORWARD -m layer7 --l7proto edonkey -j DROP
```

You can also use L7-filter in conjunction with port numbers or IP addresses. For example:

```
router:~# iptables -A FORWARD -m layer7 --l7proto edonkey -d
192.168.1.131 -j DROP
```

will drop eDonkey packets that have the destination 192.168.1.131.

Before deciding on blocking certain applications, please take a look at http://l7-filter.sourceforge.net/protocols. You will see the list of protocols supported by the L7-filter project, and how good the patterns are. If pattern matching is poor, don't use L7-filter with DROP or REJECT!

Application Bandwidth Limiting

The creators of the L7-filter project describe this as being the best way to use their project. To limit bandwidth consumed by applications or users, we will use the tc tool described in Chapter 3.

L7-filter can match some or all application data in IP packets. Therefore, we can set a mark on the packets belonging to a specific application. Due to the fact that L7-filter is a match option, we can use netfilter mark to mark the packets, TOS to set a specific type of service, or DSCP to set a DSCP value, whatever we think is best to use with tc.

As an example, we will build a script that will limit BitTorrent to 2 Mbps for all our users, and FTP traffic to 512 Kbps for one user and to 1 Mbps for another user.

First, we need to mark BitTorrent and FTP data with arbitrary integer values. We can do it like this:

```
router:~# iptables -t mangle -A POSTROUTING -m layer7 --
              l7proto bittorrent -j MARK --set-mark 5
router:~# iptables -t mangle -A POSTROUTING -m layer7 --
              l7proto ftp -d 192.168.1.100 -j MARK --set-mark 6
router:~# iptables -t mangle -A POSTROUTING -m layer7 --
              l7proto ftp -d 192.168.1.112 -j MARK --set-mark 7
```

Now, let's verify the POSTROUTING chain:

```
router:~# iptables -t mangle -L POSTROUTING -n  -v
Chain POSTROUTING (policy ACCEPT 5855K packets, 4686M bytes)
 pkts bytes target    prot opt in   out    source            destination
 3183 1404K MARK      all  --  *    *      0.0.0.0/0          0.0.0.0/0
                  LAYER7 l7proto bittorrent MARK set 0x5
  119  1012K MARK        all  --  *     *      0.0.0.0/0
                  192.168.1.100    LAYER7 l7proto ftp MARK set 0x6
   12   100K MARK        all  --  *     *      0.0.0.0/0
                  192.168.1.112    LAYER7 l7proto ftp MARK set 0x7
```

OK, it seems that packets are matched and marked with the values we want (5 for BitTorrent and 7 for FTP).

We will use CBQ in this example; so we need to create the cbq classes we want. Let's create a script called limits like this:

```
#!/bin/bash

#delete root class. When running this
#script we need to delete limits first
tc qdisc del dev eth1 root


#create the root class
tc qdisc add dev eth1 root handle 10: cbq bandwidth 100Mbit avpkt 1000
tc class add dev eth1 parent 10:0 classid 10:1 cbq bandwidth 100Mbit
rate \
   100Mbit allot 1514 weight 10Mbit prio 8 maxburst 20 avpkt 1000


#create a 2 mbps class for bittorrent
tc class add dev eth1 parent 10:1 classid 10:100 cbq bandwidth 100Mbit
rate \
   2Mbit allot 1514 weight 256Kbit prio 5 maxburst 20 avpkt 1000
bounded
tc qdisc add dev eth1 parent 10:100 sfq quantum 1514b perturb 15
tc filter add dev eth1 parent 10:0 protocol ip prio 25 handle 5 fw \
      flowid 10:100

#create a 512 kbps class for ftp for the client 192.168.1.100
tc class add dev eth1 parent 10:1 classid 10:200 cbq bandwidth 100Mbit
rate \
   512Kbit allot 1514 weight 64Kbit prio 5 maxburst 20 avpkt 1000
bounded
tc qdisc add dev eth1 parent 10:200 sfq quantum 1514b perturb 15
tc filter add dev eth1 parent 10:0 protocol ip prio 25 handle 6 fw \
         flowid 10:200

#create a 1 mbps class for ftp for the client 192.168.1.112
tc class add dev eth1 parent 10:1 classid 10:300 cbq bandwidth 100Mbit
rate \
   1Mbit allot 1514 weight 128Kbit prio 5 maxburst 20 avpkt 1000
bounded
tc qdisc add dev eth1 parent 10:300 sfq quantum 1514b perturb 15
tc filter add dev eth1 parent 10:0 protocol ip prio 25 handle 7 fw \
         flowid 10:300
```

After running the script, to verify the configuration, we need to zero the POSTROUTING chain in the mangle table and run the script.

```
router:~# chmod +x limits
router:~# iptables -t mangle -Z POSTROUTING; ./limits
```

```
RTNETLINK answers: No such file or directory
router:~#
```

The error we got when running the `limits` script was generated because no limits existed on that interface, meaning that no root class was present. If we will run it again, we will not get any errors.

Now, the commands `iptables -t mangle -L POSTROUTING -n -v` and `tc -s class show dev eth1` should generate the same number of bytes and packets matched for each rule and corresponding class.

Accounting with L7-filter

Accounting is the easiest application that you can do with L7-filter. You can set up accounting scripts to see how many bytes are consumed by applications in your network.

Let's take the following example on a building router with 11 clients connected. We want to see what the traffic looks like at the application layer; so we will set up an accounting script like this:

```
iptables -A FORWARD -m layer7 --l7proto directconnect
iptables -A FORWARD -m layer7 --l7proto bittorrent
iptables -A FORWARD -m layer7 --l7proto http
iptables -A FORWARD -m layer7 --l7proto ftp
iptables -A FORWARD -m layer7 --l7proto yahoo
iptables -Z
```

After a few minutes, we can get an idea on what type of traffic is most popular with those clients:

```
router:~# iptables -L FORWARD -n -v
Chain FORWARD (policy ACCEPT 289K packets, 209M bytes)
 pkts bytes target    prot opt in   out   source              destination
62318   55M           all  --  *    *     0.0.0.0/0           0.0.0.0/0
                              LAYER7 l7proto directconnect
 6978 1202K           all  --  *    *     0.0.0.0/0           0.0.0.0/0
                              LAYER7 l7proto bittorrent
 8037 6116K           all  --  *    *     0.0.0.0/0           0.0.0.0/0
                              LAYER7 l7proto http
    0    0            all  --  *    *     0.0.0.0/0           0.0.0.0/0
                              LAYER7 l7proto ftp
  108 10724           all  --  *    *     0.0.0.0/0           0.0.0.0/0
                              LAYER7 l7proto yahoo
```

And the winner is dc++ with about 25% of the traffic!

IPP2P: A P2P Match Option

IPP2P is an application that matches P2P data in IP traffic, mostly in the way that L7-filter does, except that IPP2P is oriented only towards P2P applications. The project home page is `http://www.ipp2p.org`.

Installing IPP2P

Installing IPP2P is much simpler than L7-filter. We need to check on its web page for the latest stable version and download it.

```
router:~# wget http://www.ipp2p.org/downloads/ipp2p-X.Y.Z.tar.gz
--19:59:51--  http://www.ipp2p.org/downloads/ipp2p-X.Y.Z.tar.gz
           => `ipp2p-X.Y.Z.tar.gz'
Resolving www.ipp2p.org... 81.169.145.64
Connecting to www.ipp2p.org[81.169.145.64]:80... connected.
HTTP request sent, awaiting response... 200 OK
Length: 18,910 [application/x-tar]

100%[=================================================================
=================>] 18,910        --.--K/s

19:59:52 (181.98 KB/s) - `ipp2p-X.Y.Z.tar.gz' saved [18910/18910]
```

Next, we extract the files from the archive:

```
router:~# tar xfvz ipp2p-X.Y.Z.tar.gz
```

The README file says "*modify the Makefile (change "IUSER = -I/usr/src/iptables/include" to wherever iptables.h is located)*". For example, we have the iptables sources in `/usr/src/iptables-1.3.4`. However, some versions don't have IUSER defined in the makefile, but they have:

```
ifndef $(IPTABLES_SRC)
IPTVER ?= \
        $(shell $(IPTABLES_BIN) --version | $(SED) -e 's/^iptables v//')
IPTABLES_SRC = $(wildcard /usr/src/iptables-$(IPTVER))
endif
```

which means that the script will check the iptables version and search for the iptables sources in `/usr/src/iptables-<VERSION>`; so, in our situation, we don't have to modify anything.

Now type `make`. The application compiles, after which we have to copy `libipt_ipp2p.so` to the iptables `lib` folder, in our case `/usr/local/lib/iptables/`, and `ipt_ipp2p.ko` to the module's directory and run `depmod -a`. In this case:

```
router:~/ipp2p-0.8.0# cp ipt_ipp2p.ko /lib/modules/2.6.12.5-home.made/
kernel/net/ipv4/
router:~# depmod -a
router:~# modinfo ipt_ipp2p
filename:        /lib/modules/2.6.12.5-home.made/kernel/net/ipv4/
                 ipt_ipp2p.ko
author:          Eicke Friedrich/Klaus Degner <ipp2p@ipp2p.org>
description:     An extension to iptables to identify P2P traffic.
license:         GPL
vermagic:        2.6.12.5-home.made preempt PENTIUMIII gcc-3.3
depends:         ip_tables
```

Next, we need to load the module, and it's all set.

```
router:~/ipp2p-0.8.0# modprobe ipt_ipp2p
```

Using IPP2P

IPP2P provides another match option for iptables; so the syntax is:

```
iptables … -m ipp2p --option ...
```

where option can be:

Option	P2P network	Protocol	Quality
--edk	eDonkey, eMule, Kademlia	TCP and UDP	very good
--kazaa	KaZaA, FastTrack	TCP and UDP	good
--gnu	Gnutella	TCP and UDP	good
--dc	Direct Connect	TCP only	good
--bit	BitTorrent, extended BT	TCP and UDP	good
--apple	AppleJuice	TCP only	(need feedback)
--winmx	WinMX	TCP only	(need feedback)
--soul	SoulSeek	TCP only	good (need feedback)
--ares	Ares, AresLite	TCP only	moderate (DROP only)

Another possibility is to use as option --ipp2p, which matches all the protocols stated earlier.

This new match option has the same rules as the L7-filter project, and it's basically the same. Let's make some tests and compare the results between IPP2P and L7-filter.

IPP2P versus L7-filter

In order to test the results of L7-filter and IPP2P matches, we will set up accounting rules and see the results. We will use three of the most popular P2P applications: DirectConnect (DC++), BitTorrent, and eDonkey.

Let's set up a script like this:

```
iptables -I FORWARD -m layer7 --l7proto directconnect
iptables -I FORWARD -m ipp2p --dc

iptables -I FORWARD -m layer7 --l7proto bittorrent
iptables -I FORWARD -m ipp2p --bit

iptables -I FORWARD -m layer7 --l7proto edonkey
iptables -I FORWARD -m ipp2p --edk
```

After a few minutes, we pick up the results:

```
router:~/ipp2p-0.8.0# iptables -L FORWARD -n -v
Chain FORWARD (policy ACCEPT 25M packets, 18G bytes)
 pkts bytes target     prot opt in     out     source               destination
 2797  253K            all  --  *      *       0.0.0.0/0            0.0.0.0/0
                ipp2p v0.8.0 --edk
 1533  434K            all  --  *      *       0.0.0.0/0            0.0.0.0/0
                LAYER7 l7proto edonkey
 6665 1069K            all  --  *      *       0.0.0.0/0            0.0.0.0/0
                ipp2p v0.8.0 --bit
 7375 1273K            all  --  *      *       0.0.0.0/0            0.0.0.0/0
                LAYER7 l7proto bittorrent
  192 36558            all  --  *      *       0.0.0.0/0            0.0.0.0/0
                ipp2p v0.8.0 --dc
 693K  640M            all  --  *      *       0.0.0.0/0            0.0.0.0/0
                LAYER7 l7proto directconnect
```

The results confirm our expectations that there are a lot of differences between these two applications.

For example, for eDonkey, IPP2P matched more packets (but less data) than L7-filter. That doesn't mean that IPP2P matches `edk` better; it means that IPP2P and L7-filter don't match the same packets. The explanation is found in the `edonkey.pat` file in `/etc/l7-protocols`:

```
edonkey

# http://gd.tuwien.ac.at/opsys/linux/sf/p/pdonkey/eDonkey-protocol-0.6
#
```

```
# In addition to \xe3, \xc5 and \xd4, I see a lot of \xe5
#
# God this is a mess.  What an irritating protocol.
# This will match about 1% of streams with random data in them!

^[\xe3\xc5\xe5\xd4].?.?.?.?([\x01\x02\x05\x14\x15\x16\x18\x19\x1a\x1b\
x1c\x20\x21\x32\x33\x34\x35\x36\x38\x40\x41\x42\x43\x46\x47\x48\x49\
x4a\x4b\x4c\x4d\x4e\x4f\x50\x51\x52\x53\x54\x55\x56\x57\x58\x5b\x5c\
x60\x81\x82\x90\x91\x93\x96\x97\x98\x99\x9a\x9b\x9c\x9e\xa0\xa1\xa2\
xa3\xa4]|\x59...............?[ -~]|\x96....$)

# matches everything and too much
# ^(\xe3|\xc5|\xd4)

# ipp2p essentially uses "\xe3....\x47", which doesn't seem at all
right to me.

# bandwidtharbitrator uses
# e0.*@.*6[a-z].*p$|e0.*@.*[a-z]6[a-z].*p0$|e.*@.*[0-
9]6.*p$|emule|edonkey
# no comments to explain what all the mush is, of course...
```

Well, they all use different patterns, which explains the difference.

BitTorrent values are closer between IPP2P and L7-filter, but we can't tell which one is closer to the truth. To be able to make such an affirmation, we have to set up a test lab and I really don't think it's worth the trouble.

DC++ data, however, has the most differences. In this case, I'm 90% sure that L7-filter was way more accurate that IPP2P, because I saw a few of the users behind that Linux router on our DC++ hub during the time that I waited for these values.

Summary

In this chapter we saw two ways of filtering Layer 7 (Application) traffic in a network.

The most popular and most stable project is L7-filter, which has pretty good matching patterns for quite a large number of protocols.

Using Layer 7 filtering with Linux is a very nice feature, but it is CPU intensive, and might not be suitable for high-traffic conditions. Dedicated, specialized hardware solutions have existed for Layer 7 filtering for quite some time now, and some of them deliver good performance.

L7-filter is a smart and ambitious project aimed at small to medium networks that need bandwidth optimization. The advantage of L7-filter over the specialized hardware solutions is, of course, the cost.

To conclude this chapter, there are two important ideas to be drawn from it, and those are:

- Use L7-filter if it doesn't affect the network performance and doesn't overload the router's CPU. The decision whether to use L7-filter must be based on the machine performance (mainly CPU speed) and the type of traffic passing through it (mainly datarates in PPS).
- L7-filter is recommended to be used for marking packets in order to queue them, and should not be used to drop or reject packets as there might be many false matches. In case of false matches, it's better to have that data slower than not to have it at all.

6

Small Networks Case Studies

In this chapter we will see some live examples about firewalls for small networks. By small networks we mean networks with a small number of users (up to 10) that can be usually found in homes or small offices.

We will try to cover some of the most common situations encountered in small networks. However, there might be some scenarios that you will face when administering a small network that cannot be found here, especially if there are some other devices in the network (like IP phones, for example). Therefore, even if your interest is only in small networks, we recommend reading the following chapters also, where we might cover the usage of such (or similar) devices.

Now, let's try to build two scenarios that can be encountered in small networks.

Linux as SOHO Router

SOHO stands for Small Offices and Home Offices, and usually refers to situations where there exists just one computer at home to a few computers in a small office.

There is a very large offer of SOHO routers on the market nowadays from various manufacturers, but from what I've tested, most of them do the same basic things (NAT, DHCP, and some port filtering). They are less expensive than any computer, but if you have an old computer that you are about to throw away, you can easily install Linux on it and make it your own SOHO router having the advantage of higher flexibility at zero cost.

Usually, a SOHO router has a WAN port that is an Ethernet port where the provider connection must be plugged in. The Provider's CPE (Customer Premises Equipment) can be of any type (xDSL modem, wireless bridge, cable modem, fiber optic media converter) that can provide an Ethernet connection. SOHO routers usually have four to eight Ethernet ports for the LAN. This is basically a small four-to-eight-port switch that's built in the SOHO router. Some SOHO routers also have a wireless access point chipset that is bridged to the built-in switch.

Our computer that will run Linux and act as SOHO router must have two Ethernet cards, one for the WAN function of a SOHO router into which the provider's CPE is plugged, and one for the LAN. If you want the LAN to be wired and wireless, the Ethernet interface for the local network will be plugged into an access point with a built-in switch. However it is, everything is basically a LAN (wired, wireless, bridged, or switched); so, from the firewall point of view, it doesn't really matter what we use at the first and second layers of the OSI model (access points, hubs, switches).

A typical SOHO configuration looks like this:

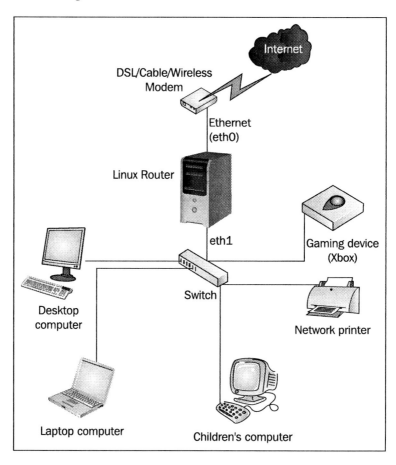

The provider usually assigns us a public IP address that can be either statically assigned or dynamically assigned using DHCP or PPPoE. Linux has support for PPPoE; this can be downloaded from `http://www.roaringpenguin.com/pppoe/`.

 It is not the purpose of this book to teach how to set up the internet connection, mainly because usually this is provider specific, and providers have a HowTo on this when you buy the service. The main idea is that you will have an Ethernet connection to the Internet and a public IP address.

Setting Up the Network

When setting up the local network, we must use a range of private IP addresses. In this example, we will use the private class C network 192.168.1.0/24; so, the best thing to do would be to assign the IP address 192.168.1.1 on the Ethernet interface `eth1` on our Linux router.

```
router:~#ifconfig eth1 192.168.1.1 netmask 255.255.255.0 up
```

In order to create a proper firewall for all devices behind NAT, we should assign them static IP addresses. However, we might want to use DHCP for the gaming device and for the laptop. To do that, first, we need to install the DHCP server. This is a distribution-specific task. For example, on Debian we run the following commands:

```
router:~# apt-get install dhcp
Reading Package Lists... Done
Building Dependency Tree... Done
The following NEW packages will be installed:
  dhcp
```

Next, we need to set up the DHCP server. We want to let the laptop acquire IP addresses from 192.168.1.2 to 192.168.1.10, for example. We set up a range just in case we have some friends visiting with their laptops. In the `/etc/dhcpd.conf` file, we need to enter the following text:

```
subnet 192.168.1.0 netmask 255.255.255.0 {
    range 192.168.1.2 192.168.1.10;
    option domain-name-servers provider.assigned.me.one;
    option routers 192.168.1.1;
    option subnet-mask 255.255.255.0;
    option broadcast-address 192.168.1.255;
    default-lease-time 600;
    max-lease-time 7200;
}
```

For the printer, desktop computer, and the children's computer, we want to assign them the same IP addresses *every* time. We find out the MAC addresses for each one, and, based on their MAC address, we assign them IP addresses by writing in the /etc/dhcpd.conf the following lines:

```
host children {
    hardware ethernet 02:03:04:05:06:07;
    fixed-address 192.168.1.55;
    option name-servers provider.assigned.me.one;
    option routers 192.168.1.1;
    option subnet-mask 255.255.255.0;
    option broadcast-address 192.168.1.255;
}
host desktop {
    hardware ethernet 02:03:04:05:06:08;
    fixed-address 192.168.1.11;
    option name-servers provider.assigned.me.one;
    option routers 192.168.1.1;
    option subnet-mask 255.255.255.0;
    option broadcast-address 192.168.1.255;
}
host printer {
    hardware ethernet 02:03:04:05:06:09;
    fixed-address 192.168.1.100;
    option name-servers provider.assigned.me.one;
    option routers 192.168.1.1;
    option subnet-mask 255.255.255.0;
    option broadcast-address 192.168.1.255;
}
host Xbox {
    hardware ethernet 02:03:04:05:06:10;
    fixed-address 192.168.1.200;
    option name-servers provider.assigned.me.one;
    option routers 192.168.1.1;
    option subnet-mask 255.255.255.0;
    option broadcast-address 192.168.1.255;
}
```

Now, we need to edit the /etc/init.d/dhcp script and set the interface to eth1:

```
# Defaults
INTERFACES="eth1"
```

and start the DHCP server by running the /etc/init.d/dhcp script with the start argument.

At this point, we have:

- The Linux router has a public IP address on eth0, the private IP address on eth1 192.168.1.1, and DHCP running.
- The laptop acquires a private IP address from the range 192.168.1.2-192.168.1.10.
- The desktop computer always acquires the private IP address 192.168.1.11.
- The children's computer always acquires the private IP address 192.168.1.55.
- The network printer always acquires the private IP address 192.168.1.100.
- The gaming device always acquires the private IP address 192.168.1.200.

Defining the Security Policy

Before building up any firewalls, we have to decide what the firewall must do by creating a security policy that can be from a document (recommended) to a piece of paper, or some thoughts in our heads.

For the simple and very common network just discussed, we can decide the following simple rules:

- The gaming device can access anything on the Internet. Also, we want to host games on it using GameSpy Arcade.
- The network printer must be accessed only from inside our network.
- The children must use the computer to browse the Internet and use Yahoo! Messenger. We don't want them to be able to access porn content or download viruses. We also don't want to let them use P2P software; so basically we limit their access to the Web and Yahoo! messenger.
- The laptop and guests laptops can access anything on the Internet (we don't want to be rude and deny them access to xxx sites, for example).
- The desktop can access anything. Also, we want to be able to log in on the desktop computer from outside using VNC (Virtual Network Computing).
- The Linux router must run SSH so that we can log in to it from the internal network and from the office.

The most difficult thing from our list is to perform all those restrictions for the children's computer. To be able to block porn sites and viruses, we must use a proxy server and make it transparent.

Building the Firewall

First, we need to set up Squid proxy server to be able to perform transparent proxy for the children's computer and deny access to porn sites and some viruses.

Squid can be found at `www.squid-cache.org`, and is the most widely used proxy server under Linux—most distributions have packages for Squid. The best documentation for Squid is the configuration file itself, which is heavily commented.

We will run Squid on its default port, 3128. To be able to use Squid as transparent proxy, we have to add the following information in the configuration file (usually `/etc/squid/squid.conf`):

```
httpd_accel_host virtual
httpd_accel_port 80
httpd_accel_with_proxy on
httpd_accel_uses_host_header on
```

Next, we need to define Squid access lists for the internal network to have access to Squid and to deny porn sites and dangerous files. We will do this for our entire internal network, but we will use the transparent proxy only for the children's computer. Any file can be a virus, and the file extensions that follow are just as an example; so please feel free to add any file extension you consider dangerous. In the `squid.conf` file, we add the following lines:

```
acl all src 0.0.0.0/0.0.0.0
acl our_network src 192.168.1.0/24
acl porn url_regex -i sex adult porn hardcore fetish
acl downloads urlpath_regex \.exe$ \.rar$ \.zip$ \.pif$ \.scr$

http_access deny porn
http_access deny downloads
http_access allow our_network
http_access deny all
```

The ACL named "porn" contains a list of names that are not allowed in the URL; so you won't be able to access a site that has one of those words in its name using the proxy server.

The ACL named "downloads" contains a list of file types that are not allowed to be accessed; so you won't be able to download files with the extensions in that list using the proxy server.

Now that we have set up the proxy server, let's implement the firewall to match the security policy we just built. First of all, because we will use NAT, we might want to load some of the connection tracking helpers described in Chapter 4:

```
modprobe ip_nat_ftp
modprobe ip_nat_irc
```

For the gaming device, we need to find out how it works when we host GameSpy Arcade games on it. We go to their websites and we see that we need to forward the following ports to the gaming device:

- 6500 UDP: for GameSpy Arcade
- 6700 UDP: for GameSpy Tunnel

Let's forward those ports:

```
iptables -t nat -A PREROUTING -p udp --dport 6500 -j DNAT --to
192.168.1.200
iptables -t nat -A PREROUTING -p udp --dport 6700 -j DNAT --to
192.168.1.200
```

For the gaming device to work, we also have to perform NAT for it, which will be included in the NAT rule for our entire network, which will be at the end.

Next, we need to deny access for the network printer to the Internet. Normally, we don't do filtering in the NAT table, but we don't want to do masquerading for the printer IP address. Since the printer has a private IP address, it won't be accessible from outside and also we will drop packets going out of eth0 in the POSTROUTING chain of the nat table so that the printer's IP address doesn't get NATed.

```
iptables -t nat -A POSTROUTING -o eth0 -s 192.168.1.100 -j DROP
```

For the children's computer, we will perform transparent proxy, meaning that the computer will use the proxy server without configuring the web browser. We have already set up the proxy server, so now we need to redirect all the traffic for port 80 TCP to the proxy server. We also want the children's computer to access port 443 TCP, which is HTTPS:

```
iptables -t nat -A PREROUTING -s 192.168.1.55 -p tcp --dport 80 -j
REDIRECT --to-port 3128
iptables -t nat -A POSTROUTING -o eth0 -s 192.168.1.55 -p tcp --dport
443 -j MASQUERADE
```

Now, requests from 192.168.1.55 to any host having the destination port 80 or 443 will go to our proxy server; so everything is done locally and we don't have to masquerade 192.168.1.55 for those requests.

Next, we need to masquerade the children's computer when it sends DNS requests to our provider:

```
iptables -t nat -A POSTROUTING -o eth0 -s 192.168.1.55 -p udp --dport
53 -j MASQUERADE
```

DNS requests use port 53 UDP; so now the children's computer can access any DNS servers.

We want to allow them to use Yahoo! Messenger only for chatting (not voice or file transfer). Reading the Yahoo! Messenger help, we see that Yahoo! Messenger uses ports 20, 23, 25, 80, 119, 5050, 8001, and 8002. Also, we see that the hosts needed for instant messaging using Yahoo! Messenger are:

- `scs.msg.yahoo.com`
- `scsa.msg.yahoo.com`
- `scsb.msg.yahoo.com`
- `scsc.msg.yahoo.com`

So it's better to masquerade the children's computer IP address when accessing those hosts; we should do like this:

```
iptables -t nat -A POSTROUTING -o eth0 -s 192.168.1.55 -d scs.msg.
yahoo.com -j MASQUERADE
iptables -t nat -A POSTROUTING -o eth0 -s 192.168.1.55 -d scsa.msg.
yahoo.com -j MASQUERADE
iptables -t nat -A POSTROUTING -o eth0 -s 192.168.1.55 -d scsb.msg.
yahoo.com -j MASQUERADE
iptables -t nat -A POSTROUTING -o eth0 -s 192.168.1.55 -d scsc.msg.
yahoo.com -j MASQUERADE
```

> When using a canonical name instead of an IP address in the syntax of iptables, the Linux router will resolve the IP address(es) of the canonical name and insert the rules in the kernel using those IP addresses. If one canonical name is resolved to multiple IP addresses, then iptables will insert in the kernel a number of rules equal to the number of IP addresses resolved, each line having one of the resolved IP addresses.

Now that we have set up access for the children's computer, we have to deny access to other ports and hosts. We do that in the POSTROUTING chain of the nat table:

```
iptables -t nat -A POSTROUTING -o eth0 -s 192.168.1.55 -j DROP
```

The laptop and desktop computer must be able to access anything, and so, no special rules are inserted for them, except the MASQUERADE rule for our network, which we will append now:

```
iptables -t nat -A POSTROUTING -o eth0 -s 192.168.1.0/24 -j MASQUERADE
```

One more configuration must be done in the `nat` table to provide the ability to log in remotely to the desktop computer using VNC. We set up VNC server to use TCP port 9112 on the desktop computer, so we have to perform DNAT for this port as follows:

```
iptables -t nat -A PREROUTING -p tcp --dport 9112 -j DNAT --to
192.168.1.11
```

This is all the configuration that we need for the local network. We need to set up some firewall rules to secure the Linux router.

First, we need SSH to run on the Linux router so we can administer it remotely. To secure the SSH access, it is best to create a chain called `SSH` in which we permit or deny access to SSH. If a vulnerability is discovered in OpenSSH, it's very likely that worms scanning for OpenSSH servers on port 22 will appear in a few hours. Therefore, we might want to run the SSH server on another port than the standard one (for example, 1234). The `SSH` chain is created by:

```
iptables -N SSH
```

Next, we insert a rule that tells the kernel to look up the `SSH` chain for all incoming TCP connections on port 1234:

```
iptables -A INPUT -p tcp --dport 1234 -j SSH
```

We must insert rules in the `SSH` chain to allow access only from trusted hosts. Let's say that the IP address at our office is 1.2.3.4:

```
iptables -A SSH -s 1.2.3.4 -j ACCEPT
iptables -A SSH -s 192.168.1.0/27 -j ACCEPT
iptables -A SSH -s 0/0 -j DROP
```

The first rule accepts connections from our office IP address 1.2.3.4. The second rule allows incoming SSH connections only from 192.168.1.0/27, which contains IP addresses from 192.168.1.1 to 192.168.1.32, as we don't want to allow SSH access from the children's computer, the printer, and the gaming device. The third rule drops all other incoming connections to port 1234.

The proxy server (Squid) has its own security by using access lists. However, the best way to secure it and the router is to drop TCP SYN packets from the Internet in the input chain. This way, no incoming connection to the Linux router can be made from the Internet, except SSH on port 1234 from 1.2.3.4, which is matched before this rule. We also want to accept all packets on the loopback interface (`lo`) for IPC (internal process communications).

```
iptables -A INPUT -i lo -j ACCEPT
iptables -A INPUT -i eth0 -p tcp --syn -j DROP
```

Dropping SYN packets offers a good protection for processes that might have bugs. However, this only drops incoming TCP connections with the SYN flag set (the request to set up a TCP connection), and will not offer any protection to software that opens UDP ports.

Setting Up the Firewall Script

On our Linux router, we create the script to contain all the rules above in the order we need to add them. We present the rules in this order, which is the order in which the kernel will analyze them.

```
#!/bin/bash

#define where iptables is
IPT=/sbin/iptables


############# Begin the NAT table operations ######

#Flush all the rules in the nat table
$IPT -t nat -F

#Load some modules needed for NAT
/sbin/modprobe ip_nat_ftp
/sbin/modprobe ip_nat_irc


#DNAT the gaming device ports 6500 and 6700 UDP for hosting games
$IPT —t nat -A PREROUTING -p udp --dport 6500 -j DNAT --to
192.168.1.200
$IPT —t nat -A PREROUTING -p udp --dport 6700 -j DNAT --to
192.168.1.200

#Deny printer access to the internet
$IPT -t nat -A POSTROUTING -o eth0 -s 192.168.1.100 -j DROP

#Transparent Proxy for the children's computer
$IPT -t nat -A PREROUTING -s 192.168.1.55 -p tcp --dport 80 -j
REDIRECT --to-port 3128

#Masquerade HTTPS for children's computer
$IPT -t nat -A POSTROUTING —o eth0 -s 192.168.1.55 -p tcp --dport 443
-j MASQUERADE
#Masquerade the children's computer for DNS requests
$IPT -t nat -A POSTROUTING -o eth0 -s 192.168.1.55 -p udp --dport 53
-j MASQUERADE
```

```
#Masquerade the children's computer to access yahoo messenger servers
$IPT -t nat -A POSTROUTING -o eth0 -s 192.168.1.55 -d scs.msg.yahoo.
com -j MASQUERADE
$IPT -t nat -A POSTROUTING -o eth0 -s 192.168.1.55 -d scsa.msg.yahoo.
com -j MASQUERADE
$IPT -t nat -A POSTROUTING -o eth0 -s 192.168.1.55 -d scsb.msg.yahoo.
com -j MASQUERADE
$IPT -t nat -A POSTROUTING -o eth0 -s 192.168.1.55 -d scsc.msg.yahoo.
com -j MASQUERADE

#Drop everything else for the children's computer
$IPT -t nat -A POSTROUTING -o eth0 -s 192.168.1.55 -j DROP

#Masquerade all our network
$IPT -t nat -A POSTROUTING -o eth0 -s 192.168.1.0/24 -j MASQUERADE

#DNAT port 9112 TCP for VNC into the desktop computer
$IPT -t nat -A PREROUTING -p tcp --dport 9112 -j DNAT --to
192.168.1.11

############# End the NAT table opperations ######

#Flush all the rules in INPUT, FORWARD and OUTPUT
$IPT -F

#Allow everything on the loopback interface
$IPT -A INPUT -i lo -j ACCEPT

#Delete the SSH chain if it exists and create it again
$IPT -X SSH
$IPT -N SSH

#Pass all tcp packets to port 1234 to the SSH chain
$IPT -A INPUT -p tcp --dport 1234 -j SSH

#Append the allow and drop rules for the SSH chain
$IPT -A SSH -s 1.2.3.4 -j ACCEPT
$IPT -A SSH -s 192.168.1.0/27 -j ACCEPT
$IPT -A SSH -s 0/0 -j DROP

#DROP all incoming TCP SYN packets on eth0
$IPT -A INPUT -i eth0 -p tcp --syn -j DROP
```

Verifying the Firewall Configuration

After running the script, we want to see how our tables and chains look. First, let's check the nat table and see how our kernel analyses our rules:

We verify the configuration using `iptables -t nat -L -n -v`.

```
router:~# iptables -t nat -L -n -v
Chain PREROUTING (policy ACCEPT 201 packets, 26363 bytes)
 pkts bytes target       prot opt in      out     source       destination
    0     0 DNAT         udp  --  eth0      *      0.0.0.0/0
0.0.0.0/0           udp dpt:6500 to:192.168.1.200
    0     0 DNAT         udp  --  eth0      *      0.0.0.0/0
0.0.0.0/0           udp dpt:6700 to:192.168.1.200
    0     0 REDIRECT     tcp  --  *         *      192.168.1.55
0.0.0.0/0           tcp dpt:80 redir ports 3128
    0     0 DNAT         tcp  --  eth0      *      0.0.0.0/0
0.0.0.0/0           tcp dpt:9112 to:192.168.1.11

Chain POSTROUTING (policy ACCEPT 47 packets, 8648 bytes)
 pkts bytes target       prot opt in     out     source        destination
    0     0 DROP         all  --  *      eth0    192.168.1.100    0.0.0.0/0
    0     0 MASQUERADE   udp  --  *      eth0    192.168.1.55     0.0.0.0/0
tcp dpt:443
    0     0 MASQUERADE   udp  --  *      eth0    192.168.1.55     0.0.0.0/0
udp dpt:53
    0     0 MASQUERADE   all  --  *      eth0    192.168.1.55
216.155.193.136
    0     0 MASQUERADE   all  --  *      eth0    192.168.1.55
216.155.193.137
    0     0 MASQUERADE   all  --  *      eth0    192.168.1.55
216.155.193.138

(... some lines missing here ...)

    0     0 DROP         all  --  *      eth0    192.168.1.55     0.0.0.0/0
    0     0 MASQUERADE   all  --  *      eth0    192.168.1.0/24   0.0.0.0/0

Chain OUTPUT (policy ACCEPT 3 packets, 250 bytes)
 pkts bytes target       prot opt in     out     source        destination
router:~#
```

When an IP packet arrives into the Linux router, in the `nat` table the PREROUTING chain is analyzed first. If the packet arrives on `eth0` and has the destination UDP port 6500, the first rule is matched and the destination IP address is rewritten to 192.168.1.200. If the packet doesn't match the first rule, the kernel will try to analyze the second rule, and so on.

After the PREROUTING chain is analyzed, the kernel does the routing process and analyzes the POSTROUTING chain rule by rule.

At the risk of repeating, you must keep in mind that when a chain is analyzed, the kernel analyzes the rules in the order they are seen with iptables -L, and if it matches one rule in the chain, no other rule in that chain will be analyzed. For example, if we had the rule that did MASQUERADE for the entire network 192.168.1.0/24 before the rule in which we drop all packets for the children's computer (192.168.1.55), then the last rule would have no effect.

After verifying the nat table, we verify the Netfilter table with iptables -L -n -v:

```
router:~# iptables -L -n -v
Chain INPUT (policy ACCEPT 86 packets, 6206 bytes)
 pkts bytes target     prot opt in      out     source
destination
    0     0 ACCEPT     all  --  lo      *       0.0.0.0/0        0.0.0.0/0
    0     0 SSH        tcp  --  *       *       0.0.0.0/0        0.0.0.0/0
tcp dpt:1234
    0     0 DROP       tcp  --  eth0    *       0.0.0.0/0        0.0.0.0/0
tcp flags:0x16/0x02

Chain FORWARD (policy ACCEPT 0 packets, 0 bytes)
 pkts bytes target     prot opt in      out     source          destination

Chain OUTPUT (policy ACCEPT 3775 packets, 776K bytes)
 pkts bytes target     prot opt in      out     source          destination

Chain SSH (1 references)
 pkts bytes target     prot opt in      out     source          destination
    0     0 ACCEPT     all  --  *       *       1.2.3.4          0.0.0.0/0
    0     0 ACCEPT     all  --  *       *       192.168.1.0/27   0.0.0.0/0
    0     0 DROP       all  --  *       *       0.0.0.0/0        0.0.0.0/0
```

The FORWARD and OUTPUT chains are empty and have the default policy ACCEPT. The first rule in the INPUT chain tells the kernel to accept all incoming packets on the loopback interface. If the packet doesn't arrive on the loopback interface, the second rule is tested, which tells the kernel that if the destination port is 1234 TCP, it should check the SSH chain to see if it should accept or drop the packet. The kernel next looks up the SSH chain and accepts or drops the packet.

If the packet is not matched by the second rule in the INPUT chain, then the kernel doesn't look up the SSH chain at all, and it checks the third rule, which states that the kernel must drop TCP SYN packets.

QoS—Bandwidth Allocation

At this point our network is protected by a firewall and we have a SOHO router that we built from a PC running Linux. With Linux we can do a lot more than this; so it's time to configure it to do more for us.

Let's say that we have a 1Mbps connection (download speed) that we want to share between the devices in this home so that everyone is happy. First, we need to decide how to split this bandwidth.

The gaming device needs a maximum of 128kbps when playing online; so we must allocate at least 128kbps for it, but we want to allow it to use the maximum bandwidth available when downloading updates, etc.

We want the children's computer and the desktop to have a 256kbps each, and we also want to leave them the possibility to use the entire bandwidth when it's available; and for the laptop and friends, we will allocate the remaining 384kbps, along with the possibility of reaching 1Mbps.

For SOHO applications, usually we don't need to do upload bandwidth allocation; so we'll just limit the download speeds.

 For teaching purposes we will use HTB in this section of the chapter and CBQ in the following section.

So, what we need is to create an HTB class of 1Mbit and four child classes for the devices.

First, we need to attach the root `qdisc` to the interface `eth1` and create a root class with the speed of the interface—100Mbps in our case:

```
tc qdisc add dev eth1 root handle 1: htb
tc class add dev eth1 parent 1:0 classid 1:10 htb rate 100Mbit
```

Next, we need to create our 1Mbps class that we'll share between the all devices:

```
tc class add dev eth1 parent 1:10 classid 1:20 htb rate 1Mbit
```

This line creates an HTB class with the ID 1:20 and the parent 1:10, which is the root class.

For the gaming device, we will create an HTB class with the ID 1:100 as a child class to 1:20:

```
tc class add dev eth1 parent 1:20 classid 1:100 htb rate 128Kbit ceil
1Mbit
```

We need to attach a queuing discipline to this class. We will use `sfq` in this section:

```
tc qdisc add dev eth1 parent 1:100 sfq quantum 1514b perturb 15
```

Now we need to add a `tc` filter to specify which packets belong to this class:

```
tc filter add dev eth1 protocol ip parent 1:0 prio 5 u32 match ip dst
192.168.1.200 flowid 1:100
```

This is all for the gaming device. For the other HTB classes, we will do the same thing.

For the children's computer:

```
tc class add dev eth1 parent 1:20 classid 1:200 htb rate 256Kbit ceil
1Mbit
tc qdisc add dev eth1 parent 1:200 sfq quantum 1514b perturb 15
tc filter add dev eth1 protocol ip parent 1:0 prio 5 u32 match ip dst
192.168.1.55 flowid 1:200
```

For the desktop:

```
tc class add dev eth1 parent 1:20 classid 1:300 htb rate 256Kbit ceil
1Mbit
tc qdisc add dev eth1 parent 1:300 sfq quantum 1514b perturb 15
tc filter add dev eth1 protocol ip parent 1:0 prio 5 u32 match ip dst
192.168.1.11 flowid 1:300
```

For the laptop and friends, we will create a class just like the others, but we want to filter all the IP addresses in the 192.168.1.0/24 network. Since we have already created the earlier classes, IP packets for 192.168.1.200, 192.168.1.55, and 192.168.1.11 will match those classes and not this one, even if the filter contains the whole network:

```
tc class add dev eth1 parent 1:20 classid 1:400 htb rate 256Kbit ceil
1Mbit
tc qdisc add dev eth1 parent 1:400 sfq quantum 1514b perturb 15
tc filter add dev eth1 protocol ip parent 1:0 prio 5 u32 match ip dst
192.168.1.0/24 flowid 1:400
```

The QoS Script

We need to put all the QoS lines in a script running at boot time, after the network is initialized. Also, we need to delete the root `qdisc` first in case we run it again manually if we make some modifications. Deleting the root `qdisc` will destroy all classes.

```
#!/bin/bash

#delete root qdisc (this will destroy all classes)
tc qdisc del dev eth1 root

#attach root qdisc and create the 100Mbps root class
tc qdisc add dev eth1 root handle 1: htb
tc class add dev eth1 parent 1:0 classid 1:10 htb rate 100Mbit

#create the 1Mbps class for the whole bandwidth
tc class add dev eth1 parent 1:10 classid 1:20 htb rate 1Mbit

#Xbox - 128kbit
tc class add dev eth1 parent 1:20 classid 1:100 htb rate 128Kbit ceil
1Mbit
tc qdisc add dev eth1 parent 1:100 sfq quantum 1514b perturb 15
tc filter add dev eth1 protocol ip parent 1:0 prio 5 u32 match ip dst
192.168.1.200 flowid 1:100

#children - 256kbit
tc class add dev eth1 parent 1:20 classid 1:200 htb rate 256Kbit ceil
1Mbit
tc qdisc add dev eth1 parent 1:200 sfq quantum 1514b perturb 15
tc filter add dev eth1 protocol ip parent 1:0 prio 5 u32 match ip dst
192.168.1.55 flowid 1:200

#desktop - 256kbit
tc class add dev eth1 parent 1:20 classid 1:300 htb rate 256Kbit ceil
1Mbit
tc qdisc add dev eth1 parent 1:300 sfq quantum 1514b perturb 15
tc filter add dev eth1 protocol ip parent 1:0 prio 5 u32 match ip dst
192.168.1.11 flowid 1:300

#all other IPs from this class - 384kbit
tc class add dev eth1 parent 1:20 classid 1:400 htb rate 256Kbit ceil
1Mbit
tc qdisc add dev eth1 parent 1:400 sfq quantum 1514b perturb 15
tc filter add dev eth1 protocol ip parent 1:0 prio 5 u32 match ip dst
192.168.1.0/24 flowid 1:400
```

Verifying the QoS Configuration

We need to verify the configuration we created by looking at the HTB classes. This is done with tc class show:

```
root@router:~# tc class show dev eth1

class htb 1:10 root rate 100000Kbit ceil 100000Kbit burst 126575b
cburst 126575b
class htb 1:100 parent 1:20 leaf 8081: prio 0 rate 128000bit ceil
1000Kbit burst 1759b cburst 2849b
class htb 1:20 parent 1:10 rate 1000Kbit ceil 1000Kbit burst 2849b
cburst 2849b
class htb 1:200 parent 1:20 leaf 8082: prio 0 rate 256000bit ceil
1000Kbit burst 1919b cburst 2849b
class htb 1:300 parent 1:20 leaf 8083: prio 0 rate 256000bit ceil
1000Kbit burst 1919b cburst 2849b
class htb 1:400 parent 1:20 leaf 8084: prio 0 rate 256000bit ceil
1000Kbit burst 1919b cburst 2849b
```

So we see the root class 1:10, and the 1000Kbit (1Mbit) class 1:20 having the parent 1:10, and the other classes with their bandwidths having the parent 1:20.

We need to see if packets match our classes. In case of zero traffic, we will verify that by pinging their IP address and seeing if they made a match for the corresponding class:

```
root@router:~# ping -f -c 10 192.168.1.200
PING 192.168.1.200 (192.168.1.200) 56(84) bytes of data.

--- 192.168.1.200 ping statistics ---
10 packets transmitted, 10 received, 0% packet loss, time 3ms
rtt min/avg/max/mdev = 0.198/0.210/0.300/0.033 ms, ipg/ewma
0.394/0.230 ms

root@router:~# tc -s class show dev eth1 | fgrep -A 4 1:100
class htb 1:100 parent 1:20 leaf 808d: prio 0 rate 128000bit ceil
1000Kbit burst 1759b cburst 2849b
 Sent 980 bytes 10 pkts (dropped 0, overlimits 0)
 lended: 10 borrowed: 0 giants: 0
 tokens: 40962 ctokens: 12387
```

What we did was to send a flood ping with 10 packets to 192.168.1.200, and then check at the 1:100 class for the gaming device to see if those packets matched the class for the gaming device, and, as we expected, they did.

Linux as Router for a Typical Small to Medium Company

In a typical small to medium business, using Linux as a router has a number of advantages, including low cost and flexibility; also, a Linux router can be used to do a lot more than just routing.

Let's analyze the following example of a typical small to medium company:

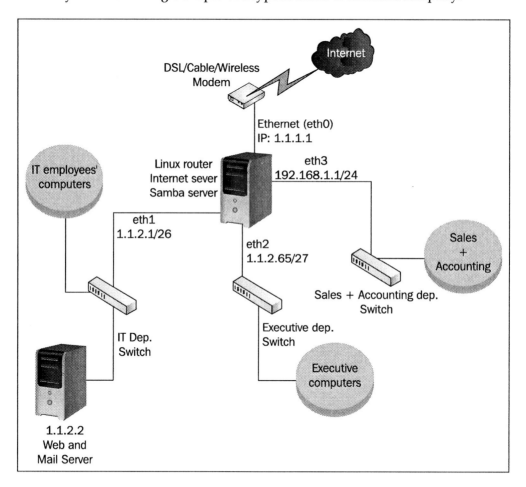

Setting Up the Router

The network above is built for a small to medium company with sales, accounting, executive, and IT departments as illustrated in the diagram.

For easy understanding of the network, we've placed three switches belonging to three separate networks, one for the sales and accounting departments, one for the executive offices, and one for the IT department. Usually, a managed switch is used in this case to create three separate VLANS.

What we have here in this network is:

- A broadband internet connection. The provider assigned us the IP 1.1.1.1 for our router and routed the class C network 1.1.2.0/24 through our router's IP address (1.1.1.1). The modem is inserted into Eth0, which is statically configured with the IP address 1.1.1.1, netmask 255.255.255.252, and default gateway 1.1.1.2, which is the provider's directly connected router.

- The Linux router has four fast Ethernet cards. Besides routing IP packets, it also runs Apache for our intranet application and Samba server; so it acts like a router, intranet server, and file server.

- The IT department has, besides the IT manager, one or more network administrators. They have a separate network and the web server and mail server (which is a single Linux machine) resides in the same network. The web and mail server needs a public IP address, and all the IT department employees have static public IP addresses. With the thought of adding more servers in the future, we reserve a 64-host subnet, the first in our class C, 1.1.2.0/26; so we assign to Eth1 on our Linux router the IP address 1.1.2.1, netmask 255.255.255.192, and configure the web and mail server to have 1.1.2.2, netmask 255.255.255.192, and default gateway 1.1.2.1. If you want, we will call this network the DMZ zone .

- The executive department network contains the computers for all the managers in the company. They expressed their need to have the least restriction possible for special chat applications and so on (and also file sharing). We assign a 32-hosts subnet from our class C for them, the 1.1.2.64/27 network. We assign the static public IP address 1.1.2.65, netmask 255.255.255.224 on Eth2 of our Linux router, and statically assign to them IP addresses from 1.1.2.66 to 1.1.2.94 using netmask 255.255.255.224 and default gateway 1.1.2.65.

- Sales and accounting departments have one big network, as the company has a large number of sales agents. This is the part of the network that requires the most of our attention since usually sales is the department with the most IT problems :-). We will run DHCP on our Linux router to serve clients on Eth3. We set up the private IP address 192.168.1.1 with netmask 255.255.255.0 on Eth3 and give our clients, through DHCP, private IP addresses from 192.168.1.2 to 192.168.1.254, netmask 255.255.255.0, and default gateway 192.168.1.1.

This is our company now, with three smaller networks. It is time to define the security policy.

Defining the Security Policy

The IT department network is our DMZ zone because the IT guys are experienced computer users and they know how to secure their computers. The web and mail server must be accessed from anywhere; so we need to open port 80 TCP for web access, ports 110 and 25 TCP for mail, and also need SSH. We need to be able to access both Linux servers in the network using SSH from the IT department computers as well as from some public IP addresses we have at home.

The intranet server must be accessed only from computers in the office, and so must the fileserver too. The two servers are on the same machine, but we are referring here to the services when we say "server".

The executive department must be able to access anything on the Internet; so it somehow resembles the DMZ zone, but we might want to create some restrictions for them:

- Deny access from people outside the executive network to see their file shares (NetBIOS file shares, shared folders, etc.)
- Use a transparent proxy for them to deny access to `.pif` and `.scr` files.

Sales and accounting departments' computers are allowed to do the following:

- Browse the Web, but not to download `.pif`, `.scr`, `.exe`, `.zip`, and `.rar` files, and also not to visit sex sites
- Access HTTPS port 443 TCP for internet banking
- Send and receive email using the company mail server
- Access the intranet and file servers

A Few Words on Applications

We described earlier in this chapter how to set up Squid for transparent proxy and how to set up access lists. In our case, the same Squid proxy server must do the following:

- Be used as transparent proxy
- Deny dangerous files (`.pif` and `.scr`) for the managers, but allow everything else for them
- Deny dangerous files and sex sites for sales and accounting, but allow everything else

The solution to this problem is the order of the access lists in the squid.conf file.

First, to be able to use Squid as transparent proxy, we have to set:

```
httpd_accel_host virtual
httpd_accel_port 80
httpd_accel_with_proxy on
httpd_accel_uses_host_header on
```

in the squid.conf file. Next, we need to set up ACLs for the managers, sales, and accounting, and the ACLs to deny malicious files, downloads, and sex sites:

```
acl all src 0.0.0.0/0.0.0.0
acl managers src 1.1.2.64/27
acl sales_accounting src 192.168.1.0/24
acl malicious urlpath_regex \.pif$ \.scr$
acl downloads urlpath_regex \.exe$ \.rar$ \.zip$
acl porn url_regex -i sex adult porn hardcore fetish
```

Now, to match our security policy, we have to set http_access to those ACLs in the following order:

```
http_access deny malicious
http_access allow managers
http_access deny downloads
http_access deny porn
http_access allow sales_accounting
http_access deny all
```

The intranet server is usually a web server that runs an application that, in most cases, is a database interface. If the intranet application uses MySQL or PostgreSQL, which can be installed on the same machine, both of them can be configured using their configuration files (my.cnf for MySQL and pg_hba.conf for PostgreSQL) to allow access only from localhost. However, we want to protect ourselves against possible bugs of this database server software by filtering the ports that listen for incoming connections, which we can find out by examining the configuration files.

Using Samba as a file server can be done in multiple ways. For the above configuration, it is recommended to use Samba as WINS server. We can see that by starting the Samba service only, we will have the following output of netstat –anp:

```
router:~# netstat -anp
Active Internet connections (servers and established)
Proto Recv-Q Send-Q Local Address     Foreign Address   State
tcp      0      0 0.0.0.0:139       0.0.0.0:*         LISTEN  3950/smbd
tcp      0      0 0.0.0.0:445       0.0.0.0:*         LISTEN  3950/smbd
udp      0      0 0.0.0.0:137       0.0.0.0:*                 3948/nmbd
udp      0      0 0.0.0.0:138       0.0.0.0:*                 3948/nmbd
```

This means that the Samba server opened TCP ports 139 and 445 and UDP ports 137 and 138.

We know that NetBIOS uses the famous trio of ports 137-138-139, so 445 TCP looks a little strange.

It was opened by Samba and is the port for **microsoft-ds** (Microsoft Directory Services); so we need to filter this port for packets coming from the Internet.

The Samba file server is very complex software. For more information on Samba, please visit `http://us2.samba.org/samba/docs/man/Samba-HOWTO-Collection/`.

Creating the Firewall Rules

Since the sales and accounting departments have a lot of people, we will use the remaining public IP addresses to SNAT those two departments, even if they have very restrictive access.

First, we need to SNAT the DNS requests made by the computers in those departments:

```
iptables -t nat -A POSTROUTING -o eth0 -s 192.168.1.0/24 -p udp
--dport 53 -j SNAT --to 1.1.2.96-1.1.2.254
```

Next, we need to redirect all the web requests to the proxy server, except those for the intranet server:

```
iptables -t nat -A PREROUTING -s 192.168.1.0/24 -d ! 192.168.1.1 -p
tcp --dport 80 -j REDIRECT --to-port 3128
```

For HTTPS (port 443 TCP) we can't redirect the requests to the proxy server; so we will SNAT those requests as well:

```
iptables -t nat -A POSTROUTING -o eth0 -s 192.168.1.0/24 -p tcp
--dport 443 -j SNAT --to 1.1.2.96-1.1.2.254
```

Next, we need to drop all packets originating from sales and accounting to the Internet:

```
iptables -t nat -A POSTROUTING -o eth0 -s 192.168.1.0/24 -j DROP
```

With these five simple rules, we solved the restrictive access for the sales and accounting departments. All they can do on the Internet is browse web pages that don't contain the words in our Squid ACL "porn" and can't download files with the extensions defined by our Squid ACLs "malicious" and they "downloads". They also can access all HTTPS sites because they work with several banks that offer internet banking and also they have to make online acquisitions using credit cards.

Now that we are adding rules in the nat table, we should redirect managers' web requests to use the proxy:

```
iptables -t nat -A PREROUTING -s 1.1.2.64/27 -p tcp --dport 80 -j
REDIRECT --to-port 3128
```

The thing we need to make sure is to allow packets on the loopback interface before we start filtering ports.

```
iptables -A INPUT -i lo -j ACCEPT
```

We will need access to SSH on both Linux servers we have from a list of allowed hosts from our network and from outside (e.g. network administrators' home IP addresses). First, we decide on a port (22 is default for SSH), let's say 61146 TCP for running SSH on both our hosts.

Next, we need to build the list of IP addresses that are authorized to access the SSH ports. Let's say those are 1.1.2.0/26, 1.1.3.192, 1.1.9.21, 1.1.19.61. The simplest way to build the rules for SSH is to create a chain called MANAGEMENT as follows:

```
iptables -N MANAGEMENT
iptables -A MANAGEMENT -s 1.1.2.0/26 -j ACCEPT
iptables -A MANAGEMENT -s 1.1.3.192 -j ACCEPT
iptables -A MANAGEMENT -s 1.1.9.21 -j ACCEPT
iptables -A MANAGEMENT -s 1.1.19.61 -j ACCEPT
iptables -A MANAGEMENT -s 0/0 -j DROP
```

On our Linux router, we need to apply the rules in the MANAGEMENT chain for incoming packets with the destination port 61146 TCP:

```
iptables -A INPUT -p tcp --dport 61146 -j MANAGEMENT
```

Also, for the web and mail server, we will run SSH on port 61146 TCP, and we need to apply the rules in the MANAGEMENT chain to packets destined to 1.1.2.2 port 61146 TCP:

```
iptables -A FORWARD -d 1.1.2.2 -p tcp --dport 61146 -j MANAGEMENT
```

Since we don't want to allow access to the Samba file server from anywhere except our networks, we will deny access to ports 137, 138, 139 UDP and TCP, and to port 445 TCP in the INPUT chain:

```
iptables -A INPUT -i eth0 -p tcp --dport 137:139 -j DROP
iptables -A INPUT -i eth0 -p udp --dport 137:139 -j DROP
iptables -A INPUT -i eth0 -p tcp --dport 445 -j DROP
```

In the security policy, we stated that we want the intranet server that runs on the Linux router to be accessed only from inside our departments' networks; so we will have to filter port 80 TCP on the Linux router:

```
iptables -A INPUT -i eth0 -p tcp --dport 80 -j DROP
```

The intranet application is coded in PHP and uses PostgreSQL as database. We run PostgreSQL on the default port 5432, and we don't need connections from outside to it; so we will filter it regardless of the interface the packet arrives on to port 5432.

```
iptables -A INPUT -p tcp --dport 5432 -j DROP
```

Next, we want to drop TCP SYN packets in the INPUT chain. This is a very useful rule in the eventuality that one of the people that have SSH access on the Linux router start a buggy service running on a TCP port. This rule also gives us protection for the Squid proxy server, because we are now not only protected by access lists, but no one can connect to port 3128 from the Internet:

```
iptables  -A INPUT -i eth0 -p tcp --syn -j DROP
```

So far, we managed to implement our security policy for the sales and accounting departments' network and for the Linux router. We also secured SSH connections from trusted hosts for the web and mail server. We want to allow access from anywhere to the web and mail server for HTTP (port 80 TCP), SMTP (port 25 TCP), and POP3 (port 110 TCP). It is important to allow the web and mail server to make DNS requests (port 53 UDP), and we will not filter any UDP traffic for now; so DNS requests will work OK.

```
iptables -A FORWARD -d 1.1.2.2 -p tcp -m multiport --dport 80,25,110
-j ACCEPT
```

Next, we will drop any TCP SYN packets for the web and mail server:

```
iptables -A FORWARD -d 1.1.2.2 -p tcp --syn -j DROP
```

Our security policy requires that no one from outside the executive offices may access their NetBIOS shares, so we will drop NetBIOS and Microsoft-DS packets for them:

```
iptables -A FORWARD -d 1.1.2.64/27 -p tcp --dport 137:139 -j DROP
iptables -A FORWARD -d 1.1.2.64/27 -p udp --dport 137:139 -j DROP
iptables -A FORWARD -d 1.1.2.64/27 -p tcp --dport 445 -j DROP
```

The only thing left in our security policy that we haven't implemented yet is limiting the bandwidth consumed by the executive computers for BitTorrent and DC++. To do that, we need the help of our little friend called `tc`, which stands for "traffic control", a tool included in the iproute package found in every Linux distribution.

Since BitTorrent and DC++ don't use standard ports, we will also need the help of the L7-filter project.

The strategy is to mark packets matched by L7-filter for BitTorrent and DC++ and to limit the bandwidth those two protocols use with `tc`.

Installation and usage of L7-filter is described in the Chapter 5 called *Layer 7 filtering*, and marking packets is done by using the mangle table described in Chapter 4. To be able to limit the bandwidth used by BitTorrent and DC++, we will mark the packets using an `nfmark`. We will use `nfmark` 5 in this example:

```
iptables -t mangle -A POSTROUTING -o eth2 -m layer7 --l7proto
bittorrent -j MARK --set-mark 5
iptables -t mangle -A POSTROUTING -o eth2 -m layer7 --l7proto
directconnect -j MARK --set-mark 5
```

At this point we've created all the firewall rules to match our security policy.

Setting Up the Firewall Script

On the Linux router, we will create the following script to add the rules we created just now, in the correct order, so that the firewall will have the desired effect:

```
#!/bin/bash

#define where iptables is
IPT=/sbin/iptables



############# Begin the NAT table opperations ######

#Flush all the rules in the nat table
$IPT -t nat -F

#SNAT sales and accounting to port 53 UDP (DNS)
$IPT -t nat -A POSTROUTING -o eth0 -s 192.168.1.0/24 -p udp --dport 53
-j SNAT --to 1.1.2.96-1.1.2.254

#Transparent Proxy for sales and accounting
$IPT -t nat -A PREROUTING -s 192.168.1.0/24 -p tcp --dport 80 -j
REDIRECT --to-port 3128

#SNAT Sales and accounting for HTTPS
$IPT -t nat -A POSTROUTING -o eth0 -s 192.168.1.0/24 -p tcp --dport
443 -j SNAT --to 1.1.2.96-1.1.2.254

#Drop everything else from sales and accouting to the internet
$IPT -t nat -A POSTROUTING -o eth0 -s 192.168.1.0/24 -j DROP
```

```
#Transparent Proxy for management
$IPT -t nat -A PREROUTING -s 1.1.2.64/27 -p tcp --dport 80 -j REDIRECT
--to-port 3128


############# End the NAT table opperations ######

#Flush netfilter table
$IPT -F

#allow packets on the loopback interface
$IPT -A INPUT -i lo -j ACCEPT

#delete MANAGEMENT chain if exists
$IPT -X MANAGEMENT
#create MANAGEMENT chain
$IPT -N MANAGEMENT

#add authorized IPs to the MANAGEMENT chain, drop all the others
$IPT -A MANAGEMENT -s 1.1.2.0/26 -j ACCEPT
$IPT -A MANAGEMENT -s 1.1.3.192 -j ACCEPT
$IPT -A MANAGEMENT -s 1.1.9.21 -j ACCEPT
$IPT -A MANAGEMENT -s 1.1.19.61 -j ACCEPT
$IPT -A MANAGEMENT -s 0/0 -j DROP

#Jump incoming packets for port 61146 TCP to the MANAGEMENT chain
$IPT -A INPUT -p tcp --dport 61146 -j MANAGEMENT

#Jump packets destined to 1.1.2.2 port 61146 TCP to the MANAGEMENT
#chain
$IPT -A FORWARD -d 1.1.2.2 -p tcp --dport 61146 -j MANAGEMENT

#drop samba (netbios and ms-ds)
$IPT -A INPUT -i eth0 -p tcp --dport 137:139 -j DROP
$IPT -A INPUT -i eth0 -p udp --dport 137:139 -j DROP
$IPT -A INPUT -i eth0 -p tcp --dport 445 -j DROP

#deny access to the intranet web server
$IPT -A INPUT -i eth0 -p tcp --dport 80 -j DROP

#filter the PostgreSQL port
$IPT -A INPUT -p tcp --dport 5432 -j DROP

#drop incoming TCP SYN packets
$IPT -A INPUT -i eth0 -p tcp --syn -j DROP
```

```
#allow http, pop3, smtp for the web and mail server
$IPT -A FORWARD -d 1.1.2.2 -p tcp -m multiport --dport 80,25,110 -j
ACCEPT

#drop all other tcp traffic for the web and mail server
$IPT -A FORWARD -d 1.1.2.2 -p tcp --syn -j DROP

#Drop netbios and ms-ds for the managers
$IPT -A FORWARD -d 1.1.2.64/27 -p tcp --dport 137:139 -j DROP
$IPT -A FORWARD -d 1.1.2.64/27 -p udp --dport 137:139 -j DROP
$IPT -A FORWARD -d 1.1.2.64/27 -p tcp --dport 445 -j DROP

#Flush the mangle table
$IPT -t mangle -F

#Mark packets belonging to dc++ and bittorrent
$IPT -t mangle -A POSTROUTING -o eth2 -m layer7 --l7proto bittorrent
-j MARK --set-mark 5
$IPT -t mangle -A POSTROUTING -o eth2 -m layer7 --l7proto
directconnect -j MARK --set-mark 5
```

Since we used the `netfilter` table, the `mangle` table, and the `nat` table, to verify all the rules, we need to see the output of `iptables -L -n -v`, `iptables -t nat -L -n -v`, and `iptables -t mangle -L -n -v`.

QoS—Bandwidth Allocation

For this example, we will perform a simple bandwidth splitting between the departments of the company. To do bandwidth sharing between them is a bit more complicated, because each department has its own interface; so, we will have to use an additional tool to do that. We will explain how to perform bandwidth sharing on multiple interfaces in the following chapter; for now, we will divide the bandwidth between the departments using CBQ.

Let's say our total bandwidth is 6Mbps. We want to give 1Mbps to sales and accounting, 2Mbps to the executive department (from which 512kbps at most goes to BitTorrent and DC++), 1Mbps to the web and mail server, and 2Mbps to the IT department.

CBQ has more parameters than HTB, and these can be tuned to adjust performance. We got the best results using the parameters that we'll use for this example.

First, for the sales and accounting departments we need to attach a CBQ `qdisc` to Eth3. After attaching the qdisc, we need to create the root class for the interface:

```
tc qdisc add dev eth3 root handle 30: cbq bandwidth 100Mbit avpkt 1000

tc class add dev eth3 parent 30:0 classid 30:1 cbq bandwidth 100Mbit
rate 100Mbit allot 1514 weight 10Mbit prio 8 maxburst 20 avpkt 1000
```

Now, for Eth3 all that needs to be done is to create a class of 1Mbps, attach an SFQ qdisc to the class, and a `tc` filter to match the IP addresses in those departments:

```
tc class add dev eth3 parent 30:1 classid 30:100 cbq bandwidth 100Mbit
rate 1Mbit allot 1514 weight 128Kbit prio 5 maxburst 20 avpkt 1000
bounded

tc qdisc add dev eth3 parent 30:100 sfq quantum 1514b perturb 15

tc filter add dev eth3 parent 30:0 protocol ip prio 5 u32 match ip dst
192.168.1.0/24 flowid 30:100
```

In the `tc` class, the `rate` parameter refers to the bandwidth in bps that we allow for this class. Most CBQ documentation recommends using the `weight` parameter as rate/10. If we do that, traffic would not exceed 100KB/s, while for 1Mbps bandwidth, the download speed should be 128KB/s; so it only seems fair to use rate/8.

The `bounded` parameter of the CBQ class tells the class NOT to exceed the specified rate. Without the `bounded` parameter, a class can borrow up to 100% of the free bandwidth in its parent class.

We will move next to limiting the bandwidth for the executive department. For them, we will create a 2Mbps CBQ class and two child classes, one of 512Kbps and one of 1.5Mbps. We won't allow the 512Kbps class to borrow bandwidth from the other class, but we'll allow the 1.5Mbps to go up to 2Mbps.

As for Eth3, we need to attach a CBQ qdisc and to create a root class for Eth2 first:

```
tc qdisc add dev eth2 root handle 20: cbq bandwidth 100Mbit avpkt 1000

tc class add dev eth2 parent 20:0 classid 20:1 cbq bandwidth 100Mbit
rate 100Mbit allot 1514 weight 10Mbit prio 8 maxburst 20 avpkt 1000
```

Next, we will create a 2Mbps class that will be the parent for the other two classes we discussed earlier:

```
tc class add dev eth2 parent 20:1 classid 20:10 cbq bandwidth 100Mbit
rate 2Mbit allot 1514 weight 256Kbit prio 5 maxburst 20 avpkt 1000
bounded
```

Now, we will create a 512Kbps class having 20:10 as parent. We will set the bounded parameter to this class so that it can't go over 512Kbps; we will attach an SFQ qdisc and a tc filter to match the nfmark 5 that we set in the firewall for BitTorrent and DC++:

```
tc class add dev eth2 parent 20:10 classid 20:100 cbq bandwidth
100Mbit rate 512Kbit allot 1514 weight 64Kbit prio 5 maxburst 20 avpkt
1000 bounded

tc qdisc add dev eth2 parent 20:100 sfq quantum 1514b perturb 15

tc filter add dev eth2 parent 20:0 protocol ip prio 5 handle 5 fw
flowid 20:100
```

For the rest of the traffic to the executive department, we will create a 1.5Mbps class with the parent class 20:10, without the bounded parameter set. We will attach an SFQ qdisc to this class and a tc filter to match the executive department subnet:

```
tc class add dev eth2 parent 20:10 classid 20:200 cbq bandwidth
100Mbit rate 1536Kbit allot 1514 weight 192Kbit prio 5 maxburst 20
avpkt 1000

tc qdisc add dev eth2 parent 20:200 sfq quantum 1514b perturb 15

tc filter add dev eth2 parent 20:0 protocol ip prio 5 u32 match ip dst
1.1.2.64/27 flowid 20:200
```

The configuration for the web server and for the IT department is done in a similar way; there's nothing new here.

```
tc qdisc add dev eth1 root handle 10: cbq bandwidth 100Mbit avpkt 1000
tc class add dev eth1 parent 10:0 classid 10:1 cbq bandwidth 100Mbit
rate 100Mbit allot 1514 weight 10Mbit prio 8 maxburst 20 avpkt 1000

tc class add dev eth1 parent 10:1 classid 10:100 cbq bandwidth 100Mbit
rate 1Mbit allot 1514 weight 128Kbit prio 5 maxburst 20 avpkt 1000
bounded
tc qdisc add dev eth1 parent 10:100 sfq quantum 1514b perturb 15
tc filter add dev eth1 parent 10:0 protocol ip prio 5 u32 match ip dst
1.1.2.2 flowid 10:100

tc class add dev eth1 parent 10:1 classid 10:200 cbq bandwidth 100Mbit
rate 2Mbit allot 1514 weight 256Kbit prio 5 maxburst 20 avpkt 1000
bounded
tc qdisc add dev eth1 parent 10:200 sfq quantum 1514b perturb 15
tc filter add dev eth1 parent 10:0 protocol ip prio 5 u32 match ip dst
1.1.2.2 flowid 10:200
```

The QoS Script

We need to place all those lines in a script, and also need to add some lines to delete the attached qdisc from all interfaces before adding it again. The script looks like this:

```
#!/bin/bash

#delete root qdisc for eth3
tc qdisc del dev eth3 root

#attach root qdisc and create the root class for eth3
tc qdisc add dev eth3 root handle 30: cbq bandwidth 100Mbit avpkt 1000
tc class add dev eth3 parent 30:0 classid 30:1 cbq bandwidth 100Mbit
rate \
   100Mbit allot 1514 weight 10Mbit prio 8 maxburst 20 avpkt 1000

#create the 1Mbps class for sales and accounting
tc class add dev eth3 parent 30:1 classid 30:100 cbq bandwidth 100Mbit
rate \
   1Mbit allot 1514 weight 128Kbit prio 5 maxburst 20 avpkt 1000
bounded
tc qdisc add dev eth3 parent 30:100 sfq quantum 1514b perturb 15
tc filter add dev eth3 parent 30:0 protocol ip prio 5 u32 match ip dst
192.168.1.0/24 flowid 30:100

#delete root qdisc for eth2
tc qdisc del dev eth2 root

#attach root qdisc and create the root class for eth2
tc qdisc add dev eth2 root handle 20: cbq bandwidth 100Mbit avpkt 1000
tc class add dev eth2 parent 20:0 classid 20:1 cbq bandwidth 100Mbit
rate \
   100Mbit allot 1514 weight 10Mbit prio 8 maxburst 20 avpkt 1000

#create the 2Mbps class for all traffic to executive dep.
tc class add dev eth2 parent 20:1 classid 20:10 cbq bandwidth 100Mbit
rate \
   2Mbit allot 1514 weight 256Kbit prio 5 maxburst 20 avpkt 1000
bounded

#the bittorrent and dc++ class - 512Kbps
tc class add dev eth2 parent 20:10 classid 20:100 cbq bandwidth
100Mbit rate \
   512Kbit allot 1514 weight 64Kbit prio 5 maxburst 20 avpkt 1000
bounded
tc qdisc add dev eth2 parent 20:100 sfq quantum 1514b perturb 15
```

```
tc filter add dev eth2 parent 20:0 protocol ip prio 5 handle 5 fw
flowid 20:100

#other traffic to executive dep.
tc class add dev eth2 parent 20:10 classid 20:200 cbq bandwidth
100Mbit rate \
   1536Kbit allot 1514 weight 192Kbit prio 5 maxburst 20 avpkt 1000
tc qdisc add dev eth2 parent 20:200 sfq quantum 1514b perturb 15
tc filter add dev eth2 parent 20:0 protocol ip prio 5 u32 match ip dst
1.1.2.64/27 flowid 20:200

#delete root qdisc for eth1
tc qdisc del dev eth1 root

#attach root qdisc and create the root class for eth1
tc qdisc add dev eth1 root handle 10: cbq bandwidth 100Mbit avpkt 1000
tc class add dev eth1 parent 10:0 classid 10:1 cbq bandwidth 100Mbit
rate \
   100Mbit allot 1514 weight 10Mbit prio 8 maxburst 20 avpkt 1000

#create the 1Mbps class for the web and mail server
tc class add dev eth1 parent 10:1 classid 10:100 cbq bandwidth 100Mbit
rate \
   1Mbit allot 1514 weight 128Kbit prio 5 maxburst 20 avpkt 1000
bounded
tc qdisc add dev eth1 parent 10:100 sfq quantum 1514b perturb 15
tc filter add dev eth1 parent 10:0 protocol ip prio 5 u32 match ip dst
1.1.2.2 flowid 10:100

#create the 2Mbps class for the IT dep.
tc class add dev eth1 parent 10:1 classid 10:200 cbq bandwidth 100Mbit
rate \
   2Mbit allot 1514 weight 256Kbit prio 5 maxburst 20 avpkt 1000
bounded
tc qdisc add dev eth1 parent 10:200 sfq quantum 1514b perturb 15
tc filter add dev eth1 parent 10:0 protocol ip prio 5 u32 match ip dst
1.1.2.2 flowid 10:200
```

The QoS configuration is verified with `tc show dev ethX` and with the options `-s` and `-d` to have a more verbose output. Whichever qdisc is used (CBQ or HTB), the configuration is verified with `tc show`, though the output differs a bit. For example, for this script, the output of `tc -s class show dev eth1` would be like this:

```
root@router:~# tc -s class show dev eth1
class cbq 10: root rate 100000Kbit (bounded,isolated) prio no-
transmit
```

```
   Sent 391984925 bytes 323636 pkts (dropped 0, overlimits 0)
     borrowed 0 overactions 0 avgidle 53 undertime 0
 class cbq 10:100 parent 10:1 leaf 8091: rate 1000Kbit (bounded)
 prio 5
   Sent 0 bytes 0 pkts (dropped 0, overlimits 0)
     borrowed 0 overactions 0 avgidle 184151 undertime 0
 class cbq 10:1 parent 10: rate 100000Kbit prio no-transmit
   Sent 0 bytes 0 pkts (dropped 0, overlimits 0)
     borrowed 0 overactions 0 avgidle 65 undertime 0
 class cbq 10:200 parent 10:1 leaf 8092: rate 2000Kbit (bounded)
 prio 5
   Sent 0 bytes 0 pkts (dropped 0, overlimits 0)
     borrowed 0 overactions 0 avgidle 91145 undertime 0
```

Of course, this output shows zero bytes and zero packets sent for the classes, but when traffic starts, you should see packets matching the classes.

Summary

In this first case-study chapter of this book, we've analyzed a couple of scenarios that we can classify as "small" networks, for which we've built firewall and QoS.

The chapter presented:

- How to make a SOHO router out of a PC running Linux
- How to secure a SOHO network
- How to use Linux as router for a small to medium office, and how to secure such a network
- How to perform transparent proxy using Squid and iptables
- How to perform NAPT to redirect traffic for certain ports to other hosts using Linux
- How to split bandwidth between the devices in a SOHO environment using HTB
- How to do bandwidth shaping using CBQ
- How to use the L7-filter project to shape traffic consumed by certain applications
- Most important, how to think, define, and apply security policies for SOHO and small-to-medium office environments

7
Medium Networks
Case Studies

In the previous chapter we learned about using Linux as a SOHO router and as a router for a medium company with internal departments.

While small networks have the most common topologies because of their simplicity, when we go further in the hierarchy of networks, there are fewer chances to find standard topologies for networks built with Linux machines as routers. This is not a bad thing at all, because, considering Linux' flexibility, network administrators can deploy networks and services using more their imagination than standardization.

Throughout this chapter we will try to describe a few medium networks we've encountered in our experience, how we deployed them, and how we built the firewall for those networks.

Example 1: A Company with Remote Locations

The following example is from a real application. It's about a hypermarket having the headquarters in one location, one store in the same city, and several stores in other cities.

The hypermarket has an application that uses MSSQL databases in each location. The remote database contains details on stocks and personnel, and needs to replicate with the headquarters database every day at closing hours. Replication is needed for stock details update, as the checkout devices query the database for prices and update stocks so that the headquarters database has all info on daily sales, and available stocks in every store. The application is developed by a third party software company that also does database administration and remote storage; so it needs access to all databases in every store.

All locations have IP Analog Telephone Adapters (IP phones in the diagram that follows) with subscriptions at the main provider (the HQ provider). In this example we will use, just as in the real application, H.323 as VoIP protocol. SIP, IAX, MGCP, or other VoIP protocols can also be used with slight modifications of the firewalls we are going to present here.

Headquarters and the store in the same city are connected to the same ISP. Given its fact that MAN access is much cheaper than an internet connection, headquarters has a 10 Mbps internet connection with 100 Mbps MAN, and for the store, they wanted only 100 Mbps MAN, with no internet connection. The rest of the stores have internet connections from other ISPs in the cities they are in.

The Network

Let's have a look at the network diagram:

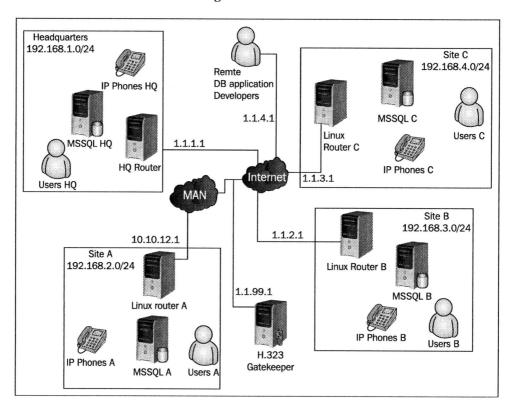

At the headquarters:

- The provider assigned the public IP address 1.1.1.1 for the internet connection. The connection is a 10 Mbps internet connection and 100 Mbps metropolitan access.

- We decided to use the private class C 192.168.1.0/24 for our internal network.

- We set the HQ router LAN interface with the private IP address 192.168.1.1.

- MSSQL HQ must have a static private IP address – 192.168.1.2.

- The IP ATA must have a static private IP address – 192.168.1.3.

Site A (Store A):

- The provider assigned the private IP address 10.10.12.1 for the MAN connection. The connection is a 100 Mbps metropolitan access, and no internet access.

- We decided to use the private class C 192.168.2.0/24 for our internal network.

- We set the Linux router A LAN interfaces with the private IP address 192.168.2.1.

- MSSQL A must have a static private IP address – 192.168.2.2.

- The IP ATA must have a static private IP address – 192.168.2.3.

Sites B and C (Stores B and C):

- Local providers assigned public IP addresses 1.1.2.1 for Store B and 1.1.3.1 for Store C. Internet connections are: 2 Mbps for Store B and 1Mbps for Store C.

- We decided to use the private class C 192.168.3.0/24 for Store B and 192.168.4.0/24 for Store C.

- We set the Linux routers B and C LAN interface with the private IP addresses 192.168.3.1 and 192.168.4.1.

- MSSQL B and C must have static private IP addresses – 192.168.3.2 and 192.168.4.2.

- The IP ATAs must have static private IP addresses – 192.168.3.3 and 192.168.3.4.

 The actual network we deployed contains more stores. However, there is no special situation for any other store than Stores B and C; so deploying this network is enough to know how to add more sites.

Building the Network Configuration

All remote locations must have an encrypted VPN connection to headquarters. This will eliminate the possibility of a MITM (Man In The Middle) attack, and sniffing of packets between locations will be impossible due to encryption.

Building encrypted VPN connections can be done in various ways: using OpenVPN software, IP tunnel contained in the iproute package, using POP-TOP (pptpd package), etc. We decided to use IP tunnel because it was most suited for this applications (IP addresses are statically assigned) in each location.

The Linux distribution used in all locations is Debian; so we will show the configuration files as they are on Debian Linux, with the remark that they can be adapted for any Linux distribution.

For the headquarters' Linux router, we will set up the network interfaces and the GRE-encrypted tunnels by modifying the `/etc/network/interfaces` file like this:

```
#eth0 - ISP inteface

auto eth0
iface eth0 inet static
        address 1.1.1.1
        netmask 255.255.255.252
        network 1.1.1.0
        broadcast 1.1.1.3
        gateway 1.1.1.2
        dns-nameservers 1.1.11.1

#eth1 - LAN interface

auto eth1
iface eth1 inet static
        address 192.168.1.1
        netmask 255.255.255.0
        network 192.168.1.0
        broadcast 192.168.1.255

#tunnel to site A

auto sitea
iface sitea inet static
    address 10.100.100.1
    netmask 255.255.255.252
    network 10.100.100.0
```

```
    broadcast 10.100.100.3
    pre-up /sbin/modprobe ip_gre
    pre-up /sbin/iptunnel add sitea mode gre local 1.1.1.1
        remote 10.10.12.1 key 111111 dev eth0
    up /sbin/route add -net 192.168.2.0/24 gw 10.100.100.2
    post-down /sbin/iptunnel del sitea

#tunnel to site B

auto siteb
iface siteb inet static
    address 10.100.200.1
    netmask 255.255.255.252
    network 10.100.200.0
    broadcast 10.100.200.3
    pre-up /sbin/modprobe ip_gre
    pre-up /sbin/iptunnel add siteb mode gre local 1.1.1.1
        remote 1.1.2.1 key 222222 dev eth0
    up /sbin/route add -net 192.168.3.0/24 gw 10.100.200.2
    post-down /sbin/iptunnel del siteb

#tunnel to site C

auto sitec
iface sitec inet static
    address 10.100.300.1
    netmask 255.255.255.252
    network 10.100.300.0
    broadcast 10.100.300.3
    pre-up /sbin/modprobe ip_gre
    pre-up /sbin/iptunnel add sitec mode gre local 1.1.1.1
        remote 1.1.3.1 key 333333 dev eth0
    up /sbin/route add -net 192.168.4.0/24 gw 10.100.300.2
    post-down /sbin/iptunnel del sitec
```

By performing a network restart, our Linux router will have five logical interfaces: eth0, eth1, sitea, siteb, and sitec. The configuration can be verified using ifconfig and ip tunnel show commands.

The network configuration for routers B and C is very similar to the HQ router's configuration. IP addresses on Eth0 need to be changed to 1.1.2.1 for site B and 1.1.3.1 for site C with their corresponding gateways. Also, the IP addresses for Eth1 in both locations need to be changed to 192.168.3.1 for site B and 192.168.4.1 for site C. The tunnel interfaces in sites B and C are configured with IP addresses 10.100.200.2 for site B and 10.100.300.2 on site C. Remember that the tunnels must be configured with the same keys used on the HQ router.

The router at site A needs a special configuration, because it only has metro access and no internet access, and therefore it needs to have as the default route the IP address of the HQ router. Here's the configuration:

```
#eth0 – ISP inteface

auto eth0
iface eth0 inet static
        address 10.10.12.1
        netmask 255.255.255.252
        network 10.10.12.0
        broadcast 10.10.12.3
        up /sbin/route add 1.1.1.1 gw 10.10.12.2


#eth1 – LAN interface

auto eth1
iface eth1 inet static
        address 192.168.2.1
        netmask 255.255.255.0
        network 192.168.2.0
        broadcast 192.168.2.255

#tunnel to HeadQuarters

auto hq
iface hq inet static
    address 10.100.100.2
    netmask 255.255.255.252
    network 10.100.100.0
    broadcast 10.100.100.3
    pre-up /sbin/modprobe ip_gre
    pre-up /sbin/iptunnel add hq mode gre local 10.10.12.1
        remote 1.1.1.1 key oursiteAkey dev eth0
    up /sbin/route add default gw 10.100.100.1
    post-down /sbin/iptunnel del hq
```

When bringing up the interface eth0, no default route is set; so, in order to set up the tunnel, we have to add the route to the IP address of the HQ router via the provider's directly connected IP address.

After bringing up the tunnel between site A and HQ, we add the default route via 10.100.100.1, which is the IP address of the HQ router on the tunnel interface.

Designing the Firewalls

At a first glance, firewalls for this network might seem complicated; however, they are pretty simple to build. The main concern is database security and with the tunnels built between the locations, the encryption gives us most of the protection we need; so data will not be intercepted when database replication occurs.

A man in the middle who wants to sniff packets between the sites sees encrypted GRE packets, and without the key can't use the captured data.

The third-party database developers can be allowed access to the database servers either by trusting their IP addresses (trusting routes to them, meaning the providers on the way) or by giving them a way to make a VPN connection to the sites or to HQ and letting them work via encrypted connections. In our real-life example, we allowed them to work directly from their IP addresses because we trust the providers in between.

We will present our real-life solution for the third-party database developers with the remark that by giving them VPN access to HQ or directly to the sites the firewalls are simplified.

Now, what we need to do is *deny* access to port 1433/TCP, which is used for MSSQL, from everyone, then allow and DNAT the trusted IP addresses from the third-party developer to each database in every location.

There's a special configuration for site A, and we can either change the port on which MSSQL is running, or we can give the developers another port and can DNAT that port to 1433/TCP. In our example, we will leave MSSQL running on 1433/TCP and we will give the developers port 9001/TCP to connect to the MSSQL server in site A, which we will then DNAT to 1433/TCP.

Another complicated situation has to do with the IP Analog Telephone Adapters (ATA). They use the protocol H.323, which is not so NAT-friendly, because it uses UDP to transport voice. Fortunately, we know that the standard call signaling port is 1720/TCP and best of all, we can set the call signaling port on every ATA to be whatever port we want. We can also set the UDP ports that every ATA uses for RTP (Real Time Protocol), which is used to transport voice over IP.

Without any firewall configuration, the IP ATA can make calls without hearing the audio from the other end, but it can't receive calls. So, for the IP ATAs to work, we have to DNAT RTP ports in our Linux routers. Also, for site A we have to change the call signaling port so we can use the IP address of the HQ router.

At a first glance at this you might say this is all, but there's one other thing that we found out only after we implemented the solution. Site A connects to the Internet over an IP tunnel. The IP tunnel interface can't inherit the MTU (Maximum Transmit

Unit) of the Ethernet interface. When we NAT the users in site A with the IP address of the HQ router, packets are transmitted over the Internet with the MTU of the Ethernet interface eth0 of the HQ router: 1500 bytes.

The problem is that when packets arrive in the HQ router having a size of 1500 bytes and the DF (Don't Fragment) bit in the TCP header set to 1, the HQ router can't send the packet to a user in site A. The Linux kernel drops that IP packet because this is how TCP works (if the IP packet size is greater than the MTU of the interface through which it needs to be sent, Linux will fragment the packet only if DF is set to 0 in the IP header; otherwise packets are dropped).

We noticed this problem when having IP tunnels with private IP addresses. If the IP addresses at the end of the tunnels are public, packets with a length greater than the MTU will be dropped, but the router in site A will send an ICMP packet to the source with the message "couldn't fragment". The source will then lower the size of the packet until a suitable size is reached. This is called PMTU-D (Path MTU Discovery), but in order for it to work, routers at the other end of the tunnel need to be able to communicate with the source of the packet, and so, ICMP must be allowed; and ICMP needs a public IP address (or the IP address should be NATed).

Please read carefully the PMTU part. PMTU uses ICMP messages. There are a lot of network administrators who block ICMP messages because they consider them as security threats because of DoS attacks that use ICMP messages. ICMP should not be filtered anywhere on the Internet. To give you an example, if Yahoo! administrators were to filter ICMP packets, over 80% of Internet users would not be able to access their web-based mail servers.

Building the Firewalls

We have a pretty clear image of what we need to do here. We will start with the firewalls for sites B and C, which are the simplest.

Sites B and C

The network administrators are all at the headquarters location and they have IP addresses from 192.168.1.32 to 192.168.1.38; so we will allow SSH on port 22 only from these IP addresses:

```
iptables -A INPUT -p tcp --dport 22 -s ! 192.168.1.32/29 -j DROP
```

For the MSSQL servers, we will create separate chains like this:

```
iptables -N SQL
iptables -A FORWARD -p tcp --dport 1433 -j SQL
```

and add the rules we want for the SQL chain:

```
iptables -A SQL -s 192.168.1.3 -j ACCEPT
iptables -A SQL -s 1.1.4.1 -j ACCEPT
iptables -A SQL -s 0/0 -j DROP
```

Now, let's DNAT the SQL server:

```
iptables -t nat -A PREROUTING -d 1.1.2.1 -p tcp --dport 1433 -j DNAT
--to 192.168.3.2
```

and for site C:

```
iptables -t nat -A PREROUTING -d 1.1.3.1 -p tcp --dport 1433 -j DNAT
--to 192.168.4.2
```

 This is the logical way to do it, but *it's wrong*. If we build the firewall this way, everyone can access our SQL servers on port 1433 by connecting to IP addresses 1.1.2.1 and 1.1.3.1 on port 1433/TCP. We especially wrote it this way so you can see the big difference. Packets for 1.1.2.1 (site B) and 1.1.3.1 (site C) are treated in the INPUT chain, even if the MSSQL server is behind the Linux router.

What we need to do is:

```
iptables -A INPUT -p tcp --dport 1433 -j SQL
```

or instead of:

```
iptables -t nat -A PREROUTING -d 1.1.3.1 -p tcp --dport 1433 -j DNAT
--to 192.168.3.2
```

we should use:

```
iptables -t nat -A PREROUTING -d 1.1.3.1 -s 1.1.4.1 -p tcp --dport
1433 -j DNAT --to 192.168.3.2
```

However, we prefer the first way because if developers want to add other IP addresses that can access the SQL servers, it would be easier in that manner.

Now, let's allow everyone access to the Internet:

```
iptables -t nat -A POSTROUTING -s 192.168.3.0/24 -d ! 192.168.1.0/24
-j
MASQUERADE
```

At this point, our VoIP device is able to place calls but it's not able to receive calls. Setting the RTP port range for our IP ATA to from 16384 to 16500, with DNAT port 1720/TCP used for call signaling, and port range 16384-16500/UDP used for RTP, everything should work fine:

```
iptables -t nat -A PREROUTING -p tcp --dport 1720 -j DNAT --to
192.168.3.3
iptables -t nat -A PREROUTING -p udp --dport 16384:16500   -j DNAT --
to 192.168.3.3
```

 At a first sight you might think that by doing DNAT for all packets coming from 1.1.99.1 to the ATA device everything works OK. This is true *only* if 1.1.99.1 is a VoIP Proxy. If it's not a proxy, then call signaling and RTP will come from an unlimited number of IP addresses; so by doing things the way we presented here it will work for sure.

This is basically all that needs to be done to sites B and C. Now, the smart way of setting up those is to create a generic script for sites in those situations. This will help a lot when adding new sites:

```
#!/bin/bash

#define the prefix for the network (where we are)
PREFIX=192.168.3

#define where iptables is
IPT=/sbin/iptables

#Flush all Rules
$IPT -F

#Flush all the rules in the nat table
$IPT -t nat -F

#Load some modules needed for NAT
/sbin/modprobe ip_nat_ftp
/sbin/modprobe ip_nat_irc
```

```
#deny SSH access except admins
$IPT -A INPUT -p tcp --dport 22 -s ! 192.168.1.0/29 -j DROP

#SQL Chain
$IPT -N SQL
$IPT -A FORWARD -p tcp --dport 1433 -j SQL
$IPT -A INPUT -p tcp --dport 1433 -j SQL

$IPT -A SQL -s 192.168.1.2 -j ACCEPT
$IPT -A SQL -s 1.1.4.1 -j ACCEPT
$IPT -A SQL -s 0/0 -j DROP

#Dnat port 1433 - SQL server
$IPT -t nat -A PREROUTING -s 1.1.4.1 -p tcp --dport 1433 -j DNAT --to
$PREFIX.2

#NAT all to the internet. Don't nat to network at HQ
$IPT -t nat -A POSTROUTING -s $PREFIX.0/24 -d ! 192.168.1.0/24 -j
MASQUERADE

#allow the IP phone to receive calls.
$IPT -t nat -A PREROUTING -p tcp --dport 1720 -j DNAT --to $PREFIX.3
$IPT -t nat -A PREROUTING -p udp --dport 16384:16500   -j DNAT --to
$PREFIX.3
```

Every time we add a site we modify the *prefix* with the network that we use at that location. For example, for site C we will copy this script and use `PREFIX=192.168.4`

Site A

Site A has a special situation due to the fact that it has no internet connection. Because of that, we have to find some ways not only to allow to access the Internet for hosts at site A, but also to allow remote DB developers access to the SQL server and the VoIP device to function.

So, the first thing we did was to bring up the tunnel and the interface. The interface looks like this:

```
hq          Link encap:UNSPEC  HWaddr C2-99-E9-C1-00-00-00-00-00-00-00-
                00-00-00-00-00
            inet addr:10.100.100.2  P-t-P:10.100.100.1
                Mask:255.255.255.252
            UP POINTOPOINT RUNNING NOARP  MTU:1472  Metric:1
            RX packets:0 errors:0 dropped:0 overruns:0 frame:0
            TX packets:0 errors:0 dropped:0 overruns:0 carrier:0
            collisions:0 txqueuelen:0
            RX bytes:0 (0.0 b)  TX bytes:0 (0.0 b)
```

We have the default route set to 10.100.100.1. Also, we can see that the hq interface doesn't have the standard Ethernet MTU of 1500, and instead has an MTU of 1472.

The funniest thing about this special configuration is that site A doesn't need much of a firewall. Think about it—it has a private IP address that can only be accessed from the provider's MAN. However, the default route is set on the tunnel so all packets will go through the HQ router, which can do the filtering. Everything behind the Linux router in site A has private IP addresses so no one has access to those.

The only thing that can go wrong would be a route to the private network 192.168.2.0/24 added by the provider via 10.10.12.1, which is the site A MAN-connection IP address. In this case a MAN user can try to attack the SQL server for example. There's a very simple way to solve this without using iptables. All you need is to do like this:

```
echo 1 > /proc/sys/net/conf/all/rp_filter
```

This will enable rp_filter on all interfaces. rp_filter is short for "Return Path Filter", and is the mechanism that Linux uses to drop all packets that come in one interface but go out on another one. This is usually used to prevent spoof attacks, and in most Linux distributions is enabled by default. In our case setting rp_filter "on" on the site A router will give us the protection we need.

The only thing we need to set up is to filter SSH access on this router:

```
iptables -A INPUT -p tcp --dport 22 -s ! 192.168.1.0/29 -j DROP
```

To our shame that's all we did the first time we deployed this configuration. Afterwards, users started to complain that several sites (e.g. mail.yahoo.com) didn't work. The problem is that those sites send data with the segment size set to the MSS (Maximum Segment Size) of Ethernet and the DF (Don't fragment) bit set to 1. MTU is the size of the entire IP packet while MSS is the size of the payload. Normally, the header of a TCP packet is 40 bytes if there aren't any TCP options expanding the header, and so MSS is equal to MTU−40. For Ethernet, MSS is 1460. For our connection the MTU is 1472; so MSS is 1432. When a packet has a segment size larger than 1432 and the DF bit set to 1, the packet is dropped and the Linux router in site A informs the sender of the packet about this by sending an ICMP message "Couldn't fragment". This is where PMTU-D (Path MTU Discovery) should come in, but Linux router A tries to send this packet from it's IP address 10.100.100.2, and so, the original sender will never receive the "Couldn't fragment" message, because 10.100.100.2 is a private IP address.

If PMTU-D fails, there are a lot of things that might not function right. The solution for this is:

```
iptables -t mangle -A POSTROUTING -o hq -j TCPMSS --clamp-mss-to-pmtu
```

The TCPMSS target of iptables is used to alter the MSS of outgoing packets. In our case, all packets going out on the hq interface are altered to use another MSS value than the original value. The --clamp-mss-to-pmtu option automatically sets MSS to the proper value of the connection. iptables changes the MSS for every packet that goes out of the hq interface to PMTU (Path Maximum Transfer Unit) minus 40 = 1432.

This is the entire configuration needed for site A.

Headquarters

The HQ Linux router seems to have a more complicated configuration, but in fact, it is pretty simple. If we look at what needs to be done step by step, we can see that it differs from sites B and C by performing almost the same functions for two networks—192.168.1.0/24 in the headquarters location, and 192.168.2.0/24 at site A.

If we take a look again at the network diagram, we can see that if the HQ Linux router had two IP addresses, the configuration would be the same as sites B and C (with a few minor changes). Because we only have one IP address, we have to manage those connections in an intelligent manner.

First, we can use some parts of the script we built for the remote sites:

```
#!/bin/bash

#define the prefix for the network (where we are)
PREFIX=192.168.1

#define where iptables is
IPT=/sbin/iptables

#Flush all Rules
$IPT -F

#Flush all the rules in the nat table
$IPT -t nat -F

#Load some modules needed for NAT
/sbin/modprobe ip_nat_ftp
/sbin/modprobe ip_nat_irc

#deny SSH access except admins
$IPT -A INPUT -p tcp --dport 22 -s ! 192.168.1.0/29 -j DROP

#SQL Chain
$IPT -N SQL
$IPT -A FORWARD -p tcp --dport 1433 -j SQL
```

```
$IPT -A INPUT -p tcp --dport 1433 -j SQL

$IPT -A SQL -s 192.168.1.2 -j ACCEPT
$IPT -A SQL -s 192.168.2.2 -j ACCEPT
$IPT -A SQL -s 192.168.3.2 -j ACCEPT
$IPT -A SQL -s 192.168.4.2 -j ACCEPT
$IPT -A SQL -s 1.1.4.1 -j ACCEPT
$IPT -A SQL -s 0/0 -j DROP

#Dnat port 1433 - SQL server
$IPT -t nat -A PREROUTING -s 1.1.4.1 -p tcp --dport 1433 -j DNAT --to
$PREFIX.2

#NAT all to the internet. Don't nat to network at HQ
$IPT -t nat -A POSTROUTING -s $PREFIX.0/24 -d 192.168.2.0/24 -j ACCEPT
$IPT -t nat -A POSTROUTING -s $PREFIX.0/24 -d 192.168.3.0/24 -j ACCEPT
$IPT -t nat -A POSTROUTING -s $PREFIX.0/24 -d 192.168.4.0/24 -j ACCEPT
$IPT -t nat -A POSTROUTING -s $PREFIX.0/24 -j MASQUERADE

#allow the IP phone to receive calls.
$IPT -t nat -A PREROUTING -p tcp --dport 1720 -j DNAT --to $PREFIX.3
$IPT -t nat -A PREROUTING -p udp --dport 16384:16500  -j DNAT --to
$PREFIX.3
```

What we did here was almost the same as in sites B and C, except that we accept SQL connections from all the SQL servers in all the locations and we don't NAT the local network 192.168.1.0/24 for all the networks in the remote locations.

We added access to the IP address 192.168.1.2 in the SQL chain because all packets that pass through the HQ router with the destination port 1433/TCP go through the SQL chain, even the packets from the SQL server in the headquarters location to the SQL server in site A.

The script doesn't end here. We have to do the same things for site A, but we can't use port 1433/TCP for SQL, port 1720/TCP for call signaling, and ports 16384-16500/UDP for RTP.

We already gave the remote DB developers the IP address 1.1.1.1 and port 9001/TCP to connect to the SQL server in site A, and so, what we need to do is to DNAT packets arriving from 1.1.4.1 with the destination port 9001/TCP to 192.168.2.2 on port 1433/TCP. We don't need to filter anything for this because we don't DNAT everyone; so, connections from other hosts to 1.1.1.1 on port 9001/TCP will be dropped because the HQ router doesn't run anything on port 9001/TCP. We will therefore add to the script the following line:

```
$IPT -t nat -A PREROUTING -s 1.1.4.1 -p tcp --dport 9001 -j DNAT --to
192.168.2.2:1433
```

Next, we need to reconfigure the VoIP device at site A to use port 1721/TCP for call signaling and ports 16501 to 16800 for RTP. After that, we need to do DNAT for it to work; so we'll add the following lines to the script:

```
$IPT -t nat -A PREROUTING -p tcp --dport 1721 -j DNAT --to 192.168.2.3
$IPT -t nat -A PREROUTING -p udp --dport 16501:16800   -j DNAT --to
192.168.2.3
```

The H.323 gatekeeper sees two terminals registered from the same IP address (1.1.1.1), one with the call signaling port 1720/TCP, and the other with 1721/TCP.

Next, we need to NAT the network in site A for Internet access; so we'll add the following line to the script:

```
$IPT -t nat -A POSTROUTING -s 192.168.2.0/24 -d ! 192.168.1.0/24 -j
MASQUERADE
```

Now everything should work fine. Path MTU Discovery should work OK from headquarters to site A, because we don't filter ICMP and there are routes to the private IP addresses from both locations. However, just to be sure everything works OK, we can add the following lines to the script:

```
#Set MSS on the tunnels
$IPT -t mangle -A POSTROUTING -o sitea -j TCPMSS --clamp-mss-to-pmtu
$IPT -t mangle -A POSTROUTING -o siteb -j TCPMSS --clamp-mss-to-pmtu
$IPT -t mangle -A POSTROUTING -o sitec -j TCPMSS --clamp-mss-to-pmtu
```

 We're all set with the basic configuration. Of course in time there will be requests such as to deny user access to some services, but most of those were explained in the previous chapter. The idea is that we can apply to this kind of network everything we learned in the previous chapters.

Make the Network Intelligent by Adding QoS

Most people want to use their resources in the optimum way they can. QoS in this case is related to iptables in the way that we need to use iptables to mark packets to differentiate services.

Without QoS, one or more users in this network, with or without intention, can slow things down and can make the use of the VoIP devices almost impossible. It doesn't matter how much bandwidth each location has; this can happen anyway.

Let's have a look at the network diagram again:

The general rules we should consider when building QoS for this network are the following:

- Voice traffic should have the highest priority because it is the most sensitive to packet loss and high delays. We will use priority 0 for voice traffic.
- Database replication is very important and it should have priority over user traffic — priority 1.
- Remote DB application developers must be able to work on the SQL servers with low latency — priority 2.
- Traffic between headquarters and the remote locations should have priority over internet traffic — priority 3.
- Internet traffic from users must have the lowest priority — priority 4.

We will create a script for QoS just as we did for the firewall so that we can ease our work when deploying new locations. When talking about QoS, there's no "best way" to do it; it's just how we think it's better and optimum for our needs. For example, for this network we allocated a bandwidth for the VoIP devices in every location, leaving the rest of the applications only able to consume less than the total available bandwidth. Some might think this is not optimum, but we know that there's a lot of voice traffic from the locations and latency is very important to VoIP.

While some applications (e.g. data replication) might eat up all bandwidth, when a call is set up from the VoIP device, it takes a few seconds for HTB or CBQ to lower the bandwidth consumed by those applications and give bandwidth to the VoIP device. For a conversation that has just started, those seconds are very bad in the way that voice quality is very poor. Our decision can be justified also with the fact that, being VoIP, the devices use low-bit codecs such as g.729 or g.723, which consume very low bandwidth for a call (about 16 kbps average).

From the total bandwidth a site has, we will allocate 32 kbps for each line of a VoIP ATA to make sure that calls don't experience problems. This bandwidth should have the highest priority over the rest of the traffic. The database replication is important and bandwidth-consuming at the same time; so we will allocate at least 3/8th of the remaining bandwidth, with the possibility of borrowing bandwidth from the other classes, except from VoIP.

The remote developers don't need to eat up so much bandwidth; so we'll allocate a minimum of 1/8 of the total bandwidth minus the voice bandwidth, with the possibility to borrow the other's bandwidth, except VoIP.

At this point we've allocated half of the total bandwidth minus the VoIP bandwidth. For the rest of the traffic that normally passes through site routers, we only have traffic between the site and headquarters, and the rest is normal internet traffic. We will divide the rest of the free bandwidth in two and allocate it to those two types of traffic, except that we'll give priority 3 to HQ traffic and priority 4 to Internet traffic. This bandwidth allocation that we described is detailed in the following figure:

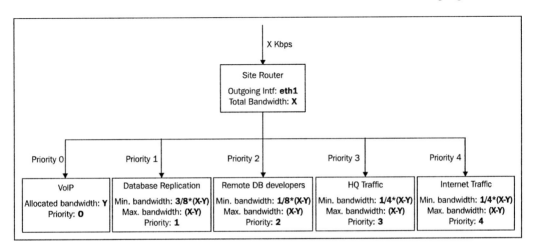

To differentiate these services we will mark packets in the `mangle` table in the `POSTROUTING` chain for every service, using the `MARK` target of iptables (module `ipt_MARK`).

Let's go back to the firewall script we created for sites B and C. We need to add the following lines to the script:

```
#Flush Mangle chain
$IPT -t mangle -F

#mark packets for the Voip Device - value 0
$IPT  -t mangle -A POSTROUTING -d $PREFIX.3 -j MARK --set-mark 1

#mark packets for Database replication - value 1
$IPT  -t mangle -A POSTROUTING -s 192.168.1.2 -d $PREFIX.2 -j MARK --
set-mark 2

#mark packets for remote DB developers - value 2
$IPT  -t mangle -A POSTROUTING -s 1.1.4.1 -d $PREFIX.2 -j MARK --set-
mark 3

#mark packets for HQ traffic - value 3
$IPT  -t mangle -A POSTROUTING -s 192.168.1.0/24 -d $PREFIX.0/24 -j
MARK --set-mark 4
```

Now, we have packets marked like this:

- 0: VoIP traffic
- 1: Database Replication
- 2: Remote DB Developers
- 3: Headquarters traffic
- 4: Everything else is Internet traffic

The `POSTROUTING` chain of the `mangle` table looks like this:

```
Chain POSTROUTING (policy ACCEPT)
target     prot opt source          destination
MARK       all  --  0.0.0.0/0       192.168.4.3      MARK set 0x1
MARK       all  --  192.168.1.2     192.168.4.2      MARK set 0x2
MARK       all  --  1.1.4.1         192.168.4.2      MARK set 0x3
MARK       all  --  192.168.1.0/24  192.168.4.0/24   MARK set 0x4
```

We will create HTB classes for this configuration using the following script:

```
#!/bin/bash

#Edit these lines to suit location

TOTALBW=1024       #Total DOWNLOAD bandwidth for the location
VBW=128            #Voice bandwidth in this location
PREFIX=192.168.4   #IP addresses in this location

#no more editing is required below this line

let BW=$TOTALBW-$VBW

#delete root qdisc - this will drop all classes
tc qdisc del root dev eth1

#create root qdisc
tc qdisc add dev eth1 root handle 1: htb default 12

#create root class
tc class add dev eth1 parent 1: classid 1:1 htb rate ${TOTALBW}kbit
ceil ${TOTALBW}kbit

#add class, Add Qdisc, Add Filter
AC="tc class add dev eth1 parent"
AQ="tc qdisc add dev eth1 parent"
AF="tc filter add dev eth1 protocol ip parent 1:0 prio 1"

#VoIP should have the highest priority
$AC 1:1 classid 1:10 htb rate ${VBW}kbit ceil ${VBW}kbit prio 0
$AQ 1:10 handle 100: pfifo limit 5
$AF handle 1 fw classid 1:10


#Database Replication
#we allow a minimum of 3/8 of total bandwidth for replication
let DBW=3*$BW/8

$AC 1:1 classid 1:20 htb rate ${DBW}kbit ceil ${BW}kbit prio 1
$AQ 1:20 handle 200: pfifo limit 5
$AF handle 2 fw classid 1:20


#Remote DB application developers
```

```
#we allow a minimum of 1/8 of total bandwidth for remote developers

let RBW=$BW/8

$AC 1:1 classid 1:30 htb rate ${RBW}kbit ceil ${RBW}kbit prio 2
$AQ 1:30 handle 300: pfifo limit 5
$AF handle 3 fw classid 1:30

#traffic between HQ and this location
#we allow a minimum of 1/4 of total bandwidth for traffic with HQ

let I=$BW/4
$AC 1:1 classid 1:40 htb rate ${I}kbit ceil ${BW}kbit prio 3
$AQ 1:40 handle 400: pfifo limit 5
$AF handle 4 fw classid 1:40

#Internet Traffic for users
#we allow a minimum of 1/4 of total bandwidth for internet traffic
$AC 1:1 classid 1:50 htb rate ${I}kbit ceil ${BW}kbit prio 4
$AQ 1:50 handle 500: pfifo limit 5
tc filter add dev eth1 protocol ip parent 1:0 prio 5 u32 match ip dst
$PREFIX.0/24 flowid 1:50
```

In this script we used $TOTALBW (X in the earlier diagram) 1024 kbps = 1 Mbps, and $VBW (Y in the same diagram) 128 kbps. We can verify the configuration using the following command:

```
sitec~# tc -s class show dev eth1
class htb 1:1 root rate 1Mbit ceil 1Mbit burst 2909b cburst 2909b
  Sent 0 bytes 0 pkts (dropped 0, overlimits 0)
  lended: 0 borrowed: 0 giants: 0
  tokens: 18187 ctokens: 18187

class htb 1:10 parent 1:1 leaf 100: prio 0 rate 128Kbit ceil 128Kbit
burst 1762b cburst 1762b
  Sent 0 bytes 0 pkts (dropped 0, overlimits 0)
  lended: 0 borrowed: 0 giants: 0
  tokens: 88149 ctokens: 88149

class htb 1:20 parent 1:1 leaf 200: prio 1 rate 336Kbit ceil 896Kbit
burst 2029b cburst 2745b
  Sent 0 bytes 0 pkts (dropped 0, overlimits 0)
  lended: 0 borrowed: 0 giants: 0
  tokens: 38666 ctokens: 19614
```

```
class htb 1:30 parent 1:1 leaf 300: prio 2 rate 112Kbit ceil 112Kbit
burst 1742b cburst 1742b
 Sent 0 bytes 0 pkts (dropped 0, overlimits 0)
 lended: 0 borrowed: 0 giants: 0
 tokens: 99599 ctokens: 99599

class htb 1:40 parent 1:1 leaf 400: prio 3 rate 224Kbit ceil 896Kbit
burst 1885b cburst 2745b
 Sent 0 bytes 0 pkts (dropped 0, overlimits 0)
 lended: 0 borrowed: 0 giants: 0
 tokens: 53885 ctokens: 19614

class htb 1:50 parent 1:1 leaf 500: prio 4 rate 224Kbit ceil 896Kbit
burst 1885b cburst 2745b
 Sent 0 bytes 0 pkts (dropped 0, overlimits 0)
 lended: 0 borrowed: 0 giants: 0
 tokens: 53885 ctokens: 19614
```

To be sure everything works OK you should make some traffic of any kind, and you should see `Sent` bytes more than `0` for the appropriate class. The number of bytes and packets sent out on any class should match the number of bytes and packets on each rule in the `POSTROUTING` chain of the `mangle` table, only of the scripts run at the same time.

We presented here how to limit and prioritize traffic that comes into one site (download only). This doesn't limit the upload. For each interface, you can limit and prioritize traffic that goes *out* on that interface but not what comes *in*; so, in order to limit the upload, we have to make another script for interface eth0.

For limiting upload, we will mark packets in the `PREROUTING` chain of the `mangle` table; so we'll add the following lines to the firewall script:

```
#mark packets from the Voip Device - value 0
$IPT  -t mangle -A PREROUTING -s $PREFIX.3 -j MARK --set-mark 1

#mark packets for Database replication - value 1
$IPT  -t mangle -A PREROUTING -d 192.168.1.2 -s $PREFIX.2 -j MARK --
set-mark 2

#mark packets for remote DB developers - value 2
$IPT  -t mangle -A PREROUTING -d 1.1.4.1 -s $PREFIX.2 -j MARK --set-
mark 3
```

```
#mark packets for HQ traffic - value 3
$IPT  -t mangle -A PREROUTING -d 192.168.1.0/24 -s $PREFIX.0/24 -j
MARK --set-mark 4
```

The QoS script should look like this:

```
#!/bin/bash

#Edit these lines to suit location

TOTALBW=1024       #Total UPLOAD bandwidth for the location
VBW=128            #Voice bandwidth in this location
PREFIX=192.168.4   #IP addresses in this location

#no more editing is required below this line

let BW=$TOTALBW-$VBW

#delete root qdisc - this will drop all classes
tc qdisc del root dev eth0

#create root qdisc
tc qdisc add dev eth0 root handle 1: htb default 12

#create root class
tc class add dev eth0 parent 1: classid 1:1 htb rate ${TOTALBW}kbit
ceil ${TOTALBW}kbit

#add class, Add Qdisc, Add Filter
AC="tc class add dev eth0 parent"
AQ="tc qdisc add dev eth0 parent"
AF="tc filter add dev eth0 protocol ip parent 1:0 prio 1"

#VoIP should have the highest priority
$AC 1:1 classid 1:10 htb rate ${VBW}kbit ceil ${VBW}kbit prio 0
$AQ 1:10 handle 100: pfifo limit 5
$AF handle 1 fw classid 1:10

#Database Replication
#we allow a minimum of 3/8 of total bandwidth for replication
let DBW=3*$BW/8

$AC 1:1 classid 1:20 htb rate ${DBW}kbit ceil ${BW}kbit prio 1
$AQ 1:20 handle 200: pfifo limit 5
$AF handle 2 fw classid 1:20
```

```
#Remote DB application developers
#we allow a minimum of 1/8 of total bandwidth for remote developers

let RBW=$BW/8

$AC 1:1 classid 1:30 htb rate ${RBW}kbit ceil ${RBW}kbit prio 2
$AQ 1:30 handle 300: pfifo limit 5
$AF handle 3 fw classid 1:30

#traffic between HQ and this location
#we allow a minimum of 1/4 of total bandwidth for traffic with HQ

let I=$BW/4
$AC 1:1 classid 1:40 htb rate ${I}kbit ceil ${BW}kbit prio 3
$AQ 1:40 handle 400: pfifo limit 5
$AF handle 4 fw classid 1:40

#Internet Traffic for users
#we allow a minimum of 1/4 of total bandwidth for internet traffic
$AC 1:1 classid 1:50 htb rate ${I}kbit ceil ${BW}kbit prio 4
$AQ 1:50 handle 500: pfifo limit 5
tc filter add dev eth0 protocol ip parent 1:0 prio 5 u32 match ip src
$PREFIX.0/24 flowid 1:50
```

This is the basic setup for QoS. More information about HTB can be found at
`http://luxik.cdi.cz/~devik/qos/htb/manual/userg.htm`.

Example 2: A Typical Small ISP

The term "typical" might not be so appropriate when talking about small ISPs. We have met a lot of network administrators and we seen a lot of small ISPs, and they all had different configurations.

The network we are going to build in this example is not specific to any provider but rather a general one. These types of networks exist in generally with a few modifications.

The network has more security breakpoints than the previous network; so we'll have more complex and complicated firewalls.

The Network

Let's take the following network as an example:

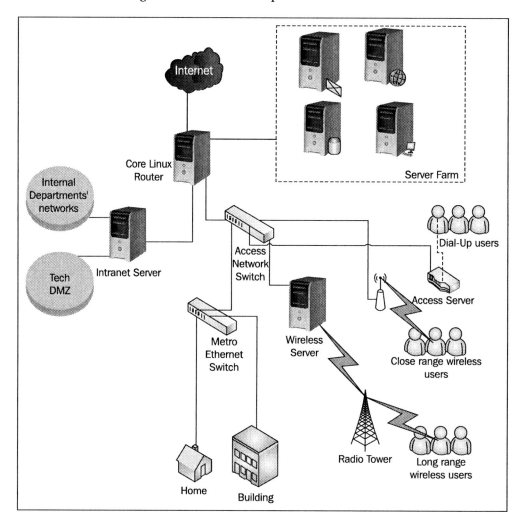

This is a small ISP that has one internet connection, an access network, a server farm, and the internal departments. This ISP uses Linux routers and servers.

The connection from the provider comes in one interface of the Linux core router. Usually, the core router should be a very stable and powerful machine because it needs to have a few network interfaces through which a significant amount of data is passed.

Depending on how powerful the core router is, we can say how many users the network can accommodate. A dual Xeon can handle easily a few hundred broadband customers and over one thousand smaller customers. You can never say "OK, this network is fit for 2000 customers", because it really depends on what kind of traffic they make or what kind of services you provide.

The intranet server is a Linux server used for intranet applications and is also used to perform routing and NAT for the internal departments. The intranet server is also responsible with the firewall for the internal departments.

There is a part of the network named the **server farm**, which contains the servers of the ISP. There is a database server, an email server, a web server that also does web hosting and a radius server used for authorization and accounting (AAA – Authentication, Authorization, and Accounting server) which also runs DNS server software. Each of these servers runs Linux as OS, and has a dedicated interface in the core router, which means that all packets arriving in this part of the network pass through the core router.

The most complicated part is the access network. When building it, you have to consider the available physical bandwidth for each connection. You can see on the diagram a server called "Wireless Server". Normally, instead of a computer there, we can use a wireless bridge. However, the wireless bridge would be connected to an access point far away in a wireless network that doesn't support very high data rates and a large number of packets per second. High traffic between users in the metro Ethernet and wireless users or a large number of broadcasts from the metro Ethernet network would affect the wireless network performance, because a wireless bridge would place the wireless network in the same broadcast domain as the metro Ethernet network, and we wouldn't be able to do anything since packets would only go through the switch. Of course this can be avoided by breaking up the network using multiple VLANs.

What we want to do is ease the core router's job and place a wireless server so that we can perform QoS for the long range wireless customers without having all the access traffic (between metro Ethernet and wireless) going through the core router.

In the close wireless user case, we won't do this. The close wireless users can connect to the access point, which is a bridge to very high data rates; so we are not in the situation where we need to limit all Metro Ethernet access to this network.

In the access part of the network, there is an access server that is used for providing dial-up access. The access server "talks" AAA with the radius server in the server farm.

Building the Network Configuration

For the internet connection, the provider assigned one public IP address (1.1.1.1). The ISP has one class C network 1.2.3.0/24 that must be divided in subnets to be able to provide public IP addresses to all these segments of the network.

The way I would subnet this class would be like this:

- 1.2.3.0/29 subnet for the servers. I would allocate 1.2.3.1 to the radius server, which also runs a DNS server. The core router would have an interface (`eth1`) with the IP address 1.2.3.6 and netmask 255.255.255.248 connected to the server farm switch.

- The intranet server has a separate interface (`eth2`) which needs a /30 subnet. I would allocate the IP address 1.2.3.9/30 (netmask 255.255.255.252) for the core router and 1.2.3.10/30 for the intranet server. The technical department needs public IP addresses; so I'll route the subnet 1.2.3.16/29 through the intranet server. The intranet server runs OpenVPN for the network administrators to connect from remote locations. We'll route the subnet 1.2.3.24/29 to the intranet server for the interfaces on OpenVPN.

- I would allocate for the access network the subnet 1.2.3.128/25 from which I would allocate 1.2.3.129 for `eth3` on the core router, 1.2.3.130 for `eth0` on the wireless server, and 1.2.3.131 for the dial-up access server.

- There are devices in the network (switches, wireless access points) that can be managed via `telnet`/`web`/`snmp`. These devices don't need public IP addresses, and we don't need to NAT them; so I bring up on the core router an alias to `eth3` (`eth3:1`) with the IP address 192.168.100.1 netmask 255.255.255.0, and set up all those devices to use IP addresses from 192.168.100.0/24.

- I would then route the subnet 1.2.3.32/27 to the long range wireless users and set 1.2.3.33 on the `wlan0` wireless interface.

- There are two E1 connections for dial-up access (60 lines in total) that can be used for analog dial-up or ISDN dial-up services. For that I would allocate the subnet 1.2.3.64/26 with a PPP pool starting from 1.2.3.65 up to 1.2.3.126.

After subnetting, the network looks like this:

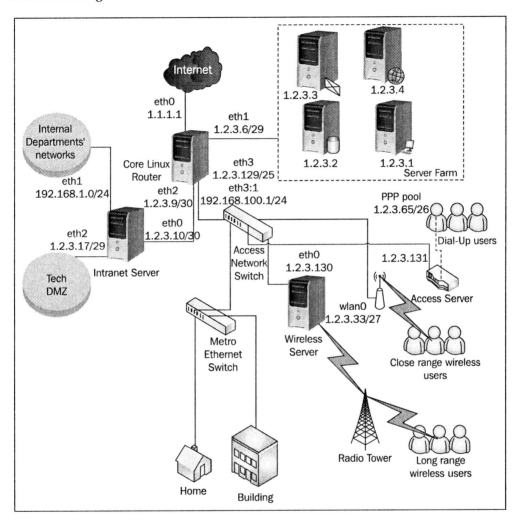

This is the network for which we will build the firewalls.

Designing and Implementing the Firewalls

Due to the fact that all the servers run Linux, they will all have their own firewall. However, the main firewall is on the core router, and so we'll have double protection and can say that we have a layered defense here. Layered defense is when we have machines and services protected by more than one firewall placed one behind the other, so that if the outer one fails, we still have protection.

The reason the intranet server exists in this network is not only for running the intranet application, but also for NATing the local network of the internal departments. If the core router did that instead of having the intranet server there, we would have to use the ip_conntrack module on the core router, which is not recommended, because at high PPS (packets per second) rates, the conntrack table would fill and drop packets.

We will build the firewall policy for each server along with the scripts.

The Intranet Server: 1.2.3.10

The intranet server runs the intranet application, which is written in PHP. It only needs to connect to the database, which has the IP address 1.2.3.2, on port 5432/TCP (PostgreSQL). It is also a file server running Samba and OpenVPN for the administrators to connect to this server from home.

We leave SSH to run on the default port (22/TCP), Apache web server on 80/TCP, and we set up OpenVPN to listen on port 6669/TCP.

We should check to see if there are other ports opened, using netstat:

```
intranet:~# netstat -an
Active Internet connections (servers and established)
Proto Recv-Q Send-Q Local Address           Foreign Address         State
tcp        0      0 0.0.0.0:139             0.0.0.0:*               LISTEN
tcp        0      0 0.0.0.0:6669            0.0.0.0:*               LISTEN
tcp        0      0 0.0.0.0:80              0.0.0.0:*               LISTEN
tcp        0      0 0.0.0.0:22              0.0.0.0:*               LISTEN
tcp        0      0 0.0.0.0:445             0.0.0.0:*               LISTEN
udp        0      0 0.0.0.0:137             0.0.0.0:*
udp        0      0 0.0.0.0:138             0.0.0.0:*
```

This looks normal; so we'll set up the filters in the INPUT chain to secure our server.

The first thing we want to do is set the INPUT policy to DROP so that all packets with the destination one of the intranet server's IP addresses will be dropped unless they match one of the ALLOW rules in the chain. We don't want to filter anything on the loopback interface.

```
iptables -P INPUT DROP
iptables -A INPUT -i lo -j ACCEPT
```

We don't want to filter any ICMP messages:

```
iptables -A INPUT -p icmp -j ACCEPT
```

Next, we want to allow our internal departments access to the web server running the intranet application:

```
iptables -A INPUT -s 192.168.1.0/24 -p tcp --dport 80 -j ACCEPT
iptables -A INPUT -s 1.2.3.16/28 -p tcp --dport 80 -j ACCEPT
```

The second line allows 1.2.3.16/28, which contains both subnets 1.2.3.16/29 (the technical department) and 1.2.3.24/29 (IP addresses for VPN connections).

We want to allow everyone to connect to OpenVPN. The authentication for OpenVPN is made using SSL certificates; so, we want to allow the network administrators with their certificates on their laptop computers or on a USB flash to connect from anywhere:

```
iptables -A INPUT -p tcp --dport 6669 -j ACCEPT
```

Only the network administrators should have SSH access on the intranet server:

```
iptables -A INPUT -s 1.2.3.16/28 -p tcp --dport 22 -j ACCEPT
```

All the internal departments must have access to the file server:

```
iptables -A INPUT -s 192.168.1.0/24 -p tcp --dport 137:139 -j ACCEPT
iptables -A INPUT -s 192.168.1.0/24 -p udp --dport 137:139 -j ACCEPT
iptables -A INPUT -s 192.168.1.0/24 -p tcp --dport 445 -j ACCEPT

iptables -A INPUT -s 1.2.3.16/28 -p tcp --dport 137:139 -j ACCEPT
iptables -A INPUT -s 1.2.3.16/28 -p udp --dport 137:139 -j ACCEPT
iptables -A INPUT -s 1.2.3.16/28 -p tcp --dport 445 -j ACCEPT
```

We want to allow the intranet server to resolve hostnames so we will allow DNS packets:

```
iptables -A INPUT -p udp --sport 53 -j ACCEPT
```

We also want to allow the intranet server to be able to initiate TCP connections (for web access, FTP, etc.):

```
iptables -A INPUT -p tcp ! --syn -j ACCEPT
```

This also allows the intranet server to connect to the database at 1.2.3.2.

The FORWARD chain must have the default policy ALLOW. We'll just filter the NetBIOS and ms-ds packets that come in on eth0, which is the "external" interface:

```
iptables -A FORWARD -i eth0 -p tcp --dport 137:139 -j DROP
iptables -A FORWARD -i eth0 -p udp --dport 137:139 -j DROP
iptables -A FORWARD -i eth0 -p tcp --dport 445 -j DROP
```

All we need to do further with the intranet server is to NAT the 192.168.1.0/24 network:

```
iptables -t nat -A POSTROUTING -s 192.168.1.0/24 -o eth0 -j MASQUERADE
```

We MASQUERADE all packets from 192.168.1.0/24 except to 1.2.3.16/28 to allow NetBIOS and remote desktop traffic between the network administrators and the rest of the internal departments.

Putting all those rules in a script that is usually executed at boot time would result in:

```
#!/bin/bash

IPT="/sbin/iptables"

#flush rules
$IPT -F

########## INPUT Chain ########
#policy Drop
$IPT -P INPUT DROP

#Accept all on the loopback interface
$IPT -A INPUT -i lo -j ACCEPT

#Accept icmp
$IPT -A INPUT -p icmp -j ACCEPT

#Allow internal departments to local web server
$IPT -A INPUT -s 192.168.1.0/24 -p tcp --dport 80 -j ACCEPT
$IPT -A INPUT -s 1.2.3.16/28 -p tcp --dport 80 -j ACCEPT

#Allow users to connect to openvpn
$IPT -A INPUT -p tcp --dport 6669 -j ACCEPT

#Allow admins SSH access
$IPT -A INPUT -s 1.2.3.16/28 -p tcp --dport 22 -j ACCEPT

#Allow internal departments SAMBA connections
$IPT -A INPUT -s 192.168.1.0/24 -p tcp --dport 137:139 -j ACCEPT
$IPT -A INPUT -s 192.168.1.0/24 -p udp --dport 137:139 -j ACCEPT
$IPT -A INPUT -s 192.168.1.0/24 -p tcp --dport 445 -j ACCEPT

#Allow admins SAMBA connections
$IPT -A INPUT -s 1.2.3.16/28 -p tcp --dport 137:139 -j ACCEPT
```

```
$IPT -A INPUT -s 1.2.3.16/28 -p udp --dport 137:139 -j ACCEPT
$IPT -A INPUT -s 1.2.3.16/28 -p tcp --dport 445 -j ACCEPT

#Allow the intranet server to receive DNS packets
$IPT -A INPUT -p udp --sport 53 -j ACCEPT

#Allow non syn packets (connections initiated by this machine)
$IPT -A INPUT -p tcp ! --syn -j ACCEPT

########## FORWARD Chain ########
#Drop SAMBA and ms-ds comming in eth0
$IPT -A FORWARD -i eth0 -p tcp --dport 137:139 -j DROP
$IPT -A FORWARD -i eth0 -p udp --dport 137:139 -j DROP
$IPT -A FORWARD -i eth0 -p tcp --dport 445 -j DROP

########## NAT table ########
#Flush Nat Rules
$IPT -t nat -F

#load some modules for nat to work better
/sbin/modprobe ip_nat_ftp
/sbin/modprobe ip_nat_irc

#MASQ internal departments
$IPT -t nat -A POSTROUTING -s 192.168.1.0/24 -o eth0 -j MASQUERADE
```

To verify the configuration, we should use `iptables -L -n` and `iptables -t nat -L -n`.

```
intranet:~# iptables -L -n
Chain INPUT (policy DROP)
ACCEPT     icmp --  0.0.0.0/0          0.0.0.0/0
ACCEPT     tcp  --  192.168.1.0/24     0.0.0.0/0          tcp dpt:80
ACCEPT     tcp  --  1.2.3.16/28        0.0.0.0/0          tcp dpt:80
ACCEPT     tcp  --  0.0.0.0/0          0.0.0.0/0          tcp dpt:6669
ACCEPT     tcp  --  1.2.3.16/28        0.0.0.0/0          tcp dpt:22
ACCEPT     tcp  --  192.168.1.0/24     0.0.0.0/0          tcp dpts:137:139
ACCEPT     udp  --  192.168.1.0/24     0.0.0.0/0          udp dpts:137:139
ACCEPT     tcp  --  192.168.1.0/24     0.0.0.0/0          tcp dpt:445
ACCEPT     tcp  --  1.2.3.16/28        0.0.0.0/0          tcp dpts:137:139
ACCEPT     udp  --  1.2.3.16/28        0.0.0.0/0          udp dpts:137:139
ACCEPT     tcp  --  1.2.3.16/28        0.0.0.0/0          tcp dpt:445
ACCEPT     udp  --  0.0.0.0/0          0.0.0.0/0          udp spt:53
ACCEPT     tcp  --  0.0.0.0/0          0.0.0.0/0          tcp flags:!0x16/0x02

Chain FORWARD (policy ACCEPT)
```

```
target      prot opt source        destination
ACCEPT      all  --  0.0.0.0/0     0.0.0.0/0
DROP        tcp  --  0.0.0.0/0     0.0.0.0/0         tcp dpts:137:139
DROP        udp  --  0.0.0.0/0     0.0.0.0/0         udp dpts:137:139
DROP        tcp  --  0.0.0.0/0     0.0.0.0/0         tcp dpt:445

Chain OUTPUT (policy ACCEPT)
target      prot opt source        destination
intranet:~#
intranet:~# iptables -t nat -L -n
Chain PREROUTING (policy ACCEPT)
target      prot opt source        destination

Chain POSTROUTING (policy ACCEPT)
target      prot opt source        destination
MASQUERADE  all  --  192.168.1.0/24     !1.2.3.16/28

Chain OUTPUT (policy ACCEPT)
target      prot opt source        destination
```

Everything looks OK, and if everything works OK for the internal departments, then it means we did a good job. More than that, we built a very restrictive firewall; so we should be safe with the intranet server.

The Wireless Server: 1.2.3.130

The wireless server is more like a router. It doesn't need much of a firewall, and it doesn't perform NAT for anyone. Its basic function is to route the subnet 1.2.3.33/27 on its wireless interface and to perform QoS for the wireless users connected to it. It only needs to run SSH; so we'll build a firewall like this:

```
#!/bin/bash

IPT="/sbin/iptables"

#flush rules
$IPT -F

######### INPUT Chain ########
#policy Drop
$IPT -P INPUT DROP

#Accept all on the loopback interface
$IPT -A INPUT -i lo -j ACCEPT
```

```
#Accept icmp
$IPT -A INPUT -p icmp -j ACCEPT

#Allow admins SSH access
$IPT -A INPUT -s 1.2.3.16/28 -p tcp --dport 22 -j ACCEPT

#Allow the wireless server to receive DNS packets
$IPT -A INPUT -p udp --sport 53 -j ACCEPT

#Allow non syn packets (connections initiated by this machine)
$IPT -A INPUT -p tcp ! --syn -j ACCEPT
```

So, what we did for this server was to set the policy for the INPUT chain to DROP. Then we allowed ICMP messages, SSH for the network administrators, and also let it access the Internet (for updates, etc.).

The AAA Server: 1.2.3.1

The AAA server runs radius for Authentication, Authorization, and Accounting for dial-up users, and also for the email users who are stored in the database at 1.2.3.2.

It also runs a DNS server. As we learned in the previous chapters, DNS is a service exposed to attacks, and bugs often appear in different DNS server implementations. The worst thing about DNS servers is that we can't filter their traffic because they wouldn't function anymore.

The most popular DNS server is BIND, which is one of the programs with a very high number of remotely exploitable bugs compromising security.

My advice is to use other DNS servers than BIND (e.g. djbdns, at http://tinydns.org/). However, if you decide on using BIND, please *don't* use any precompiled executables or installation packages. If you use BIND, you must download the latest version of BIND from http://www.isc.org/sw/bind/ and place it in a chroot jail. Please read the chroot-BIND HowTo found at http://tldp.org/HOWTO/Chroot-BIND-HOWTO.html.

We will use the FreeRADIUS server for AAA with database support. FreeRADIUS also had some security issues in the past, but we can solve that by creating an appropriate firewall for it. However, it is recommended that you run FreeRADIUS in a chroot jail too.

So, we must have SSH, DNS, and Radius running on this server:

```
AAA:~# netstat -an
Active Internet connections (servers and established)
Proto Recv-Q Send-Q Local Address     Foreign Address     State
```

```
tcp        0        0 0.0.0.0:22          0.0.0.0:*             LISTEN
tcp        0        0 0.0.0.0:53          0.0.0.0:*             LISTEN
udp        0        0 0.0.0.0:53          0.0.0.0:*
udp        0        0 0.0.0.0:1812        0.0.0.0:*
udp        0        0 0.0.0.0:1813        0.0.0.0:*
udp        0        0 0.0.0.0:1814        0.0.0.0:*
```

We will leave the INPUT chain policy as ACCEPT. First, we need to filter SSH to drop all TCP packets arriving on port 22 except from 1.2.3.16/28:

```
iptables -A INPUT -s ! 1.2.3.16/28 -p tcp --dport 22 -j DROP
```

For radius packets, we will create a chain called RADIUS and add a firewall rule in the INPUT chain to forward all packets on ports 1812-1814 UDP to the RADIUS chain:

```
iptables -N RADIUS
iptables -A INPUT -p udp --dport 1812:1814 -j RADIUS
```

Next, we want to allow Radius access to the access server, the mail server, and the Radius server itself. So we'll add the following rules to the RADIUS chain:

```
iptables -A RADIUS -i lo -j ACCEPT
iptables -A RADIUS -s 1.2.3.131 -j ACCEPT
iptables -A RADIUS -s 1.2.3.3 -j ACCEPT
```

Now we just need to drop Radius packets arriving from other hosts:

```
iptables -A RADIUS -j DROP
```

 Using the netstat command, we see that our server listens on port 53/TCP. This is used by the DNS server for zone transfer. Since we don't have a secondary DNS server, we might disable that or just filter it.

We will leave UDP traffic untouched, but since we don't need to receive any TCP connections to this server, and only initiate TCP connections, we'll drop SYN packets:

```
iptables -A INPUT -i ! lo -p tcp --syn -j DROP
```

Putting it up together, the script should look like this:

```
#!/bin/bash

IPT="/sbin/iptables"
```

```
#flush rules
$IPT -F

#Drop SSH packets except from admins
$IPT -A INPUT -s ! 1.2.3.16/28 -p tcp --dport 22 -j DROP

#Create the RADIUS Chain
$IPT -N RADIUS

#All incoming radius packets jump to RADIUS chain
$IPT -A INPUT -p udp --dport 1812:1814 -j RADIUS

#Allow some hosts to the RADIUS chain
$IPT -A RADIUS -i lo -j ACCEPT
$IPT -A RADIUS -s 1.2.3.131 -j ACCEPT
$IPT -A RADIUS -s 1.2.3.3 -j ACCEPT

#Drop everything else in the RADIUS chain
$IPT -A RADIUS -j DROP

#Drop incoming TCP SYN packets except on loopback
$IPT -A INPUT -i ! lo -p tcp --syn -j DROP
```

The Database Server: 1.2.3.2

The database server is the most important servers because it holds the database with all customer details and the business operations from the intranet application.

It is very important for us to secure the database server, and this is not even very difficult. Although we can combine the other three servers in two or even one server that can run Radius, DNS, web, FTP, and email, this ISP should keep the database on a separate machine. They can all be on the same machine, but it's strongly recommended that the database be on a different machine, as DNS, web, FTP, email, and even Radius are open to remote exploits.

We stated that it's not very difficult to secure the database server. Assuming we run PostgreSQL on the default port 5432, we have only a few steps to be taken. First, we want to set the INPUT chain policy to DROP:

```
iptables -P INPUT DROP
```

Next, we want to allow packets on the loopback interface:

```
iptables -A INPUT -i lo -j ACCEPT
```

We will accept incoming SSH connections from the network administrators:

```
iptables -A INPUT -s 1.2.3.16/28 -p tcp --dport 22 -j ACCEPT
```

Next, we need to create a chain named SQL and pass all packets arriving with the destination port 5432/TCP to this chain:

```
iptables -N SQL
iptables -A INPUT -p udp --dport 5432 -j SQL
```

In the SQL chain we need to allow packets from the Radius server and from the intranet server:

```
iptables -A SQL -s 1.2.3.1 -j ACCEPT
iptables -A SQL -s 1.2.3.10 -j ACCEPT
iptables -A SQL -j DROP
```

We want to give access to the SQL server to the Internet for updates. We will allow DNS packets and TCP packets except SYN. To be more restrictive, we can allow DNS packets only from our DNS server.

```
iptables -A INPUT -s 1.2.3.1 -p udp --sport 53 -j ACCEPT
iptables -A INPUT -p tcp ! --syn -j ACCEPT
```

Now, let's set the script for the database server:

```
#!/bin/bash

IPT="/sbin/iptables"

#flush rules
$IPT -F

#INPUT chain policy DROP
$IPT -P INPUT DROP

#Accept packets on loopback
$IPT -A INPUT -i lo -j ACCEPT

#Accept SSH from Admins
$IPT -A INPUT -s 1.2.3.16/28 -p tcp --dport 22 -j ACCEPT

#Create SQL chain and jump packets for 5432/tcp to it
$IPT -N SQL
$IPT -A INPUT -p udp --dport 5432 -j SQL

#Allow SQL connections from AAA and intranet servers
```

```
$IPT -A SQL -s 1.2.3.1 -j ACCEPT
$IPT -A SQL -s 1.2.3.10 -j ACCEPT
$IPT -A SQL -j DROP

#Allow outgoing TCP connections
$IPT -A INPUT -s 1.2.3.1 -p udp --sport 53 -j ACCEPT
$IPT -A INPUT -p tcp ! --syn -j ACCEPT
```

The Email Server: 1.2.3.3

Sendmail is the most popular SMTP server. Sendmail had some security issues in the past, and it's very probable for it to have such issues in the future. For this server, we have firewalls similar to the others. The SMTP server running on port 25 must not be filtered, because then it would not be able to receive emails anymore. chrooting Sendmail is not a good idea because most probably you won't be able to receive mail.

Therefore you can either choose another SMTP server (I would recommend Postfix) or have your Sendmail server up to date all the time.

Running the xinetd POP3 server is a good idea and it has been pretty stable over the years. There is no reason to filter POP3 unless you don't want to allow users to get their email from other locations than within the ISP network. Some may call it paranoia, but there's a good reason for why others do this—POP3 is unencrypted, and it's is very easy to sniff POP3 passwords, and so, getting your email from outside your ISP network might bring some risks for your email account. We can also encrypt POP3 (e.g. on Debian Linux package `courier-pop-ssl`) to eliminate this concern.

Since the email server has a firewall somewhat similar to the others, we'll present the script with the appropriate comments:

```
#!/bin/bash

IPT="/sbin/iptables"

#flush rules
$IPT -F

#INPUT chain policy DROP
$IPT -P INPUT DROP

#Accept packets on loopback
$IPT -A INPUT -i lo -j ACCEPT

#Accept SSH from Admins
```

```
$IPT -A INPUT -s 1.2.3.16/28 -p tcp --dport 22 -j ACCEPT


#Accept UDP radius packets from the AAA server
$IPT -A INPUT -s 1.2.3.1 -p udp --sport 1812:1814 -j ACCEPT


#Accept SMTP traffic
$IPT -A INPUT -p tcp --dport 25 -j ACCEPT


#Accept POP3 traffic
$IPT -A INPUT -p tcp --dport 110 -j ACCEPT


#Allow outgoing TCP connections
$IPT -A INPUT -s 1.2.3.1 -p udp --sport 53 -j ACCEPT
$IPT -A INPUT -p tcp ! --syn -j ACCEPT
```

Please note that once we set the INPUT chain policy to DROP, even if the mail server initiates connections to the Radius server, if we don't specify the rule:

```
$IPT -A INPUT -s 1.2.3.1 -p udp --sport 1812:1814 -j ACCEPT
```

those packets will be dropped because Radius uses UDP packets and not TCP. As we learned in Chapter 3, UDP is not connection-oriented; there is no SYN ACK handshake, and therefore we need this rule for Radius communication to work.

The Web Server: 1.2.3.4

The web server is running Apache with PHP and MySQL for web hosting. It also runs an FTP server for users to upload their web pages.

We need to make sure that Apache and PHP are up to date and they are configured in a secure manner so that people for whom we offer web-hosting solutions can't gain unauthorized access. Please read carefully the instructions at http://httpd.apache.org/docs/2.2/misc/security_tips.html and http://www.php.net/manual/en/security.php to secure the two products.

MySQL should be accessed on the loopback interface for security; so the server string in each MySQL connection should be 127.0.0.1.

There are a lot of FTP servers that can be used, out of which we recommend ProFTPD and Pure-FTPd. Also, we need to be sure that we have the latest version. Running an FTP server on our host raises up a new problem we didn't encounter so far.

FTP is a different protocol from the others in the way that it uses a 'control' port and a 'data' port. FTP runs only on TCP, and by standard, it uses port 21 (FTP) for control (connecting and issuing commands to the server) and port 20 (FTP data) for actual data transfer. However, FTP has two modes:

- **Active mode**: The client initiates the connection to the server on port 21 using an unprivileged port N (N>1024). After the connection is established, the client listens on port N+1 and sends the FTP server the command PORT N+1. The FTP server will initiate a connection from port 20/TCP to the client on port N+1/TCP for data transfer.
- **Passive mode**: The client initiates the connection to the server on port 21 using an unprivileged port N like in the active mode. At this point, the FTP server opens an unprivileged port Y (Y>1024) and sends to the client the command "PORT Y". Then, the client will open a connection from its port N+1 to the FTP server's port Y.

To toggle between active/passive modes of FTP, a client must issue the command PASV to the server.

In the first case (active mode), at one point, the server is trying to initiate a TCP connection from port 20 to an unprivileged port of the client. If the client is behind NAT, there is a high chance that the connection won't work, and this is mainly why passive mode is used.

Considering we offer web hosting on this server, we may think that we might have a lot of clients behind NAT that want to access the FTP server. Both ProFTPD and Pure-FTPd have configuration directives to specify what port range to use for passive connections.

We should set the FTP passive port range to 50000-52000. Now, the firewall script would look like this:

```
#!/bin/bash

IPT="/sbin/iptables"

#flush rules
$IPT -F

#INPUT chain policy DROP
$IPT -P INPUT DROP

#Accept packets on loopback
$IPT -A INPUT -i lo -j ACCEPT

#Accept SSH from Admins
$IPT -A INPUT -s 1.2.3.16/28 -p tcp --dport 22 -j ACCEPT

#Accept FTP connections
$IPT -A INPUT -p tcp --dport 21 -j ACCEPT
```

```
#Active connections initiate the requests
#So we only have to accept passive connections
$IPT -A INPUT -p tcp --dport 50000:52000 -j ACCEPT

#Accept web connections
$IPT -A INPUT -p tcp --dport 80 -j ACCEPT

#Allow outgoing TCP connections
$IPT -A INPUT -s 1.2.3.1 -p udp --sport 53 -j ACCEPT
$IPT -A INPUT -p tcp ! --syn -j ACCEPT
```

A Few Words on the Access Server: 1.2.3.131

While there are a lot of linecards that can be used on Linux to provide computers with interfaces such as E1 or T1, it seems more feasible to use a dial-up access server built by a telecom hardware supplier such as Cisco, Lucent, Alcatel, etc.

These access servers usually have a built-in web server and Telnet server for configuration, and most of them support configuration via SNMP. Even if we have a firewall on the core router, it would be good to be able to build a firewall on the access server itself as the last line of defense against attackers as well as for the dial-up users.

If the access server is Cisco, then you can build an extended access list like this:

```
access-list 101 permit tcp 1.2.3.16 0.0.0.15 host 1.2.3.131 eq telnet
access-list 101 permit tcp 1.2.3.16 0.0.0.15 host 1.2.3.131 eq www
access-list 101 permit udp 1.2.3.16 0.0.0.15 host 1.2.3.131 eq snmp
access-list 101 permit icmp any host 1.2.3.131
access-list 101 deny ip any host 1.2.3.131
```

You can then apply the access list on the network interface (FastEthernet 0) and on the dialer groups you created for dial-up users.

The Core Router—First Line of Defense

We left the core router to last for the simple reason that most of the firewall on the core router contains pieces from the firewalls on the other servers.

Now, let's refresh our memory with the network diagram:

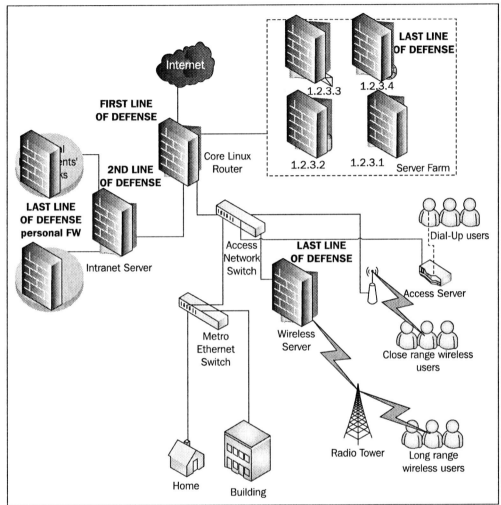

From a security point of view, the core router is the first line of defense. The first line of defense should stop all attacks coming from outside. However, if the firewall at the core router fails, then the firewall on each server is responsible for the security of that server.

If a user gains unauthorized access due to a bug in one of the services running on one server, the core router firewall or the firewall on that server are useless. In this case, the attacker has access to a server directly connected to the other servers in the server farm, and so the first line of defense has failed.

To get back to the reason we implemented security on the core router last, we think it's better this way because we already explained a lot of features that will be use in this firewall, and we did that by specifying the services for each situation.

The INPUT chain for the core router is the simplest of all the firewalls so far. We need to set the policy to DROP, allow SSH, ICMP, and DNS, and disallow SYN packets — that's all!

In the FORWARD chain, we will do most of the operations we already did on the servers. Let's set up the script:

```
#!/bin/bash

IPT="/sbin/iptables"

#flush rules
$IPT -F

########## INPUT Chain begin ########
#policy Drop
$IPT -P INPUT DROP

#Accept all on the loopback interface
$IPT -A INPUT -i lo -j ACCEPT

#Accept icmp
$IPT -A INPUT -p icmp -j ACCEPT

#Allow admins SSH access
$IPT -A INPUT -s 1.2.3.16/28 -p tcp --dport 22 -j ACCEPT

#Allow the core router to receive DNS packets
$IPT -A INPUT -p udp --sport 53 -j ACCEPT

#Allow non syn packets (connections initiated by this machine)
$IPT -A INPUT -p tcp ! --syn -j ACCEPT

########## INPUT Chain end    ########

########## FORWARD Chain begin ########
########## policy ACCEPT - default

#Deny Access to switches and wireless equipment
$IPT -A FORWARD -s ! 1.2.3.16/28 -d 192.168.100.0/24 -j DROP
```

```
#Allow SSH access to everything from admins
$IPT -A FORWARD -s ! 1.2.3.16/28 -p tcp --dport 22 -j ACCEPT

#Allow established tcp packets out eth1 and eth2
$IPT -A FORWARD -o eth1 -p tcp ! --syn -j ACCEPT
$IPT -A FORWARD -o eth2 -p tcp ! --syn -j ACCEPT

#Create a chain for the intranet server
#Intranet server
$IPT -N INTRANET
$IPT -A FORWARD -d 1.2.3.10 -j INTRANET

###### INTRANET Chain
#DROP web packets for the intranet application
$IPT -A INTRANET -p tcp --dport 80 -j DROP

#DROP SSH (Packets from ADMINS don't pass through here)
$IPT -A INTRANET -p tcp --dport 22 -j DROP

#Drop Samba and ms-ds for packets on eth2
$IPT -A FORWARD -o eth2 -p tcp --dport 137:139 -j DROP
$IPT -A FORWARD -o eth2 -p udp --dport 137:139 -j DROP
$IPT -A FORWARD -o eth2 -p tcp --dport 445 -j DROP

#wireless server - simple, we don't need a chain
$IPT -A FORWARD -d 1.2.3.130 -p udp --sport 53 -j ACCEPT
$IPT -A FORWARD -d 1.2.3.130 -p ICMP -j ACCEPT
$IPT -A FORWARD -d 1.2.3.130 -j DROP

#AAA server
$IPT -A FORWARD -d 1.2.3.1 -s ! 1.2.3.131 -p udp --dport 1812:1814 -j
DROP
$IPT -A FORWARD -d 1.2.3.1 -p tcp --dport 23 -j DROP

#SQL server
$IPT -A FORWARD -d 1.2.3.2 -s ! 1.2.3.10 -p tcp --dport 5432 -j DROP
$IPT -A FORWARD -d 1.2.3.2 -p ICMP -j ACCEPT
$IPT -A FORWARD -d 1.2.3.2 -j DROP

#MAIL server
$IPT -A FORWARD -d 1.2.3.3 -p tcp --dport 25 -j ACCEPT
$IPT -A FORWARD -d 1.2.3.3 -p tcp --dport 110 -j ACCEPT
$IPT -A FORWARD -d 1.2.3.3 -p udp --sport 53 -j ACCEPT
$IPT -A FORWARD -d 1.2.3.3 -p ICMP -j ACCEPT
```

```
$IPT -A FORWARD -d 1.2.3.3 -j DROP


#WEB server
$IPT -A FORWARD -d 1.2.3.4 -p tcp --dport 50000:52000 -j ACCEPT
$IPT -A FORWARD -d 1.2.3.4 -p tcp --dport 80 -j ACCEPT
$IPT -A FORWARD -d 1.2.3.4 -p tcp --dport 21 -j ACCEPT
$IPT -A FORWARD -d 1.2.3.4 -p ICMP -j ACCEPT
$IPT -A FORWARD -d 1.2.3.4 -j DROP


#Access Server
$IPT -A FORWARD -d 1.2.3.131 -s 1.2.3.1 -p udp --sport 1812:1814 -j
ACCEPT
$IPT -A FORWARD -d 1.2.3.131 -s 1.2.3.1 -p udp --sport 53 -j ACCEPT
$IPT -A FORWARD -d 1.2.3.131 -s 1.2.3.16/28 -j ACCEPT
$IPT -A FORWARD -d 1.2.3.131 -p ICMP -j ACCEPT
$IPT -A FORWARD -d 1.2.3.131 -j DROP
```

As you might've expected, the firewall rules from the core router differ from the ones on the servers. Let's take the SQL server for example. We have the line:

```
$IPT -A FORWARD -d 1.2.3.2 -s ! 1.2.3.10 -p tcp --dport 5432 -j DROP
```

This will drop packets from other sources than 1.2.3.10 (the intranet server) to the database server on port 5432/TCP. However, on the database server we have a chain named SQL in which we allow connections from 1.2.3.10 and 1.2.3.1 (the AAA server). The reason why we didn't add a rule in the core router for packets with the source 1.2.3.1 to pass to 1.2.3.2 is that those servers are in the same subnet (directly connected) and packets from one to another don't pass through the core router.

At this point we should verify the configuration and see if everything is OK. We will do this with iptables -L -n:

```
root@core:~# iptables -L -n
Chain INPUT (policy DROP)
ACCEPT     all   --  0.0.0.0/0         0.0.0.0/0
ACCEPT     icmp  --  0.0.0.0/0         0.0.0.0/0
ACCEPT     tcp   --  1.2.3.16/28       0.0.0.0/0        tcp dpt:22
ACCEPT     udp   --  0.0.0.0/0         0.0.0.0/0        udp spt:53
ACCEPT     tcp   --  0.0.0.0/0         0.0.0.0/0        tcp flags:!0x16/0x02


Chain FORWARD (policy ACCEPT)
target     prot opt source            destination
DROP       all   --  !1.2.3.16/28      192.168.100.0/24
ACCEPT     tcp   --  !1.2.3.16/28      0.0.0.0/0        tcp dpt:22
ACCEPT     tcp   --  0.0.0.0/0         0.0.0.0/0        tcp flags:!0x16/0x02
ACCEPT     tcp   --  0.0.0.0/0         0.0.0.0/0        tcp flags:!0x16/0x02
```

```
INTRANET    all  --  0.0.0.0/0       1.2.3.10
DROP        tcp  --  0.0.0.0/0       0.0.0.0/0       tcp dpts:137:139
DROP        udp  --  0.0.0.0/0       0.0.0.0/0       udp dpts:137:139
DROP        tcp  --  0.0.0.0/0       0.0.0.0/0       tcp dpt:445
ACCEPT      udp  --  0.0.0.0/0       1.2.3.130       udp spt:53
ACCEPT      icmp --  0.0.0.0/0       1.2.3.130
DROP        all  --  0.0.0.0/0       1.2.3.130
DROP        udp  --  !1.2.3.131      1.2.3.1         udp dpts:1812:1814
DROP        tcp  --  0.0.0.0/0       1.2.3.1         tcp dpt:23
DROP        tcp  --  !1.2.3.10       1.2.3.2         tcp dpt:5432
ACCEPT      icmp --  0.0.0.0/0       1.2.3.2
DROP        all  --  0.0.0.0/0       1.2.3.2
ACCEPT      tcp  --  0.0.0.0/0       1.2.3.3         tcp dpt:25
ACCEPT      tcp  --  0.0.0.0/0       1.2.3.3         tcp dpt:110
ACCEPT      udp  --  0.0.0.0/0       1.2.3.3         udp spt:53
ACCEPT      icmp --  0.0.0.0/0       1.2.3.3
DROP        all  --  0.0.0.0/0       1.2.3.3
ACCEPT      tcp  --  0.0.0.0/0       1.2.3.4         tcp dpts:50000:52000
ACCEPT      tcp  --  0.0.0.0/0       1.2.3.4         tcp dpt:80
ACCEPT      tcp  --  0.0.0.0/0       1.2.3.4         tcp dpt:21
ACCEPT      icmp --  0.0.0.0/0       1.2.3.4
DROP        all  --  0.0.0.0/0       1.2.3.4
ACCEPT      udp  --  1.2.3.1         1.2.3.131       udp spts:1812:1814
ACCEPT      udp  --  1.2.3.1         1.2.3.131       udp spt:53
ACCEPT      all  --  1.2.3.16/28     1.2.3.131
ACCEPT      icmp --  0.0.0.0/0       1.2.3.131
DROP        all  --  0.0.0.0/0       1.2.3.131

Chain OUTPUT (policy ACCEPT)
target      prot opt source          destination

Chain INTRANET (1 references)
target      prot opt source          destination
DROP        tcp  --  0.0.0.0/0       0.0.0.0/0       tcp dpt:80
DROP        tcp  --  0.0.0.0/0       0.0.0.0/0       tcp dpt:22
```

Overall, this looks like a pretty secure network. There's one thing that we did here that might compromise security (although it's very unlikely)—a little hole in the firewall. I'm talking about -p udp --sport 53 -j ACCEPT. Starting at one point, an unpatched service on UDP might give an attacker the possibility to pass our firewalls by using port 53 as source port.

Let's say for example we start a TFTP server on the mail server used to save the configuration from the access server. Now, we might think that the DROP policy of the INPUT chain will protect us; so we think about adding to the INPUT chain the rule:

```
iptables -A INPUT -s 1.2.3.131 -p udp --dport 69 -j ACCEPT
```

This will give access to the TFTP server for 1.2.3.131, which is OK. Due to the INPUT policy DROP, no other TFTP clients can access the TFTP server. However, an attacker might emulate a TFTP client and bind his or her local port to 53/UDP. At this point, he or she will pass our filters and will have access to the TFTP server, which would be a major security breach.

We have two solutions for that:

- The first is to allow packets with the source port 53/UDP only from trusted DNS servers; so we can modify the rules to be -s 1.2.3.1 -p udp --sport 53 -j ACCEPT.

- The second solution would be to insert the rules for TFTP using iptables -I INPUT -s ! 1.2.3.131 -p udp --dport 69 -j DROP.

Of course, we strongly recommend the first solution.

QoS for This Network

There are three Linux machines that will do QoS in this network—the intranet server, the wireless server, and the core router.

Let's take another look at our network

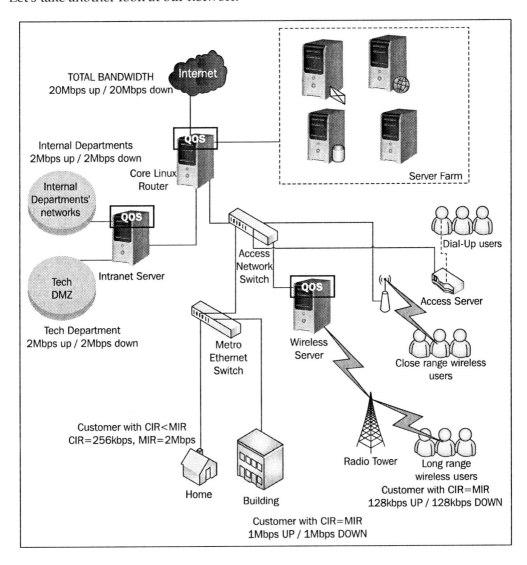

The total bandwidth we have on our internet connection is 20Mbps upload and 20Mbps download.

The core router will do bandwidth shaping for all customers except the long range wireless users for whom we'll do bandwidth allocation on the wireless server. QoS for the internal departments will be done on the intranet server.

On the metro Ethernet network and the wireless network served by the access point connected in the Access Network Switch, some users could have malicious intentions and try to escape their bandwidth allocation by changing their IP address and using some unallocated IP addresses.

To address this problem, we'll introduce a new concept in this example—the default class. The default class will be an HTB class that will have a low bandwidth limit (12 kbps), which will handle all traffic that doesn't match any other HTB class. This means that anyone's traffic that doesn't have some bandwidth allocated will fall into this 12 kbps class.

Using a default HTB class will force us to add bandwidth allocation for all IP addresses used in our network, including the servers and the dial-up users.

QoS on the Wireless Server for Long-Range Wireless Users

The wireless server has two network interfaces—eth0 with the IP address 1.2.3.130, and wlan0 with the IP address 1.2.3.33. On wlan0 there are some wireless customers connected with IP addresses from the 1.2.3.32/27 subnet.

In the previous picture, we've annotated CIR=MIR for those users. CIR means Committed Information Rate, and it's the minimum guaranteed bandwidth, and MIR means Maximum Information Rate, and it's the maximum bandwidth a user can get.

We will show in this example how to make bandwidth allocation for one user, having the first available IP address from the 1.2.3.32/27 subnet—1.2.3.34. In this case, the interface on which we do shaping for download speed for the user is wlan0 and that for upload is eth0. We'll create default classes for both interfaces so that unallocated IP addresses not to eat up our bandwidth.

The default class is specified when attaching the HTB root qdisc.

```
tc qdisc add dev wlan0 root handle 1: htb default 9999
```

When building the download limit for the users on wlan0, we will create tc filters to match the *destination* IP address—the user's IP address:

```
tc class add dev wlan0 parent 1:10 classid 1:100 htb rate 128Kbit
tc qdisc add dev wlan0 parent 1:100 sfq quantum 1514b perturb 15
tc filter add dev wlan0 protocol ip parent 1:0 prio 5 u32 match ip dst
1.2.3.34 flowid 1:100
```

When we create the upload limit for the users—on eth0 this time—we will create tc filters to match the *source* IP address as the user's IP address:

```
tc class add dev eth0 parent 1:10 classid 1:100 htb rate 128Kbit
tc qdisc add dev eth0 parent 1:100 sfq quantum 1514b perturb 15
tc filter add dev eth0 protocol ip parent 1:0 prio 5 u32 match ip src
1.2.3.34 flowid 1:100
```

The entire QoS script on the wireless server (with the limits for this user only) looks like this:

```
#!/bin/bash

#download speed first - on wlan0

#delete root qdisc (this will destroy all classes)
tc qdisc del dev wlan0 root

#attach root qdisc and create the 100Mbps root class
tc qdisc add dev wlan0 root handle 1: htb default 9999
tc class add dev wlan0 parent 1:0 classid 1:10 htb rate 100Mbit

#1st client - 128 kbps
tc class add dev wlan0 parent 1:10 classid 1:100 htb rate 128Kbit
tc qdisc add dev wlan0 parent 1:100 sfq quantum 1514b perturb 15
tc filter add dev wlan0 protocol ip parent 1:0 prio 5 u32 match ip dst
1.2.3.34 flowid 1:100

#default class
tc class add dev wlan0 parent 1:10 classid 1:9999 htb rate 16Kbit


#Upload speed - on eth0
#delete root qdisc (this will destroy all classes)
tc qdisc del dev eth0 root

#attach root qdisc and create the 100Mbps root class
tc qdisc add dev eth0 root handle 1: htb default 9999
tc class add dev eth0 parent 1:0 classid 1:10 htb rate 100Mbit

#1st client - 128 kbps
tc class add dev eth0 parent 1:10 classid 1:100 htb rate 128Kbit
tc qdisc add dev eth0 parent 1:100 sfq quantum 1514b perturb 15
tc filter add dev eth0 protocol ip parent 1:0 prio 5 u32 match ip src
1.2.3.34 flowid 1:100

#default class
tc class add dev eth0 parent 1:10 classid 1:9999 htb rate 16Kbit
```

QoS on the Intranet Server for the Internal Departments

On this server, we don't need a default class as it holds the internal departments and there are no fraud attempts here. We will limit the technical department to 2Mbps download / 2Mbps upload, but it would be wise to leave it 98Mbps speed within our network.

We can do that in two ways. The first one would be to add two classes with two `tc` filters—one with a selector to match source IP addresses 1.2.3.0/24, and one to match source IP addresses 192.168.1.0/24. The second way would be to mark the traffic from 192.168.1.0/24 and 1.2.3.0/24 with the same value and add a single class with a `tc` filter having an nfmark selector.

To choose one of these two options, we'll think further on how to create the limits for the other internal departments that are Masqueraded. They also have a 2Mbps limit, but the problem with them is that, being under NAT, a selector to match source IP addresses 192.168.1.0/24 for packets going out through Eth0 will not match any packets. The only way to limit the NATed internal departments is to mark the packets before they are NATed (in the PREROUTING chain of the mangle table) and create a filter to match the nfmark.

Now, since we already mark the packets from 192.168.1.0/24, it's easier to add another rule to the firewall and mark packets from 1.2.3.0/24 to 1.2.3.16/29 and create a single `tc` class for traffic from our network to the technical department. We'll therefore choose the second option, which consumes less resources.

So, first of all we have to go back to the firewall for the intranet server and add the line:

```
iptables -t mangle -A PREROUTING -s 192.168.1.0/24 -j MARK --set-mark 1
```

which marks all packets from 192.168.1.0/24 with the nfmark value 1.

We also need to add a line to mark packets from 1.2.3.0/24 going out on Eth2 with the same nfmark value:

```
iptables -t mangle -A POSTROUTING -s 1.2.3.0/24 -o eth2 -j MARK
--set-mark 1
```

Now, we'll create the QoS script for the intranet server:

```
#!/bin/bash

#eth2 - technical department
#delete root qdisc (this will destroy all classes)
```

```
tc qdisc del dev eth2 root

#attach root qdisc and create the 100Mbps root class
tc qdisc add dev eth2 root handle 1: htb
tc class add dev eth2 parent 1:0 classid 1:10 htb rate 100Mbit

#download limit 98Mbps from our network
tc class add dev eth2 parent 1:10 classid 1:100 htb rate 98Mbit
tc qdisc add dev eth2 parent 1:100 sfq quantum 1514b perturb 15
tc filter add dev eth2 protocol ip parent 1:0 prio 5 handle 1 fw
flowid 1:100

#The rest is internet traffic - 2Mbps
tc class add dev eth2 parent 1:10 classid 1:200 htb rate 2Mbit
tc qdisc add dev eth2 parent 1:200 sfq quantum 1514b perturb 15
tc filter add dev eth2 protocol ip parent 1:0 prio 5 u32 match ip dst
1.2.3.16/29 flowid 1:200


#eth1 - internal departments under nat
#delete root qdisc (this will destroy all classes)
tc qdisc del dev eth1 root

#attach root qdisc and create the 100Mbps root class
tc qdisc add dev eth1 root handle 1: htb
tc class add dev eth1 parent 1:0 classid 1:10 htb rate 100Mbit

#download limit 98Mbps from our network
tc class add dev eth1 parent 1:10 classid 1:100 htb rate 98Mbit
tc qdisc add dev eth1 parent 1:100 sfq quantum 1514b perturb 15
tc filter add dev eth1 protocol ip parent 1:0 prio 5 u32 match ip src
1.2.3.0/24 flowid 1:100

#The rest is internet traffic - 2Mbps
tc class add dev eth1 parent 1:10 classid 1:200 htb rate 2Mbit
tc qdisc add dev eth1 parent 1:200 sfq quantum 1514b perturb 15
tc filter add dev eth1 protocol ip parent 1:0 prio 5 u32 match ip dst
1.2.3.16/29 flowid 1:200

#Upload speed - on eth0
#delete root qdisc (this will destroy all classes)
tc qdisc del dev eth0 root

#attach root qdisc and create the 100Mbps root class
tc qdisc add dev eth0 root handle 1: htb
```

```
tc class add dev eth0 parent 1:0 classid 1:10 htb rate 100Mbit

#upload to our network
tc class add dev eth0 parent 1:10 classid 1:100 htb rate 96Mbit
tc qdisc add dev eth0 parent 1:100 sfq quantum 1514b perturb 15
tc filter add dev eth0 protocol ip parent 1:0 prio 5 u32 match ip dst
1.2.3.0/24 flowid 1:100

#Upload to the internet from the tech department - 2Mbps
tc class add dev eth0 parent 1:10 classid 1:200 htb rate 2Mbit
tc qdisc add dev eth0 parent 1:200 sfq quantum 1514b perturb 15
tc filter add dev eth0 protocol ip parent 1:0 prio 5 u32 match ip src
1.2.3.16/29 flowid 1:200

#Upload to the internet from the other departments - 2Mbps
tc class add dev eth0 parent 1:10 classid 1:300 htb rate 2Mbit
tc qdisc add dev eth0 parent 1:300 sfq quantum 1514b perturb 15
tc filter add dev eth0 protocol ip parent 1:0 prio 5 handle 1 fw
flowid 1:300
```

For Eth2, we created the class 1:100 of 98Mbps and attached a `tc` filter to match our nfmark 1, which matches all traffic from our network and the internal departments' networks. The rest of the traffic going to 1.2.3.16/29 is internet traffic; so the 1:200 class of Eth2 has a 2Mbps limit.

The packets that go out of Eth1 are either from our class C 1.2.3.0/24 or from other hosts on the Internet; so we created the 1:100 class of 98Mbps for traffic from our network to the internal departments and the 1:200 class of 2Mbps for internet traffic.

The upload is limited on Eth0, for which we created the 96Mbps class 1:100 with a filter to match all packets going to hosts in our network. If packets going out of Eth0 are not destined to 1.2.3.0/24, then they will not match the 1:100 class, and if they are from 1.2.3.16/29, they will match the 1:200 class of 2Mbps, and it means that this is upload traffic from the technical department to the Internet.

Traffic going out of Eth0 that is marked with nfmark 1 is from the NATed internal departments and is matched on the 1:300 class of 2Mbps.

QoS on the Core Router

The core router has four interfaces:

- `eth0`, connected to the upstream provider
- `eth1`, connected to the servers LAN
- `eth2`, connected with the intranet server
- `eth3`, connected to the customers

We will not perform traffic shaping on eth1 (servers) and on eth2, because we want as much bandwidth as we can get for the servers, and the internal departments are limited locally on the intranet server.

The interfaces that will have HTB qdiscs will be eth0 for upload and eth3 to shape the customers' download.

We will start with eth3, which will have a 16kbit default class. First, we will create a 100Mbps class for the access server IP address, the wireless server, and 192.168.100.0/24, which is used for switches and access points' management IP addresses. For the dial-up customers, we will allocate 1Mbps of bandwidth.

We'll create a 2Mbps class in which we will add customers who buy our service with CIR/MIR 256kbps/2Mbps. If the number of customers who buy this service grows, we can always increase the limit of this class, which is the parent class for each customer's class.

For the upload interface, the classes will look about the same, except that in the first 100Mbps class, we will add the IP addresses of the servers and the subnets for which we perform shaping on the wireless and intranet servers.

The script looks like this:

```
#!/bin/bash

#download speed first - on eth3

#delete root qdisc (this will destroy all classes)
tc qdisc del dev eth3 root

#attach root qdisc and create the 100Mbps root class
tc qdisc add dev eth3 root handle 1: htb default 9999
tc class add dev eth3 parent 1:0 classid 1:10 htb rate 100Mbit

#access server and wireless server
tc class add dev eth3 parent 1:10 classid 1:100 htb rate 100Mbit
tc qdisc add dev eth3 parent 1:100 sfq quantum 1514b perturb 15
tc filter add dev eth3 protocol ip parent 1:0 prio 5 u32 match ip dst
1.2.3.130 flowid 1:100
tc filter add dev eth3 protocol ip parent 1:0 prio 5 u32 match ip dst
1.2.3.131 flowid 1:100
tc filter add dev eth3 protocol ip parent 1:0 prio 5 u32 match ip dst
192.168.100.0/24 flowid 1:100

#dialup users
tc class add dev eth3 parent 1:10 classid 1:200 htb rate 1Mbit
```

```
tc qdisc add dev eth3 parent 1:200 sfq quantum 1514b perturb 15
tc filter add dev eth3 protocol ip parent 1:0 prio 5 u32 match ip dst
1.2.3.64/26 flowid 1:200


#1st Customer with CIR=MIR - 1.2.3.133
tc class add dev eth3 parent 1:10 classid 1:300 htb rate 1Mbit
tc qdisc add dev eth3 parent 1:300 sfq quantum 1514b perturb 15
tc filter add dev eth3 protocol ip parent 1:0 prio 5 u32 match ip dst
1.2.3.133 flowid 1:300


#2Mbps class for CIR=256, MIR=2Mbps service
tc class add dev eth3 parent 1:10 classid 1:1000 htb rate 2Mbit


#1st client for the CIR=256, MIR=2Mbps service - 1.2.3.134
tc class add dev eth3 parent 1:10 classid 1:1001 htb rate 256Kbit ceil
2Mbit
tc qdisc add dev eth3 parent 1:1001 sfq quantum 1514b perturb 15
tc filter add dev eth3 protocol ip parent 1:0 prio 5 u32 match ip dst
1.2.3.134 flowid 1:1001


#default class
tc class add dev eth3 parent 1:10 classid 1:9999 htb rate 16Kbit


#Upload speed - on eth0
#delete root qdisc (this will destroy all classes)
tc qdisc del dev eth0 root


#attach root qdisc and create the 100Mbps root class
tc qdisc add dev eth0 root handle 1: htb default 9999
tc class add dev eth0 parent 1:0 classid 1:10 htb rate 100Mbit


#access server and wireless server
tc class add dev eth0 parent 1:10 classid 1:100 htb rate 100Mbit
tc qdisc add dev eth0 parent 1:100 sfq quantum 1514b perturb 15
tc filter add dev eth0 protocol ip parent 1:0 prio 5 u32 match ip src
1.2.3.130 flowid 1:100
tc filter add dev eth0 protocol ip parent 1:0 prio 5 u32 match ip src
1.2.3.131 flowid 1:100
tc filter add dev eth0 protocol ip parent 1:0 prio 5 u32 match ip src
1.2.3.0/29 flowid 1:100
tc filter add dev eth0 protocol ip parent 1:0 prio 5 u32 match ip src
1.2.3.8/30 flowid 1:100
tc filter add dev eth0 protocol ip parent 1:0 prio 5 u32 match ip src
1.2.3.16/29 flowid 1:100
tc filter add dev eth0 protocol ip parent 1:0 prio 5 u32 match ip src
```

```
1.2.3.32/27 flowid 1:100

#dialup users
tc class add dev eth0 parent 1:10 classid 1:200 htb rate 1Mbit
tc qdisc add dev eth0 parent 1:200 sfq quantum 1514b perturb 15
tc filter add dev eth0 protocol ip parent 1:0 prio 5 u32 match ip src
1.2.3.64/26 flowid 1:200

#1st Customer with CIR=MIR - 1.2.3.133
tc class add dev eth0 parent 1:10 classid 1:300 htb rate 1Mbit
tc qdisc add dev eth0 parent 1:300 sfq quantum 1514b perturb 15
tc filter add dev eth0 protocol ip parent 1:0 prio 5 u32 match ip src
1.2.3.133 flowid 1:300

#2Mbps class for CIR=256, MIR=2Mbps service
tc class add dev eth0 parent 1:10 classid 1:1000 htb rate 2Mbit

#1st client for the CIR=256, MIR=2Mbps service - 1.2.3.134
tc class add dev eth0 parent 1:10 classid 1:1001 htb rate 256Kbit ceil
2Mbit
tc qdisc add dev eth0 parent 1:1001 sfq quantum 1514b perturb 15
tc filter add dev eth0 protocol ip parent 1:0 prio 5 u32 match ip src
1.2.3.134 flowid 1:1001

#default class
tc class add dev eth0 parent 1:10 classid 1:9999 htb rate 16Kbit
```

It looks like we didn't miss anything; so we should be happy with this configuration.

After applying this script, everything runs OK, but after a while we see some service interruptions on our upstream provider link. The upstream provider tells us everything is OK on its side, but the packet loss is very high between us, and after about 20-30 seconds, the provider can't see our MAC address for another 20-30 seconds, and this cycle repeats itself forever.

Since we haven't modified anything for a long time and this has just started happening, we might think it's a hardware problem. Well, it isn't. Since packet loss might come from a faulty cable or NIC, the strange part is that they don't see our MAC address for a while. Looking at the default class on eth0, we see that it's full, and so, someone in our network might have changed their IP address, but that shouldn't affect us.

If we take a closer look at the QoS script, we see that we don't find the IP address assigned by the provider—1.1.1.1. After 20-30 seconds, the ARP cache of the provider for our IP address expires, and so, its router sends a request to our IP address (1.1.1.1) and asks for our MAC address. Since we didn't add 1.1.1.1 anywhere in the QoS script, the reply from our router to that requests has to wait inline on the default class.

So, the solution to this problem is to add the IP address 1.1.1.1 in the filters for the 100Mbps class 1:100 of the `eth0` interface.

The reason we left this out on purpose is that we have seen a lot of network administrators doing that and taking a lot of time to troubleshoot this problem.

Summary

We saw in this chapter some pretty complicated networks. We also saw that building firewalls and QoS for such networks is not so complicated. However, it is very important to draw the network and identify security breakpoints to be able to create a firewall that will protect your network.

In my opinion, the most important things about security are knowing your network, building it in an intelligent manner and with security in mind, and most of all, understanding *how* packets flow in your network.

Understanding the flow of the packets in the network is essential for people who want to build good firewalls and intelligent QoS. I've seen simpler networks than the ones presented here with very complicated firewalls, which had rules that didn't belong there or that could be reduced to much simpler ones.

I've also seen some networks that were badly thought out from the beginning. For instance, think about the second example of this chapter and how it would be if we place one server on the customer interface, some customers in the server farm switch, etc. This would complicate our firewalls a lot. Also, a badly thought out subneting of the network would mean generating kilometers of firewall rules and a lot of `tc` filters.

It may happen at some point that you have to administer a network badly subneted and badly thought out by others. To be honest, taking each part of it and building security is way more difficult and time consuming than redrawing the network, renumbering IP address, and rebuilding the firewalls. Of course, all of these operations must be done always thinking about minimal downtime for servers and customers.

8

Large Networks Case Studies

There are different points of view in designing and deploying large networks using Linux routers or dedicated routers that can handle very high data rates.

While some prefer to pay a large amount of money for dedicated routers for which they have technical support and well-defined technical characteristics and limitations, others want to reduce the costs by building such networks using powerful computers running Linux, offering a much larger flexibility in deployment.

This is not an easy choice at all. The business point of view has ups and downs when considering the two options. The biggest advantage of using dedicated routers from the business point of view is that the value of the network rises considerably if the network is built to be sold. What I mean is that if you build a large network using Cisco routers, you have more chance of selling it to a bigger provider than if you've build the network with Linux routers.

Using dedicated routers you will have the following advantages:

- Wide range of network interfaces (ATM, SDH/SONET, Ge, Fe, etc.)
- Less likely software bugs, and technical support from producers
- Well-known and well-defined technical limitations
- Standard protocol implementations
- High market value of the network

and the following disadvantages:

- High costs for implementation, upgrade, and personnel training
- Less application flexibility

Using Linux routers has its advantages and disadvantages also. From the advantages, we can mention:

- Low deployment costs and low costs for upgrades
- Personnel cost less, and are easier to find
- High application flexibility—large open source repository that can be implemented

and from the disadvantages, we can mention:

- Low value on the market if the network is sold
- A smaller range of network interfaces available
- Higher probability of software bugs

Experienced network administrators usually prefer using dedicated routers because of well-known technical limitations and protocol standardizations. However, from my experience, the best way of implementing large networks is as a combination between those two; however, we prefer using Linux as much as we can because of the lower costs and higher application flexibility.

The biggest disadvantage in using Linux is that there are fewer options about the network interfaces that can be used in a Linux router. To give a simple example, we had to decide on using a router for the following application:

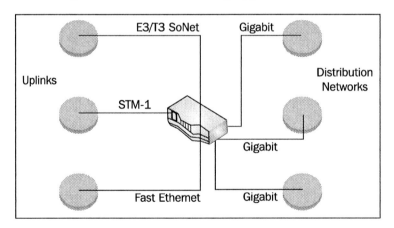

The router we had to choose had three uplink connections to other backbones of our network in a geographically distanced place. We rented an STM-1 connection from a carrier, an E3 connection from another carrier, and a FastEthernet connection from a third carrier. The router had to have three Gigabit connections to three distribution networks.

As you can probably guess, there is a large amount of traffic passing through this router. Because of the variety of interfaces, our first thought was to buy a high-capacity router with one E3, one STM-1, one FastEthernet, and three Gigabit interfaces that can handle a high number of packets per second; so the first choice would be to buy a router equivalent to (or an actual) a Cisco 7206 VXR with NPE (Network Processor Engine) running at at least 300 Mhz.

This raises the problem that we have to have other equivalent routers in the backbones with the STM-1 and E3 connections. Such a router costs at least $30,000, and adding the extra costs for the backbone routers, we would have deployment costs of over $50,000. More than that, we can think about value-added services such as dynamically allocating bandwidth for customers in the access networks, which would require dedicated machines.

There are some network hardware manufacturers that offer media converters for applications in which you need E3/T3 over SoNet or STM-1 over SoNet. These media converters have one E3/T3 or STM-1 interface, and one FastEthernet or Gigabit Ethernet; so we decided to see how they handle large traffic.

We bought a 3 GHz dual-Xeon Intel server with 2 Gigabit Ethernet onboard and a NIC with 4 Gigabit Ethernet for about $3,500, a pair of E3-to-FastEthernet converters, and a pair of STM-1 to Gigabit Ethernet converters, all of them for less $10,000. We installed Linux on the server and discovered that it could very well handle the amount of traffic we needed.

At the exact moment this chapter was written, it was forwarding a total of:

```
total:    299.61 Mb/s In    293.28 Mb/s Out  -   80742.2 p/s In    78790.2
p/s Out
```

on all interfaces with a load average: 0.95, 0.94, 0.72. It also has a total of 2700 HTB classes and 3,000 filters for those classes.

> The optimum way of building large networks in my opinion is to choose Linux as often as you can. There are some applications in which you can't use Linux, and so I think is better to reserve the budget for buying high-cost routers for those applications and try to use Linux in the applications in which you can.

Thinking Large, Thinking Layered Models

At the risk of sounding repetative, I will state the fact that the key of building a good and secure firewall is to design the network in an intelligent way, identify points of security, and understand how packets are flowing through the network.

When designing and deploying large networks, it's recommended to identify how and where routers must be placed in the network and how to scale the routers for the functions they must perform.

Large networks are often built in layers. The largest networks use a three-layered hierarchy consisting of the following three layers:

- Core layer
- Distribution layer
- Access layer

The three-layer network hierarchy is not always suited for all large networks, and some routers can perform functions of more than one layer.

Usually, a three-layered network design looks something like this:

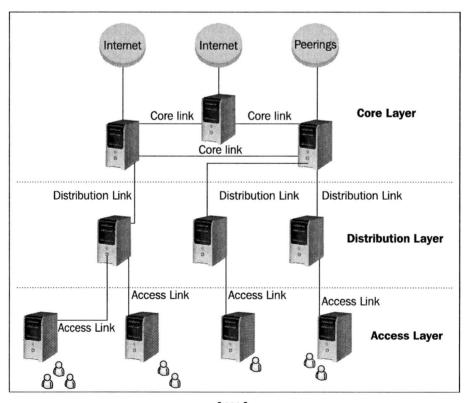

The core layer usually contains routers that have internet or local peering connections. There are high-speed links between them, and routes are distributed between them for better load balancing of internet and peering connections.

The distribution layer contains routers that route several customers in different locations, while the access layer contains routers at the customer premises, which can even be SOHO routers for smaller customers.

Of course you can have customers connected directly to a core router, which means that the core router also performs distribution and access layer functions. This is not a bad thing if the customer is a large one, because you might want to distribute them a large routing table without passing it through a distribution router, but usually it's better to pass customers through distribution routers where you do QoS so that the core routers are not overloaded with QoS functions.

A Real Large Network Example

The network we are going to present here is actually working in real life. Of course, we will replace the real IP addresses of the routers and servers.

The network is deployed at a large provider of Internet and IP telephony services. The point is to understand how packets flow through the network, to identify the security breakpoints, and build proper firewalls for the network.

We will present here only the important parts of the network as it is.

Let's start by looking at the network architecture and explain how the network is built and what's in the network.

A Brief Network Overview

The core of the network is represented in the following figure:

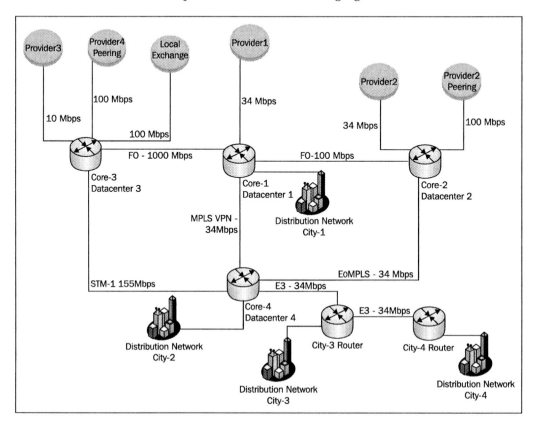

Core-1 is a router that has one FastEthernet connection to an ISP from which we buy 34Mbps of internet services. It is located in the main datacenter of this company and has a fiber optic connection at 100Mbps to Core-2 located in another datacenter. Core-1 also has a fiber optic connection at 1000Mbps (1Gbps) to Core-3.

Core-2 has one internet connection of 34Mbps connected to Provider2. Provider2 also has a large national network; so we have a peering connection with it on a 100Mbps interface. Core-2 is connected to Core-1 via a 100Mbps link.

Core-3 has a backup internet connection of 10 Mbps. It is also connected to a local exchange network for local peerings on a 100Mbps interface and to another provider (Provider4) on another 100Mbps interface. The connection with Provider4 is only for peering.

Core-4 is physically located in City-2, which is a considerable geographical distance away from City-1. It has an STM-1 connection to Core-3 (Gigabit interface using STM-1 to GE converter), one FastEthernet connection to a provider that offers us a service of MPLS VPN (34 Mbps), and another FastEthernet to a provider offering an Ethernet Over MPLS connection (34 Mbps). The City-3 router is connected through Core-4 using an E3 to FastEthernet converter.

All core routers are Linux machines and run Zebra, which is a routing software package distributed under GNU General Public License for BGP connections. Zebra can be found at http://www.zebra.org.

City-1

Datacenter-1 is the place for most voice interconnections for this provider; so it's the most important voice node in the network.

The City-1 part of this ISP network has the following particularities:

- It holds most of the voice equipment of the network.
- Customers of Internet services are only broadband customers with large bandwidth needs.
- It holds most of the web hosting and database servers (the server farm).
- Datacenter-1 is located in a building where there's an office with tech, sales, marketing, and commercial people, but it's not the Headquarters of the ISP.

The network looks like this:

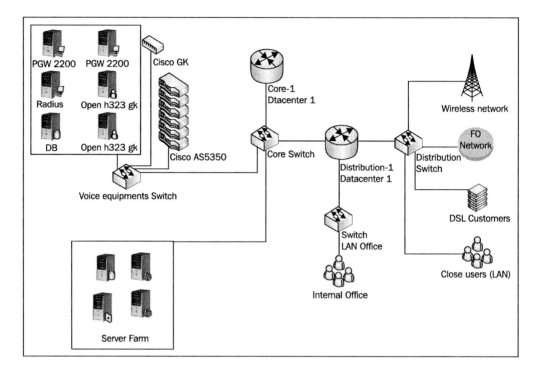

Core-1 has one interface connected to the core switch of Datacenter-1. The voice equipment has special designated racks, and it has its own switch and their own VLAN.

Another VLAN is created on the core switch for the server farm, which has web, email, and database servers.

The Distribution-1 router is a Linux machine with three FastEthernet cards: one connected to the core switch, one connected to a LAN switch for the office, and one to a distribution switch from which the distribution network begins.

City-2

Datacenter-4 is located in City-2 in the same building as the ISP Headquarters.

The City-2 part of the network has the following particularities:

- It has a very large and complex self-owned fiber optics network.
- It has one high-density DSLAM operating ADSL2+ (192 ports).
- It has a large and complex wireless network.

- It has a wireless link that connects a smaller nearby city (City-5).
- Datacenter-4 hosts voice equipment for local interconnections.
- Datacenter-4 hosts a server farm for web, mail, database, and intranet servers.
- The City-2 network has over 2000 home-users and over 100 broadband customers.
- Over 30% of the clients are subscribed to the IP telephony network of this ISP.

The network looks like this:

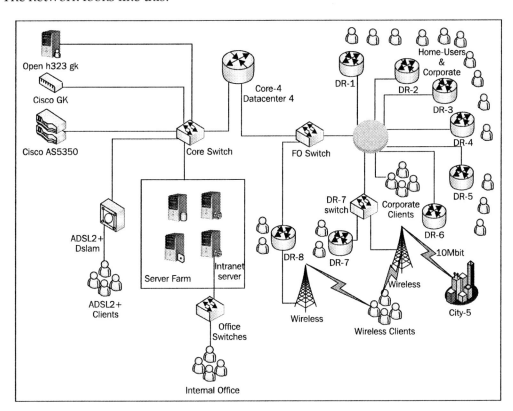

Core-4 is a Linux router that handles a lot of network traffic. It has six network interfaces, three of them connected to the other core routers, two connected to a core switch in Datacenter-4, and one to the fiber optics switch also located in Datacenter-4.

Into the core switch of Datacenter-4 are connected some voice equipment, a server farm, and an ADSL2+ DSLAM. The server farm and the voice equipment are in the same VLAN as one of Core-4's NICs, and the DSLAM is in a VLAN with the second NIC of Core-4 connected to the core switch. ADSL clients have modems that function in bridge mode; so it shouldn't be in the same VLAN with the servers or voice equipment. For the same reason, we didn't place the DSLAM in the FO switch, because high broadcast data rates may affect the performance of ADSL clients with poor lines.

The fiber optic network covers the entire city and has a ring topology at Layer 2. Some corporate clients are connected directly to the FO network, meaning they use Core-4 as the default gateway. Throughout the network, distribution routers annotated in the figure with DR-1…DR-8 are placed in distribution points to route subnets used for home users and companies connected to the distribution network.

In some of the distribution points, there are a few wireless access points used to connect wireless customers.

In the same VLAN with the DSLAM, there's an E3 to FastEthernet converter that connects City-3 and City-4.

City-3 and City-4

City-3 is located at about 40 km from City-2 and City-4 is located at 20km from City-3 (60km from City-2).

They are smaller cities and both have fiber optics distribution networks. City-3 has a wireless distribution network and a Cisco AS5350 for voice interconnection with local telcos.

The network looks like this:

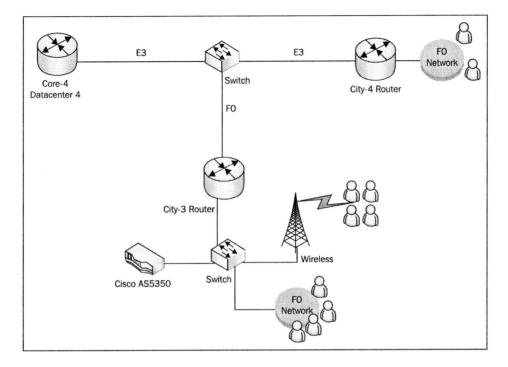

The Core Network Configuration

As we did in the earlier chapters of the book when we explained other firewall scenarios, we will present how the network configuration is built to fully understand how packets travel in the network. Without a good understanding of this process, good firewall and QoS configurations are practically impossible to achieve.

We will build the network configuration first on the core and distribution levels, and only afterwards will we build firewalls and QoS .

All routers in the core level run the BGP routing protocol (Border Gateway Protocol) described in RFC1771. With Linux, BGP is very well implemented using the Zebra router project found at http://www.zebra.org.

Zebra has support for other routing protocols and has a modular architecture having a daemon for each routing protocol it supports. The Zebra daemon is used to talk to the kernel in the way of adding and removing routes received from its routing daemons. Each daemon (protocol) has a status port that can be used for configuration and troubleshooting with commands very similar to Cisco IOS.

BGP version 4 (BGP-4) described in RFC1771 is the routing protocol used between ISPs to exchange routing information, so we can definitely say that BGP-4 is the routing protocol that gets the Internet to work. BGP is a very complex protocol and we can't cover even a short introduction in a few pages; so if you are not familiar with BGP, we suggest reading an introduction from Cisco at `http://www.cisco.com/univercd/cc/td/doc/cisintwk/ito_doc/bgp.htm`.

For obvious security reasons, we replaced the IP addresses in the real situations and the AS numbers with private AS numbers. The private AS number block is from AS64512 to AS65534.

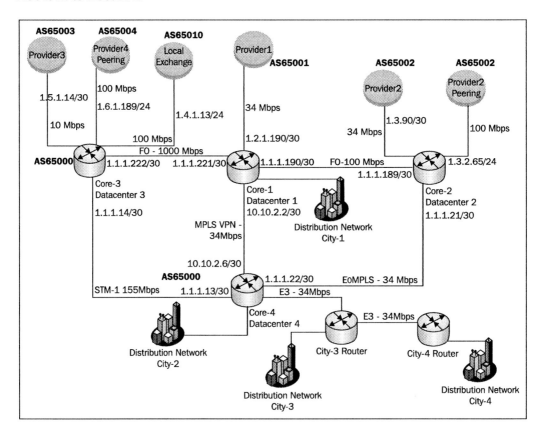

Our AS number is AS65000, as presented in the figure. The IP addresses we have are:

- 1.1.1.0/24, which we use for our routers
- 1.1.10.0/24, which we use for the voice equipment
- 1.1.48.0/20 and 1.1.96.0/20, which we use in City-2 to provide internet services
- 1.1.168.0/22, which we use in City-1 to provide internet services

1.1.48.0/20 and 1.1.96.0/20 being used in City-2 will be advertised by the Core-4 router, and 1.1.160.0/22 will be advertised by Core-1. Since most of the voice equipment is in City-1, the network 1.1.10.0/24 will be advertised by Core-1, and a subnet of 1.1.10.0/27 by Core-4.

1.1.1.0/24 can be advertised by any routers, but we will use Core-1 for the job because it's one of the routers with the most core links (three, same as Core-4) and it's a border router and closest to the other border routers.

To load-balance the links, we will use AS-path prepends for the external links and metrics for the core links.

Core-2

Core-2 has four BGP connections: two iBGP (internal BGP) and two eBGP (external BGP). We will use the internet connection to Provider-2 as the main connection for 1.1.48.0/20, which has more traffic than 1.1.96.0/20, and we will use prepends for 1.1.96.0/20 and 1.1.168.0/22.

The BGP configuration is like this:

```
core-2-bgpd# sh run

Current configuration:
!
hostname core-2-bgpd
password password
enable password enable
log file /var/log/bgpd.log
service advanced-vty
!
router bgp 65000
 neighbor 1.1.1.190 remote-as 65000
 neighbor 1.1.1.22  remote-as 65000
 neighbor 1.3.1.89  remote-as 65002
 neighbor 1.3.2.1   remote-as 65002
!
 address-family ipv4
!
 neighbor 1.1.1.190 activate
 neighbor 1.1.1.190 route-reflector-client
 neighbor 1.1.1.190 default-originate
 neighbor 1.1.1.190 route-map core-1-in in
 neighbor 1.1.1.190 route-map core-1-out out
!
```

```
 neighbor 1.1.1.22 activate
 neighbor 1.1.1.22 route-reflector-client
 neighbor 1.1.1.22 default-originate
 neighbor 1.1.1.22 route-map core-4-in in
 neighbor 1.1.1.22 route-map core-4-out out
 !
 neighbor 1.3.1.89 activate
 neighbor 1.3.1.89 next-hop-self
 neighbor 1.3.1.89 route-map provider-2-inet-in in
 neighbor 1.3.1.89 route-map provider-2-inet-out out
 !
 neighbor 1.3.2.1 activate
 neighbor 1.3.2.1 next-hop-self
 neighbor 1.3.2.1 route-map provider-2-peering-in in
 neighbor 1.3.2.1 route-map provider-2-peering-out out
 !
 network 1.1.48.1/32
 !
 exit-address-family
 !
access-list prefer-provider-2 permit 1.1.48.0/20 exact-match
access-list prefer-provider-2 permit 1.1.10.0/24 exact-match
access-list prefer-provider-2 permit 1.1.1.0/24 exact-match
 !
access-list prepend-provider-2 permit 1.1.96.0/20 exact-match
access-list prepend-provider-2 permit 1.1.168.0/22 exact-match
 !
access-list flood permit 1.1.48.1/32 exact-match
 !
access-list defaultgw permit 0.0.0.0/0 exact-match
 !
access-list permitany permit any
access-list denyany deny any
 !
route-map core-1-in permit 9
 match ip address prepend-provider-2
 set metric +2
 !
route-map core-1-in permit 10
 match ip address prefere-provider-2
 set metric +1
 !
route-map core-1-out permit 10
 match ip address permitany
```

```
!
route-map core-4-in permit 9
 match ip address prepend-provider-2
 set metric +1
!
route-map core-4-in permit 10
 match ip address prefere-provider-2
 set metric +4
!
route-map core-4-out permit 10
 match ip address permitany
!
route-map provider-2-inet-in permit 10
 match ip address defaultgw
!
route-map provider-2-inet-in deny 11
 match ip address denyany
!
route-map provider-2-inet-out permit 9
 match ip address flood
 set community 65002:6666
!
route-map provider-2-inet-out permit 10
 match ip address prefere-provider-2
!
route-map provider-2-inet-out permit 11
 match ip address prepend-provider-2
 set as-path prepend 65000 65000
!
route-map provider-2-inet-out deny 12
 match ip address denyany
!
route-map provider-2-peering-out permit 10
 match ip address prefere-provider-2
!
route-map provider-2-peering-out permit 11
 match ip address prepend-provider-2
!
route-map provider-2-peering-out deny 12
 match ip address denyany
!
route-map provider-2-peering-in deny 10
 match ip address defaultgw
!
```

```
route-map provider-2-peering-in permit 11
 match ip address permitany
!
line vty
!
end
```

This is a simple BGP configuration for Core-2 that has four BGP peers each with a route map for input and route map for output.

Core-2 originates the default route to Core-1 and Core-4. It receives the default route from the external peer 1.3.1.89, but it shouldn't receive the default route from 1.3.2.1, which is a peering BGP connection.

The configuration has an example on how to filter an IP address (1.1.48.1) on an upstream link. The upstream provider Provider-2 has the community 6666 for filtering IP addresses. In case of a flood attack to one of our IP addresses (in this case 1.1.48.1), we advertise the IP address to the provider setting the community to 65002:6666 so they filter the IP address without affecting our 34Mbps connection.

Routes to our networks are received by Core-2 from Core-1 and Core-4. We will set metric +1 for the routes found in ACL `prefer-provider-2` for the Core-1 iBGP and metric +4 for the Core-4 iBGP. Since the route with the lowest metric is preferred, Core-2 will prefer Core-1 for the networks in the `prefer-provider-2` ACL.

We also mangled metrics for the networks in the ACL `prepend-provider-2` to have the lowest metric for those routes on the EoMPLS connection with Core-4. However, metrics sum together and we have to set a metric of minimum +1 for the network 1.1.168.0/22 somewhere from Core-1 to Core-2 through Core-4 because that network must be preferred to the direct link between Core-2 and Core-1.

Core-1, Core-3, and Core-4

We picked Core-2 first to show the configuration because it has the simplest configuration. However, starting from the BGP configuration for Core-2 we can build the other core routers configurations.

Core-3 has two peering eBGP peers, one internet eBGP peer used for backup, and two iBGP peers (Core-1 and Core-4).

Since the core link from Core-3 to Core-4 has the largest bandwidth of all core links to Core-4, this link normally carries most of the traffic to Core-4; so we should play with metrics to route most of the traffic to Core-4 on this link. Other BGP attributes can also be used (local preference, prepends, weights, or communities) but we prefer using metric for this job.

Core-3 has the particularity that the internet connection to Provider3 is for backup only; so what we should do is to create an access list that contains all of our networks, and use prepends in the route map, as follows:

```
access-list ournetworks permit 1.1.48.0/20 exact-match
access-list ournetworks permit 1.1.10.0/24 exact-match
access-list ournetworks permit 1.1.1.0/24 exact-match
access-list ournetworks permit 1.1.96.0/20 exact-match
access-list ournetworks permit 1.1.168.0/22 exact-match
!
route-map provider-3-out permit 10
 match ip address ournetworks
 set as-path prepend 65000 65000 65000
```

Core-1 and Core-4 have a few particularities more because the core link between them is MPLS VPN. If all the other core links are Layer 2 connections, MPLS VPN is a Layer 3 connection, meaning that there some routers between Core-1 and Core-4 that don't belong to us.

You can see in the figure that the IP addresses are 10.10.2.2/30 on the Core-1 interface to Core-4 and 10.10.2.6/30 on the Core-4 interface to Core-1. Those IP addresses are private IP addresses, and they are not in the same subnet. So, what we need to do is to make BGP connections to the routers 10.10.2.1 and 10.10.2.5, which belong to Provider-1 (from which we acquired the MPLS VPN service) from Core-1 and Core-4, and a multi-hop BGP connection between Core-1 and Core-4.

On Core-1, we will place a static route to Core-4 through 10.10.2.1:

```
route add 10.10.2.6 gw 10.10.2.1
```

and configure the two BGP peers as follows:

```
router bgp 65000
 neighbor 10.10.2.1 remote-as 65001
 neighbor 10.10.2.6  remote-as 65000
 ...
 !
 address-family ipv4
 !
 neighbor 10.10.2.1 next-hop-self
 neighbor 10.10.2.1 allow-as-in 1
 neighbor 10.10.2.1 route-map core-4-in in
 neighbor 10.10.2.1 route-map core-4-out out
 !
 neighbor 10.10.2.6 disable-connected-check
 neighbor 10.10.2.6 route-map core-4-in in
```

```
 neighbor 10.10.2.6 route-map core-4-out out
!
...
!
route-map core-4-in permit 10
 set ip next-hop 10.10.2.1
!
...
```

On Core-4, we will set a static route to 10.10.2.2 through 10.10.2.5 and build a similar configuration.

 This summarized example configuration is taken from an existing network configuration. Building the entire BGP configurations for all routers is beyond the scope of this book. However, we hope this example gives you a starting point for your BGP configurations.

Security Threats

So far, we have built the core network configuration. Now, for all core routers we need to secure SSH, BGPd, Zebra, and SNMP (in such networks, SNMP is a must because we need to create graphs for traffic, load average, and so on).

Core Routers INPUT Firewalls

The INPUT policy of the core routers should be DROP. We should accept SSH, SNMP, Zebra, and BGPd status from the network administrators, DNS packets from our DNS servers, ICMP packets, packets on the loopback interface, and TCP packets to port 179 from our BGP peers.

The following example script is designated for all core routers. What needs to be changed is the IP addresses of the BGP peers. This example is for the Core-2 router:

```
#!/bin/bash

I=/sbin/iptables
#INPUT policy ACCEPT and at the end DROP
$I -P INPUT ACCEPT

#Flush and zero chains
$I -F
$I -X
```

```
$I -N manag

#Lo + dns + icmp + !syn
$I -A INPUT -i lo -j ACCEPT
$I -A INPUT -p tcp ! --syn -j ACCEPT
$I -A INPUT -p icmp -j ACCEPT
$I -A INPUT -p UDP  --sport 53 -s our.dns.server.ourcompany.
     org -j ACCEPT
$I -A INPUT -p UDP  --sport 53 -s our.dns.server2.ourcompany.
     org -j ACCEPT

#Management chain - ssh, snmp, zebra, BGPD
$I -A INPUT -p TCP --dport 22 -j manag    #ssh
$I -A INPUT -p UDP --dport 161 -j manag  #snmp
$I -A INPUT -p TCP --dport 2601 -j manag #zebra
$I -A INPUT -p TCP --dport 2605 -j manag #bgpd

#Network Administrators IP addresses
$I -A manag -s 1.1.40.0/27 -j ACCEPT
$I -A manag -s 1.1.169.0/27 -j ACCEPT
$I -A manag -j DROP

#Our BGP peers (core-2 example)
$I -A INPUT -s 1.3.2.1   -p TCP --dport 179 -j ACCEPT #provider-2
peering
$I -A INPUT -s 1.3.1.89  -p TCP --dport 179 -j ACCEPT #provider-2
internet
$I -A INPUT -s 1.1.1.190 -p TCP --dport 179 -j ACCEPT #core-1
$I -A INPUT -s 1.1.1.22  -p TCP --dport 179 -j ACCEPT #core-4

#policy DROP for INPUT chain
$I -P INPUT DROP
```

Protecting the Networks behind the Core Routers

The core routers offer the first protection for devices in our datacenters and in our distribution networks. For some (e.g. voice equipment in Datacenter-1), the core routers are the only external protection.

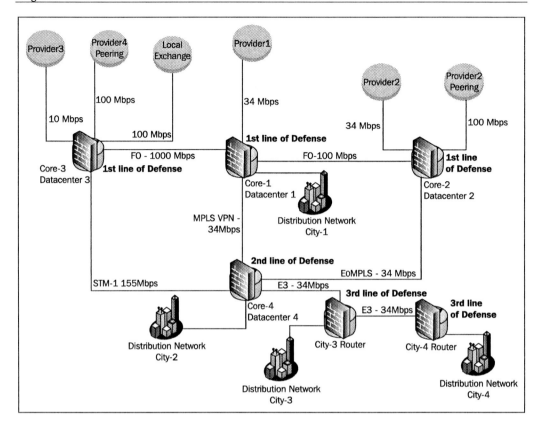

For this topology, we have to keep in mind that at any time some links may fail. At that point, the way we made the packets travel through the core links using metrics in our BGP configuration will change, and so, we have to try to unify the forward firewalls of the core routers.

In the previous figure, we state that Core-1, Core-2, and Core-3 are on the first line of defense. Even if packets from the Internet to some hosts in City-2 will go on the route Core-2 to Core-1 to Core-3 to Core-4, this only offers us a bit more protection, but the core routers that have eBGP connections are always the first line of defense.

Core-4 is the second line of defense for the networks behind it, because it only has core links to other core routers and no direct link to an external network.

We placed City-3 and City-4 Routers in the third line of defense because any packet from an other network destined to a device in City-3 or City-4 must travel through at least one of the core routers in the first line of defense *and* through Core-4.

We have already discussed in the previous chapters how to protect devices behind Linux routers; so we won't give actual examples on this topic here. It matters to see where and what we should filter. The point is that there should be a unified `FORWARD` chain on all core routers, because packets can go through any of them.

Denial of Service Attacks

DoS or DDoS (Distributed Denial of Service) attacks are every network administrator's nightmare.

When a DDoS attack is aimed at a host in our network, there can be three scenarios that can affect the entire network:

- Very high PPS (packet per second) rates that affect routers' CPUs thus resulting in high packet loss

- Very high data rates (Mbps), which creates bottlenecks on our external links

- Very high data rates and very high PPS rates — the worst kind of attack — congesting our external links *and* affecting our routers' CPUs

A DDoS attack usually comes from multiple spoofed IP addresses and is aimed at one IP address in our network. The worst effect such an attack has on our network is that all VoIP calls will be affected by bottlenecks and packet loss. If the attack lasts more than 20 seconds, then all the VoIP calls will be disconnected resulting in great revenue loss.

So, how should we deal with these types of attacks?

We saw in the example configuration that Provider-2 has a filtering community. Provider-1 doesn't have a filtering community, but if we advertise a /32 network, it will automatically be filtered. Provider-3 has the same filtering mechanism.

All our providers have some sort of flood-detection mechanisms. Usually flood detection mechanisms are pieces of software that analyze Cisco netflows and detect unusually high PPS rates towards an IP address behind the router and stop all the packets aimed at the destination IP address.

The providers' filters don't detect all DDoS attacks, and so we have to create our own filters.

At the beginning when DDoS attacks were very rare, one used to manually filter the destination IP addresses (after discovering them with tcpdump). So, what we did was to telnet on the core routers BGPd status port (2605) and issue the commands manually. For example, to filter the IP address 1.1.48.1, we did something like:

```
telnet core-2

User Access Verification

Password:
core-2-bgpd> ena
Password:
core-2-bgpd# conf t
core-2-bgpd(config)# access-list flood permit 1.1.48.1/32 exact-match
core-2-bgpd(config)# router bgp 28720
core-2-bgpd(config)# router bgp 65000
core-2-bgpd(config-router)# network 1.1.48.1/32
core-2-bgpd# clear ip bgp 1.3.1.89 out
core-2-bgpd# wr me
```

You have to do a clear ip bgp <neighbor> out to advertise the new network after adding it in the config.

With the growth of the network, DDoS attacks started occurring more often, and manually filtering the destinations became more difficult and resulted in a revenue loss. Also, a big problem with manually adding filters is that for a large PPS datarate, the CPU load grows a lot, and it takes a lot of time to be able to telnet on that machine. The actual process can take a long time from the time when the flood actually starts to when network engineers realize there's a problem, afterwards finding out the destination IP address of the flood and actually filtering the destination IP address.

So, when dealing with DDoS attacks in a network that transports live applications, we have to find a way to automatically detect and filter DDoS attacks. Since we are using Linux, Perl's PCAP libraries can be a good idea.

Here's a snapshot of a flood-detection tool created by Claudiu Filip, a very good network engineer with good Perl programming skills (this might just be the first tool of this kind ever published):

```
#!/usr/bin/perl

#Flood detection tool by Claudiu Filip - claudiu@mysql.ro

use Net::Pcap;
```

```perl
sub loop_exit { Net::Pcap::breakloop($pcap); }
sub fail() { print STDERR "$IP telnet FAILED!\n"; };

local $pcap;
my @exceptions = ('1.1.10.');  # Exceptions list
my $bgp_peer    = '1.3.1.89';  # BGP Peer that needs to be cleared
my $dev         = 'eth0';       # Monitorized interface
my $threshold   = 6500;         # Maximum limit of pps
my $timeinterval= 10;          # Time Interval to read from the interface
my $nr_packets  = 50000;        # Max number of packets to read
my $max_loss    = 3000 * $timeinterval; # Max number of lost packets
my $snap_length = 128;          # How much to read from a packet
my $pktsnapshot = 20;           # Number of captured packets
my $snapshotto  = 4;            # Snapshot timeout
my $promisc     = 1;            # Put interface in Promiscuous mode
my $to_ms       = 0;
my $filter_str  = '';           # Some tcpdump filter if we need any
my $optimize    = 1;            # Optimize filter
my $netmask     = 0;
my $log_path    = '/tmp/';      # Where we should save the tcpdump
                                # snapshots
my $IP          = '127.0.0.1';  # bgpd IP address
my $err;
my %count;
my $filter      = '';

local $dumper;
$pcap = Net::Pcap::open_live($dev, $snap_length, $promisc, $to_ms,
\$err);
$pcap || die "Can't create packet descriptor.  Error was $err";

if ( Net::Pcap::compile($pcap, \$filter, $filter_str, $optimize,
$netmask) == -1) {
        $err = Net::Pcap::geterr($pcap);
        die "Invalid filter: $filter_str (error was: $err)\n";
} else {
        Net::Pcap::setfilter($pcap, $filter);
};

local $SIG{ALRM} = \&loop_exit;
my $start_time = time;
alarm $timeinterval;
my $exitcode = Net::Pcap::loop($pcap, $nr_packets,
   \&process_packet, '');
my $end_time = time;
```

```perl
$timeinterval = $end_time - $start_time;
alarm 0;
my %stats; Net::Pcap::stats($pcap, \%stats);
my $message = '';
my @add2bgp = ();
my $subject = 'FLOOD';
my $maxx = 0; my $loss_ip = '';
while (($key, $value) = each %count) {
        $key2 = sprintf("%d.%d.%d.%d",
        ord( substr($key, 0, 1) ),
        ord( substr($key, 1, 1) ),
        ord( substr($key, 2, 1) ),
        ord( substr($key, 3, 1) ));
        $key = $key2;

        my $nr = map { $key =~ /$_/x } @exceptions;
        next if $nr > 0;
        if ($value > $maxx) {
                        $maxx = $value;
                        $loss_ip = $key;
        };

    if (($value/$timeinterval) > $threshold) {
            ####### FLOOOOOOOOOOOOD
            $subject .= ' '.$key;
            $message .= "\nFlood TO ". $key . "\t(".int($value/
                $timeinterval).' pps - Max. limit '.$threshold.')';
            push @add2bgp, $key;
    };
};

if ($message eq '') {
        if ( ($stats{ps_drop}+$stats{ps_ifdrop}) > $max_loss ){
            ## Flood to $loss_ip
            $subject .= ' '.$loss_ip;
            $message .= "\nFlood TO ". $loss_ip . "\t(".int($maxx/
                $timeinterval).' pps - Max. limit '.$threshold.
                    ")\npackets loss by filter \t".$stats{ps_drop}.
                        "\npackets loss by the interface:\
                            t".$stats{ps_ifdrop}..
                        "\nAllowed Max number of lost packets
                            ".$max_loss;
            push @add2bgp, $loss_ip;
        };
};
```

```
if ($message ne '') {

use Net::Telnet::Cisco;
my $session = Net::Telnet::Cisco->new(Host => $IP,
                Port => '2605',
                Timeout => 20,
                Errmode => \&fail);
$ok = $session->cmd(String   => 'p[',
                Prompt  => '/bgpd[\$#>]/');
$ok = $session->cmd(String   => 'enable',
                Prompt  => '/assword/',
                Timeout => 20);
$ok = $session->cmd(String   => 'p[',
                Prompt  => '/bgpd[\$#>]/',
                Timeout => 20);
$ok = $session->cmd(String      => "conf t",
                Timeout => 20,
                Prompt  => '/bgpd\(config\)[\$#>]/');
for ($i=0; $i<=$#add2bgp; $i++) {

        $key = $add2bgp[$i];

        $ok = $session->cmd(String      => "access-list flood permit
$key/32 exact-match",
                Timeout => 20,
                Prompt  => '/bgpd\(config\)[\$#>]/');
        $ok = $session->cmd(String      => "router bgp 65000",
                Timeout => 20,
                Prompt  => '/bgpd\(config\-router\)[\$#>]/');
        $ok = $session->cmd(String      => "network $key/32",
                    Timeout => 20,
                    Prompt  => '/bgpd\(config\-router\)[\$#>]/');
        $ok = $session->cmd(String      => "exit",
                Timeout => 20,
                Prompt  => '/bgpd\(config\)[\$#>]/');
};
$ok = $session->cmd(String      => "exit",
                Timeout => 20,
                Prompt  => '/bgpd[\$#>]/');
$ok = $session->cmd(String      => "clear ip bgp $bgp_peer out",
                Timeout => 20,
                Prompt  => '/bgpd[\$#>]/');
$ok = $session->cmd(String      => "wr me",
                Timeout => 20,
```

```
               Prompt  => '/bgpd[\$#>]/');
    $ok = $session->cmd(String      => "exit",
                  Timeout => 20);
    $session->close();

    };
```

This Perl script runs every 20 seconds from crontab and captures flows from the defined interface. If any host (other than the ones in the exception list) has a traffic of more than 6500 PPS (defined in `$threshold`), then the destination IP address is filtered.

City-1 Firewall for Business-Critical Voice Equipment

The City-1 network contains servers that store very sensitive data, which in the wrong hands could be very bad for business. A very fast example of how sensitive the data is, would be calling cards details stored in the database of the VoIP billing system.

If someone gains access to the database server of the VoIP billing system, they can use the calling cards that are already on the market—the company must redraw all those cards, cancel them, and generate others for market distribution. This would generate thousands of USD loss for the business.

From the security point of view, the City-1 network looks like this:

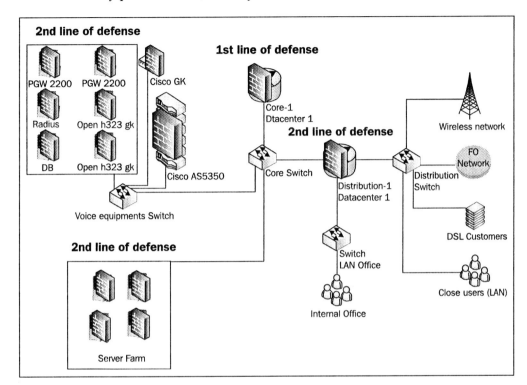

The first line of defense is Core-1, where we'll implement the firewall for all equipment in City-1. However, there can be scenarios where Core-1 is the second, third, and even fourth line of defense, depending on where the attack comes from; so we will replicate the firewall rules from Core-1 to all other core routers.

The figure shows a connection between Core-1 and the core switch, but on the physical layer, we have two interfaces from Core-1 to the core switch and two separate VLANs—one for the voice equipment, and one for the server farm and the distribution router.

For the voice equipment, the last line of defense is the local firewall implemented on each machine. The PGW2200 machines run Solaris OS and the database for the billing software is MSSQL, so the OS is Windows 2003 server. Firewalls run on both OS, but it would be off-topic to talk about those. Firewalls on the Cisco equipment are built with IOS access lists.

Securing the Voice Network

We saw earlier in this chapter that we are using IP addresses 1.1.10.0/24 for the voice network. We will allocate 1.1.10.224/27 for the equipment in City-1, and we will have:

- 1.1.10.254: interface Eth1 on Core-1
- 1.1.10.225: PGW2200 machine 1
- 1.1.10.226: PGW2200 machine 2
- 1.1.10.227: Radius Server
- 1.1.10.228: Database Server
- 1.1.10.240: Open h323 GK server 1
- 1.1.10.241: Open h323 GK server 2
- 1.1.10.242: Cisco GK
- 1.1.10.243 to 1.1.10.253: Cisco AS5350

First of all, we need to allow SSH, Telnet, and VNC access to these machines. For SSH, we change the default port 22 to 39999. We will use port 39999 for VNC as well, but Telnet is default on port 23 for Cisco. We already created the manag chain earlier when we built the input firewalls for the core routers; so we will jump target for those ports to the manag chain:

```
iptables -A FORWARD -d 1.1.10.224/27 -p tcp --dport 39999 -j manag
iptables -A FORWARD -d 1.1.10.224/27 -p tcp --dport 23 -j manag
```

We need to allow the machines running Cisco PGW2200 to communicate with Cisco AS5350 machines that are not in the same subnet for the SIGTRAN protocol to work. We will do that based on the way the voice network was provisioned. In our case, we have 1.1.10.3 ports 3000 and 3001 TCP and 1.1.10.50 ports 5000 and 5001 TCP.

This is all we need for the PGW2200 machines. We will be a bit paranoid and will deny all other traffic to and from these machines. We don't need browsing or anything from those machines.

We will create a chain named PGW, jump all packets to and from the PGW2200 machines to this chain, and we will perform all the earlier operations in the PGW chain:

```
iptables -N PGW
iptables -A FORWARD -d 1.1.10.225 -j PGW
iptables -A FORWARD -d 1.1.10.226 -j PGW
iptables -A FORWARD -s 1.1.10.225 -j PGW
iptables -A FORWARD -s 1.1.10.226 -j PGW

iptables -A PGW -s 1.1.10.3  -p udp --dport 3000:3001 -j ACCEPT
```

```
iptables -A PGW -s 1.1.10.50 -p udp --dport 5000:5001 -j ACCEPT

iptables -A PGW -d 1.1.10.3  -p udp --sport 3000:3001 -j ACCEPT
iptables -A PGW -d 1.1.10.50 -p udp --sport 5000:5001 -j ACCEPT

iptables -A PGW -j DROP
```

The Radius server runs on UDP ports 1812 (authentication) and 1813 (accounting). The only hosts that need to communicate with the Radius server, besides the Ciscos in the same subnet, are 1.1.10.3 and 1.1.10.50. We will drop all other packets to the Radius server:

```
iptables -N RADIUS
iptables -A FORWARD -d 1.1.10.227 -p udp --dport 1812:1813 -j RADIUS
iptables -A FORWARD -s 1.1.10.227 -p udp --sport 1812:1813 -j RADIUS
iptables -A FORWARD -d 1.1.10.227 -j DROP
iptables -A FORWARD -s 1.1.10.227 -j DROP

iptables -A RADIUS -s 1.1.10.3 -j ACCEPT
iptables -A RADIUS -s 1.1.10.50 -j ACCEPT
iptables -A RADIUS -d 1.1.10.3 -j ACCEPT
iptables -A RADIUS -d 1.1.10.50 -j ACCEPT
iptables -A RADIUS -j DROP
```

 This practice might seem a little bit paranoid to most people. For instance, the PGW machines and the Radius server don't have internet access, needed, for example, for automatic updates, etc. In a critical part of the network like this, we prefer not to have automatic updates, but rather perform the updates ourselves. Some automatic updates failed/rebooted/halted the machines. Also, automatic updates give the possibility of a MIM attack—it's safer to not have internet access all the time, and temporarily open it when needed.

The database server needs to communicate mainly with the Radius server, which is on the same subnet, and local firewalls on both machines need to be configured for this. However, billing applications like reports, credit control, etc., run on another Linux machine running the Apache web server, and so, this machine has to communicate with the database.

We choose to run the billing application on a dedicated Linux machine and not on a web-hosting machine for the obvious reason that it's more probable for a web-hosting machine to be hacked when some vulnerabilities are discovered. We will change the port for MSSQL server from 1433/TCP to 38888/TCP as another security measure and will allow the Linux machine in the server farm with the IP address 1.1.168.4 to communicate with the MSSQL server:

```
iptables -A FORWARD -s 1.1.168.4 -d 1.1.10.228 -p tcp --dport 38888 -j
ACCEPT
iptables -A FORWARD -s 1.1.10.228 -d 1.1.168.4 -p tcp --sport 38888 -j
ACCEPT
iptables -A FORWARD -d 1.1.10.228 -j DROP
iptables -A FORWARD -s 1.1.10.228 -j DROP
```

The open H.323 gatekeepers, the Cisco gatekeeper, and the Cisco AS5350 access servers are used for voice communication. The voice network is built using the H.323 protocol, all gatekeepers running in proxy mode, for which we have:

- Port 1718/UDP used for unicast gatekeeper discovery
- Port 1719/UDP used for H.225 RAS messages
- Port 1720/TCP used for Q.931
- Any UDP port above 1024 used for RTP

We allocated IP addresses from 1.1.10.240 to 1.1.10.253 to this equipment so that we can include it all in a subnet 1.1.10.240/28. We will create a chain VOIP in which we will allow H.323 communication for the ports we've just described:

```
iptables -N VOIP
iptables -A FORWARD -d 1.1.10.240/28 -j VOIP

iptables -A VOIP -p udp --dport 1718:1719 -j ACCEPT
iptables -A VOIP -p udp --dport 1024: -j ACCEPT
iptables -A VOIP -p tcp --dport 1720 -j ACCEPT
iptables -A VOIP -j DROP
```

At this point we are done with the security policies for the voice equipment and we need to replicate those rules on the other core routers and on Distribution-1 router.

Please note that the method presented here is the basic way to make this network secure and working. In real life, there are some other services that we might need for improving/monitoring the voice network. Those services can easily be unfiltered by adding simple rules to the firewall we just created. For example, we might want to use an external (not in the same subnet) NTP server for time synchronization, SNMP for monitoring and configuration, SNMP traps for alarms, ICMP for monitoring, TFTP to store configurations/IOS images, etc.

The real-life example contains a few of these services, but it's always good to use this example as a starting point and add services along the way.

QoS Implementation

There are three data services that this ISP can provide to its customers:

- Internet access
- National network access
- Metropolitan network access

Because there are so many peering interconnections, we have fast access to most of the national networks; so, we can offer our clients a separate bandwidth from the internet bandwidth they buy. Also, because most of the metropolitan networks are built with fiber optics, we can give our clients different metropolitan bandwidth.

To do this, we have to mark the packets on every external connection. The most reasonable things to do are:

- Mark the packets that come on the internet links with a DSCP value.
- Mark the packets that come on the peering connections with another DSCP value.
- All packets with different DSCP values than those two should be metro traffic.

Provider-1 has its own national network, and since there's a physical link of 100Mbps between us, it will mark internet traffic that we can consume up to 34Mbps and leave the rest for traffic coming from its own networks.

When we design, this it's good to have in front of us a clear picture of what the TOS byte looks like:

DSCP Differentiated Service Code Point Bits						Diffserv Flow control	
0	1	2	3	4	5	6	7
PRECEDENCE			Type Of Service - TOS				MBZ

So, Provider-1 tells us it will mark the internet traffic with precedence 2 and leave the rest of the traffic unmarked. When it says precedence 2 it is referring to the decimal value.

We should do the math and see that precedence 2 is:

- Precedence bits: 010 = 2 (in hex)
- DSCP bits: 010000 = 10 (in hex)
- TOS bits: 01000000 = 40 (in hex)

So if we look at the packets coming on the interface with Provider-1 using `tcpdump -qntvvi eth2`, we should see the packets with TOS 0x40.

If we already receive packets marked on the connection with Provider-1 with DSCP 10, we should use DSCP 10 for packets coming on our internet links, but historically speaking, we were already using DSCP value 21 (in hex) for our internet connections.

DSCP 21 in hex is DSCP 33 in decimal and 100001 in binary; so the TOS byte is 10000100 in binary, meaning 84 in hex, and therefore we should see the packets with TOS 0x84 at `tcpdump`.

So, what we need to do on Core-1 is to rewrite the DSCP field for packets with DSCP 10. The interface connected to Provider-1 is `eth2`.

```
iptables -t mangle -I PREROUTING -i eth2 —m dscp --dscp 0x10 -j DSCP
--set-dscp 0x21
```

On Core-2, the interface to Provider-2 internet is `eth0`; so we will add the following line:

```
iptables -t mangle -I PREROUTING -i eth0  -j DSCP --set-dscp 0x21
```

On Core-3, we have to do the same thing for `eth3`, which is connected to Provider-3.

```
iptables -t mangle -I PREROUTING -i eth3  -j DSCP --set-dscp 0x21
```

At this point, packets coming from the Internet all have TOS 0x84 (DSCP 21).

Next, we need to mark packets from our peering connections. We choose DSCP 22 for packets from the national network; so we have to set it for our peering connections.

On Core-2 we will set DSCP 22 for packets coming into Eth1 (Provider-2 peering interface):

```
iptables -t mangle -I PREROUTING -i eth1  -j DSCP --set-dscp 0x22
```

We also have to set DSCP 22 for packets coming from City-2 to our clients in City-1. So we will be tempted to do it as follows: on Core-2, we will set DSCP 22 for packets coming into `eth2` (Core-4 interface) and going out of `eth3` (Core-1 interface) and to 1.1.168.0/22:

```
iptables -t mangle -I FORWARD -i eth2 -o eth3 -d 1.1.168.0/22 -j DSCP
--set-dscp 0x22
```

This is wrong, because Core-2's interfaces `eth2` and `eth3` are *both* core links. This means that any traffic can pass through those links—not just the traffic from the City-2 network to City-1. For example, internet packets coming from Provider-3 to 1.1.168.0/22 can go on the route Core-3 to Core-4 to Core-2 to Core-1. The last command line will mark this traffic with DSCP 22 (national traffic) and that's not OK.

For the previous command line, we can also add sources to solve this problem, but the most elegant way to mark the packets from City-2 to City-1 is doing that in Core-4. Core-4 has `eth0` connected to the distribution network in City-2, `eth1` to City-3, `eth2` to Core-3, `eth3` to Core-1, and `eth4` to Core-2. So, to mark the packets from the networks behind Core-4 (this includes City-3 and City-4) to City-1, we will do the following:

```
iptables -t mangle -I FORWARD -i eth0 -d 1.1.168.0/22 -j DSCP --set-
dscp 0x22
iptables -t mangle -I FORWARD -i eth1 -d 1.1.168.0/22 -j DSCP --set-
dscp 0x22
```

 It is always recommended to mark the packets on the border router (the router in the network that packets reach first).

For Core-1, we have to mark the packets coming into `eth2` (Provider-2 interface) that are not marked with precedence 2:

```
iptables -t mangle -I PREROUTING -i eth2 -m dscp --dscp ! 0x10 -j DSCP
--set-dscp 0x22
```

This line must be placed in the firewall above the line where we rewrite the marking for packets having DSCP 10 (precedence 2). We present those lines here using -I (INSERT) and one after the other; so this is their correct sequence in the firewall script.

Core-1 has one interface to the City-1 distribution network (eth0); so we will mark packets from that interface to the networks in City-2, City-3, and City-4:

```
iptables -t mangle -I FORWARD -i eth0 -d 1.1.48.0/20 -j DSCP --set-
dscp 0x22
iptables -t mangle -I FORWARD -i eth0 -d 1.1.96.0/20 -j DSCP --set-
dscp 0x22
```

The local exchange peering connection in Core-3 is connected to Core-3's eth1 NIC, and the Provider-4 peering connection is connected to Core-3's eth2 NIC. All this traffic is national traffic (traffic from networks within the country); so we will mark these packets with DSCP 22:

```
iptables -t mangle -I PREROUTING -i eth1 -j DSCP --set-dscp 0x22
iptables -t mangle -I PREROUTING -i eth2 -j DSCP --set-dscp 0x22
```

 At this point, we have all packets coming from the Internet marked with DSCP 21, and all packets coming from the national networks with DSCP 22.

This wasn't hard at all. Knowing how packets travel through the network makes the tasks we have a lot simpler.

Now it is time to verify the configuration. This can be done using tcpdump -qntvvi ethX to see if packets have the right TOS—but, to our surprise, they *don't*.

Using tcpdump on Core-4, we see that the packets coming in through two core links—EoMPLS and MPLS VPN—all have TOS 0x0. The next logical thing to do is to verify the other ends of those core links, but using tcpdump on Core-1 and on Core-2, we see that the packets leave those routers with the correct DSCP marks, but they come into Core-4 with the TOS byte 0x0.

So what do those links have in common? They are both MPLS services, and most MPLS-enabled switches and routers clear the TOS byte.

Talking to Provider-2's engineers and explaining the problems, they could solve the issue, and the EoMPLS connection keeps our DSCP marks. However, Provider-1's engineers could not do the same thing for the MPLS VPN connection, but they managed to keep the precedence 2 mark (DSCP 10) on the MPLS VPN connection. So, for the MPLS VPN connection we have:

- Packets leaving one end with precedence 2 (DSCP 10) arrive at the other end with the same precedence (DSCP) value.

- Packets leaving one end with any TOS byte value (except 0x40 = DSCP 10 = precedence 2) arrive to the other end with TOS 0x0.

Given these facts, we have to do some more operations with the TOS byte of the packets so that we can have the packets marked with the wanted values.

First of all, on Core-1 we have to rewrite the TOS byte of all packets leaving eth4 (the MPLS VPN interface) from 0x84 (DSCP 21) to 0x40 (DSCP 10 = precedence 2); so we'll do the following:

```
iptables -t mangle -I POSTROUTING -o eth4 -m dscp --dscp 0x21 -j DSCP
--set-dscp 0x10
```

We should do the same thing with packets leaving eth3 on Core-4:

```
iptables -t mangle -I POSTROUTING -o eth3 -m dscp --dscp 0x21 -j DSCP
--set-dscp 0x10
```

We also have to change the DSCP from 0x10 to 0x21 when the packets come in through the MPLS VPN interface. On Core-1 we will do the following:

```
iptables -t mangle -I PREROUTING -i eth4 -m dscp --dscp 0x10 -j DSCP
--set-dscp 0x21
```

and the same on Core-4:

```
iptables -t mangle -I PREROUTING -i eth3 -m dscp --dscp 0x10 -j DSCP
--set-dscp 0x21
```

The packets that come in the MPLS VPN connection (at any end of the connection) and that are destined to our networks, if not marked with DSCP 21, are national traffic; so we should mark them with DSCP 22. On Core-1, we will do the following:

```
iptables -t mangle -I PREROUTING -i eth4 -m dscp --dscp 0x0 -d
1.1.168.0/22 -j DSCP --set-dscp 0x22
```

and on Core-4:

```
iptables -t mangle -I PREROUTING -i eth3 -m dscp --dscp 0x0 -d
1.1.48.0/20 -j DSCP --set-dscp 0x22
iptables -t mangle -I PREROUTING -i eth3 -m dscp --dscp 0x0 -d
1.1.96.0/20 -j DSCP --set-dscp 0x22
```

Now everything is all set. The packets are marked with TOS 0x84 (DSCP 21) if they come from the Internet, and 0x88 (DSCP 22) if they come from the national network. Packets marked with other DSCP values are from the metropolitan network.

Traffic Shaping for Clients

We've managed to differentiate three services by marking the packets with DSCP values, and so, we can offer our clients different bandwidth for the Internet, the national network, and the metropolitan network.

However, there might be customers who are not interested in different services, and just want to buy internet bandwidth. This doesn't mean that we won't give them access in the national or metropolitan networks; it just means that they will not have different bandwidth for these networks.

For example, to limit the entire bandwidth for 1.1.49.10 to 512kbps, we will do the following:

```
#limit the entire bandwidth for 1.1.49.10 to 512kbps

tc class add dev eth0 parent 1:10 classid 1:100 htb rate 512kbps

tc qdisc add dev eth0 parent 1:100 sfq quantum 1514b perturb 15

tc filter add dev eth0 protocol ip parent 1:0 prio 5 u32 match ip dst
1.1.49.10 flowid 1:100
```

If the customer wants to have an internet bandwidth of 512kbps and national network bandwidth of 1Mbps, but doesn't care about the national network, then the metropolitan traffic is considered to be from the metropolitan network. For example, to give this service to 1.1.49.11, we will do the following:

```
#limit the internet bandwidth for 1.1.49.11 to 512kbps

tc class add dev eth0 parent 1:10 classid 1:200 htb rate 512kbps

tc qdisc add dev eth0 parent 1:200 sfq quantum 1514b perturb 15

tc filter add dev eth0 protocol ip parent 1:0 prio 5 u32 match ip dst
1.1.49.11 match ip tos  0x84 0xfc flowid 1:200

#limit the national traffic (including metro) for 1.1.49.11 to 1Mbps

tc class add dev eth0 parent 1:10 classid 1:1200 htb rate 1Mbps

tc qdisc add dev eth0 parent 1:1200 sfq quantum 1514b perturb 15

tc filter add dev eth0 protocol ip parent 1:0 prio 5 u32 match ip dst
1.1.49.11 flowid 1:1200
```

Most customers will want different bandwidth for the three services; so, for example, if we want to give 512kbps of internet to 1.1.49.12, 1Mbps of national network, and 10Mbps of metropolitan network traffic, we will do the following:

```
#limit the internet bandwidth for 1.1.49.12 to 512kbps

tc class add dev eth0 parent 1:10 classid 1:300 htb rate 512kbps

tc qdisc add dev eth0 parent 1:300 sfq quantum 1514b perturb 15

tc filter add dev eth0 protocol ip parent 1:0 prio 5 u32 match ip dst
1.1.49.12 match ip tos  0x84 0xfc flowid 1:300

#limit the national traffic  for 1.1.49.12 to 1Mbps

tc class add dev eth0 parent 1:10 classid 1:1300 htb rate 1Mbps

tc qdisc add dev eth0 parent 1:1300 sfq quantum 1514b perturb 15

tc filter add dev eth0 protocol ip parent 1:0 prio 5 u32 match ip dst
1.1.49.12 match ip tos  0x88 0xfc flowid 1:1300

#limit the metropolitan traffic  for 1.1.49.12 to 10Mbps

tc class add dev eth0 parent 1:10 classid 1:9300 htb rate 10Mbps

tc qdisc add dev eth0 parent 1:9300 sfq quantum 1514b perturb 15

tc filter add dev eth0 protocol ip parent 1:0 prio 5 u32 match ip dst
1.1.49.12 flowid 1:9300
```

For more accessibility, you can make a bash script in which you can write the following lines:

```
A="tc class add dev eth0 parent 1:10 classid"

Q="tc qdisc add dev eth0 parent"
P="sfq quantum 1514b perturb 15"

F_NET="tc filter add dev eth0 parent 1:0 protocol ip prio 25 u32 match
ip tos  0x84 0xfc match ip dst"
F_NAT="tc filter add dev eth0 parent 1:0 protocol ip prio 25 u32 match
ip tos  0x84 0xfc match ip dst"
F_METRO="tc filter add dev eth0 parent 1:0 protocol ip prio 25 u32
match ip dst"
```

and use those variables as follows:

```
$A <classid> rate <rate>
$Q <classid> $P
$F_NET <dest_IP> flowid <classid>
or
$F_NAT <dest_IP> flowid <classid>
or
$F_METRO <dest_IP> flowid <classid>
```

As for the example above for 1.1.49.12 with internet access 512 kbps, national access 1Mbps, and metropolitan access 10Mbps, we can do the following:

```
$A 1:300 rate 512Kbit
$Q 1:300 $P
$F_NET 1.1.49.12 flowid 1:300

$A 1:1300 rate 1Mbit
$Q 1:1300 $P
$F_NAT 1.1.49.12 flowid 1:1300

$A 1:9300 rate 10Mbit
$Q 1:9300 $P
$F_METRO 1.1.49.12 flowid 1:9300
```

This is much simpler and easier to follow when the traffic shaping script becomes enormous.

The question that follows is "where" we should place those scripts. If we place them on the core routers it would be OK, but with so many core links, we won't be able to do much shaping for the customer upload bandwidth. However, for some customers who are directly connected to Core-4, we must place the script on Core-4; so, we'll have to limit the upload bandwidth on three interfaces.

Our concern is not for the clients directly connected to Core-4 as they are big companies, but rather for the home users and smaller clients who use P2P applications all the time. Those clients pass through one core router (Core-1 or Core-4) and through one distribution router.

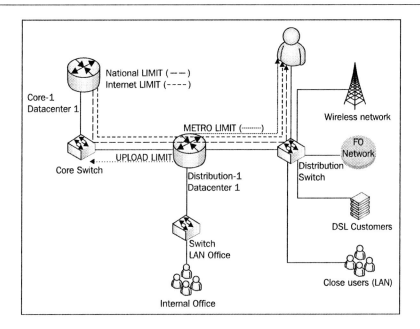

For clients that pass through a distribution router (as in the previous figure), the optimum way to shape their traffic (from the point of view of the average load of the routers) is as follows:

- Internet limit: on the core router
- National network limit: on the core router
- Metropolitan network limit: on the distribution router
- Upload limit: on the distribution router

Summary

In this chapter we saw a large network with four core routers and five core links, and discussed:

- How to build a configuration for a large network—how to create BGP connections
- What kind of security threads we should expect
- How to filter DDoS attacks with a good script that detects and filters them
- How to secure business-critical services like VoIP and billing databases
- How to differentiate services by marking packets with different values for those services

- How to solve a problem when one of the core links doesn't keep the mark of the packets
- How to perform traffic shaping for customers who buy one, two, or three services that we created
- Where to place the limit scripts for the customers

Index

M

MAC address spoofing 43
MAC attack 42, 43
mail Transport Agents. *See* **MTA**
Masquerade
  about 92
  with iptables 92
  working 93
Maximum Information Rate 216
MIM attack 41
MTA
  about 54
  problems 54
  Sendmail 54

N

NAPT. *See* **PAT**
NAT
  about 89
  connection tracking 91
  DNAT 94
  Full NAT 95
  many-to-many scenarios 91
  many-to-one scenarios 91
  Masquerade 92
  one-to-many scenarios 91
  one-to-one scenarios 91
  private IP addresses, used by hosts 90
  router 89
  scenarios 91
  SNAT 92
  SOHO routers 89
  working 90, 91
NAT using iptables
  about 97
  chains, netfilter nat table 100
  configuration, verifying 108, 109
  DNAT with iptables 105
  double NAT 109, 110
  Ethernet interfaces, SNAT with iptables 102
  Kernel, setting up 97
  Linux router configuring, double NAT 111, 112
  Netfilter Configuration section 3, 98-100
  netfilter nat table 100

OUTPUT chain, netfilter nat table 100
POSTROUTING chain, netfilter nat table 100
PREROUTING chain, netfilter nat table 100
  script, setting up 106, 108
  SNAT with iptables 102, 104
  transparent proxy 105
  VPN creating, double NAT 110
netfilter
  about 1, 63
  chains, default table 64
  default table 64
  features 63
  front-end 63
  iptables 63
  mangle modules 64
  mangle tables 64
  NAT 64
  packets, flow 65, 66
  working 64, 66
Network Address and Port Translation. *See* **PAT**
Network Address Translation. *See* **NAT**
networks
  access layer 229
  core layer 229
  distribution layer 229
  for company with remote locations 169
  large network example 229
  medium networks 169
  security 41
  setting up, Linux as SOHO router 139
  three-layered hierarchy 228
network security
  about 41
  MIM attack 41
  OSI layers 42

O

Open Secure Socket Layer. *See* **OpenSSL**
OpenSSL
  about 56
  protecting 56
  vulnerabilities 56
OSI model
  layers 119

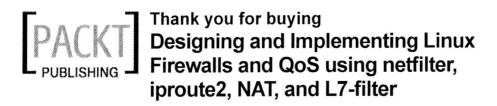

Thank you for buying
Designing and Implementing Linux Firewalls and QoS using netfilter, iproute2, NAT, and L7-filter

Packt Open Source Project Royalties

When we sell a book written on an Open Source project, we pay a royalty directly to that project. Therefore by purchasing Designing and Implementing Linux Firewalls and QoS using netfilter, iproute2, NAT, and L7-filter, Packt will have given some of the money received to the netfilter/iptables project.

In the long term, we see ourselves and you—customers and readers of our books—as part of the Open Source ecosystem, providing sustainable revenue for the projects we publish on. Our aim at Packt is to establish publishing royalties as an essential part of the service and support a business model that sustains Open Source.

If you're working with an Open Source project that you would like us to publish on, and subsequently pay royalties to, please get in touch with us.

Writing for Packt

We welcome all inquiries from people who are interested in authoring. Book proposals should be sent to authors@packtpub.com. If your book idea is still at an early stage and you would like to discuss it first before writing a formal book proposal, contact us; one of our commissioning editors will get in touch with you.

We're not just looking for published authors; if you have strong technical skills but no writing experience, our experienced editors can help you develop a writing career, or simply get some additional reward for your expertise.

About Packt Publishing

Packt, pronounced 'packed', published its first book "Mastering phpMyAdmin for Effective MySQL Management" in April 2004 and subsequently continued to specialize in publishing highly focused books on specific technologies and solutions.

Our books and publications share the experiences of your fellow IT professionals in adapting and customizing today's systems, applications, and frameworks. Our solution-based books give you the knowledge and power to customize the software and technologies you're using to get the job done. Packt books are more specific and less general than the IT books you have seen in the past. Our unique business model allows us to bring you more focused information, giving you more of what you need to know, and less of what you don't.

Packt is a modern, yet unique publishing company, which focuses on producing quality, cutting-edge books for communities of developers, administrators, and newbies alike. For more information, please visit our website: www.PacktPub.com.

Configuring IPCop Firewalls

ISBN: 1-904811-36-1   Paperback: 154 pages

How to setup, configure and manage your Linux firewall, web proxy, DHCP, DNS, time server, and VPN with this powerful Open Source solution

1. Learn how to install, configure, and set up IPCop on your Linux servers

2. Use IPCop as a web proxy, DHCP, DNS, time server, and VPN

3. Advanced add-on management

OpenVPN: Building and Integrating Virtual Private Networks

ISBN: 1-904811-85-X   Paperback: 258 pages

Learn how to build secure VPNs using this powerful Open Source application

1. Learn how to install, configure, and create tunnels with OpenVPN on Linux, Windows, and MacOSX

2. Use OpenVPN with DHCP, routers, firewall, and HTTP proxy servers

3. Advanced management of security certificates

Please check **www.PacktPub.com** for information on our titles

PUBLISHING

Building Telephony
Systems with Asterisk

An easy introduction to using and configuring Asterisk to build
feature-rich telephony systems for small and medium businesses

David Gomillion   Barrie Dempster   PACKT

Building Telephony Systems With Asterisk

ISBN: 1-904811-15-9   Paperback: 180 pages

An easy introduction to using and configuring
Asterisk to build feature-rich telephony systems for
small and medium businesses

1. Install, configure, deploy, secure, and
    maintain Asterisk

2. Build a fully-featured telephony system and
    create a dial plan that suits your needs

3. Learn from example configurations for different
    requirements

Linux Email
Set up and Run a Small Office Email Server

Magnus Back   Alistair McDonald
Patrick Ben Koetter   David Rusenko
Ralf Hildebrandt   Carl Taylor   PACKT

Linux Email: Set up and Run a Small Office Email Server

ISBN: 1-904811-37-X   Paperback: 295 pages

A simple step-by-step guide to setting up a
Linux email server using the most popular free
Open Source tools

1. All the information you need to easily set up
    your own Linux email server

2. Shows how to provide web access to email,
    virus and spam protection, and more

3. Techniques to backup and protect your data

4. Applications used include PostFix, Courier,
    SquirrelMail, SpamAssassin, ProcMail, and
    ClamAV

Please check **www.PacktPub.com** for information on our titles

Printed in the United States
65251LVS00004B/335-336